I0037532

Banking Terms

Financial Education Is Your Best Investment

Published February 24, 2019

Revision 2.1

Financial Terms Dictionary

Copyright And Trademark Notices

Limits of Liability and Disclaimer of Warranties

The materials in this book are provided "as is" and without warranties of any kind either express or implied. The Author disclaims all warranties, express or implied, including, but not limited to, implied warranties of merchantability and fitness for a particular purpose.

The Author does not warrant that defects will be corrected, or that that the site or the server that makes this eBook available are free of viruses or other harmful components. The Author does not warrant or make any representations regarding the use or the results of the use of the materials in this book in terms of their correctness, accuracy, reliability, or otherwise. Applicable law may not allow the exclusion of implied warranties, so the above exclusion may not apply to you.

Under no circumstances, including, but not limited to, negligence, shall the Author be liable for any special or consequential damages that result from the use of, or the inability to use this eBook, even if the Author or his authorized representative has been advised of the possibility of such damages.

Applicable law may not allow the limitation or exclusion of liability or incidental or consequential damages, so the above limitation or exclusion may not apply to you. In no event shall the Author's total liability to you for all damages, losses, and causes of action (whether in contract, tort, including but not limited to, negligence or otherwise) exceed the amount paid by you, if any, for this eBook.

Facts and information are believed to be accurate at the time they were placed in this book. All data provided in this book is to be used for information purposes only. The information contained within is not intended to provide specific legal, financial or tax advice, or any other advice whatsoever, for any individual or company and should not be relied upon in that regard. The services described are only offered in jurisdictions where they may be legally offered. Information provided is not all-inclusive and is limited to information that is made available and such information should not be relied upon as all-inclusive or accurate.

You are advised to do your own due diligence when it comes to making business decisions and should use caution and seek the advice of qualified professionals. You should check with your accountant, lawyer, or professional advisor, before acting on this or any information. You may not consider any examples, documents, or other content in this eBook or otherwise provided by the Author to be the equivalent of professional advice.

The Author assumes no responsibility for any losses or damages resulting from your use of any link, information, or opportunity contained in this book or within any other information disclosed by the author in any form whatsoever.

About the Author

Thomas Herold is a successful entrepreneur, mediator, author, and personal development coach. He published over 20 books with over 200,000 copies distributed worldwide and the founder of seven online businesses.

For over ten years Thomas Herold has studied the monetary system and has experienced some profound insights on how money and wealth are related. After three years of successful investing in silver, he released 'Building Wealth with Silver - How to Profit From The Biggest Wealth Transfer in History' in 2012. One of the first books that illustrate in a remarkable, simple way the monetary system and its consequences.

He is the founder and CEO of the 'Financial Terms Dictionary' book series and website, which explains in detail and comprehensive form over 1000 financial terms. In his financial book series, he informs in detail and with practical examples all aspects of the financial sector. His educational materials are designed to help people get started with financial education.

In his 2018 released book 'The Money Deception', Mr. Herold provides the most sophisticated insight and shocking details about the current monetary system. Never before has the massive manipulation of money caused so much economic inequality in the world. In spite of these frightening facts, 'The Money Deception' also provides remarkable and simple solutions to create abundance for all people, and it's a must read if you want to survive the global monetary transformation that's underway right now.

For more information please visit:

Financial Terms Dictionary

Financial Dictionary Series

There are 12 books in this financial terms series available. Click the link below to see an overview and available formats on Amazon.

Thomas Herold Author page on Amazon

Please leave your review on Amazon:

This book is self-published and the author does not have a contract with one of the five largest publishers, which are able to support the author's work with advertising. If you like this book, please consider leaving a solid 5-star review on Amazon.

Table Of Contents

American Bankers Association (ABA)

The American Bankers Association, or ABA, is a trade association of the U.S. banks large and small conveniently located in Washington, D.C. This powerful lobbying organization hails back to 1875 when it was established by several bankers.

Today, the ABA has grown to represent banks of all stripes and sizes and encompasses more than 95% of all bank assets in the nation. This means that money center banks, regional banks, community thrift banks, mutual savings banks, savings and loans associations, trust companies, and large commercial banks all count the ABA as their voice before the federal government. The typical sized member bank boasts around $250 million in assets.

This trade and industry group proves to be the biggest banking trade association by far within the U.S. today. It is also known as the biggest financial trade group anywhere in the United States. The American Bankers Association thrives and prospers because of its impressive range of both services and products it delivers to member institutions. This includes help in such diverse industry segments as insurance, staff training and education, asset management, capital management, consulting, and risk-compliance endeavors.

Probably the most famous creation of the American Bankers Association remains the all important nine digit routing numbers which designate all banks everywhere within the U.S. These routing numbers are pictured on every single check and are also necessary identification for wire transfer transactions. The ABA can truthfully boast that it created this system over a hundred years ago, way back in 1910.

Today's American Bankers Association keeps extremely busy lobbying with Congress for its banking members and their common interests. The group has concentrated its efforts in the last several years on banning the so-called unfair tax exempt status enjoyed by credit unions. Credit unions originally catered to selective and tiny targeted memberships, as with a particular company's own employees. This did not threaten commercial banks and other similar financial institutions.

More recently though, to bank's undying enmity and impotency in the face of this real and rising threat, credit unions found the means to vastly expand their roles of membership and possible pools of customers. It is no exaggeration to state that numerous credit unions can boast over $1 billion in assets nowadays. This makes them as big as some of the larger and even too big to fail banks.

The ABA strenuously maintains that such credit unions have morphed into a structure and operations which are so similar to the traditional commercial banks that they no longer deserve this special favor of tax exempt status. It was actually the infamous Panic of 1873 that gave rise to the initial founding of the American Bankers Association. A banker James Howenstein of St. Louis, Missouri, one day discovered that he was up against a proverbial wall in his bank. He only possessed several hundred dollars in cash against his millions of deposits he needed to return back to panicking depositors.

By falling back on assistance and knowledge willingly provided by his peers in the banking business via rapid and frequent correspondence, Mr. Howenstein escaped from his business-threatening dilemma to survive. He then knew that he had been saved by this informal network and fraternal organization of fellow bankers and wanted to expand on this successful construct.

To this effect, Mr. Hownestein convened his first meeting of 17 different bankers on May 24, 1875 in New York City. Together they made plans for an initial American Bankers Association convention that did successfully take place on July 20, 1875 in Saratoga Springs, New York. Fully 349 different bankers who hailed from 31 states as well as the nation's capital attended.

Chief among the first endeavors of the ABA proved to be setting up the American Institute of Banking. They founded this in 1903 in order to offer certificates and examinations as professional banking education in their local branch chapters. This AIB offered interested participants a different way to pursue a banking career than by going to university for a degree in law and finance.

American Institute of Banking (AIB)

The American Institute of Banking (AIB) is a venerable educational and training institution for the United States based banking industry which was established by the American Bankers Association (ABA) back in 1907.

This AIB offers continuing training and a full range of banking career education for parties who are interested in the banking field or who are already participants within it. Over 150,000 existing bankers take part in their extensive range of continuing educational programs every year. As such, the AIB is the definitive and universally recognized continuing education curriculum for those within the fields of financial services.

American Institute of Banking programs were created to boost, refresh, and improve the job skills and knowledge base of those working in or seeking to work within the financial services industry. Completing some of these degreed programs can provide a path to AIB certificates and even diplomas which are universally recognized within the banking realm. They can also help with obtaining required professional licenses.

These programs encompass more than the traditional open enrollment programs provided throughout all of the various states. The AIB of today also offers convenient digital format purchase of its services and products, training provided in-house and Internet-based provision of online classes and coursework, tests, and study teams classes. These are only a few of the many options for its in-depth and extensive industry-wide programs.

The American Institute of Banking falls under the umbrella of the founder American Bankers Association. This means that all AIB programs and courses are provided through the local area branches of the ABA and its providers. Among its many classes and programs are core courses in such fields as business fundamentals; general banking; consumer, commercial, and mortgage lending; retail banking; asset management; compliance issues; and marketing.

In-bank branch training utilizes instructions and resources to offer specifically tailored delivery of the various ABA training regimens within a banker's own branch. It might also be offered off site in the immediate area, depending on demand.

In recent years, the American Institute of Banking has moved aggressively into the digital age with its instructional offerings. Thanks to this decision, they now offer Internet-based online versions of their best selling, traditional instructor-driven AIB courses. They provide extensive information, schedules, and enrollment forms for this mode of education on their website.

The American Institute of Banking offers certificate programs which it tailored to help participants boost their knowledge of and performance in banking utilizing course curriculum which has been bank tested for a specific bank focus. These courses run the gamut across a variety of skill sets and content and each complement the other. Certificate-driven courses are shorter in length and typically run from one to three weeks in total duration.

The American Institute of Banking also provides full-scale banking diplomas. These are awarded for successfully completing both required and elective option courses. Courses which provide at least two hours of credit award traditional grade levels of A, B, C, or D. In order for courses to count towards one of the AIB diplomas, students must receive a C or higher overall average. One course can be utilized towards one or multiple certificates or diplomas.

The ABA has recently decided to roll up the separately branded AIB into its own proprietary programs. All American Institute of Banking courses are now provided as a division of ABA Training. These courses, whether offered in person or online, generally meet the requirements mandated by the ICB Institute of Certified Bankers for continuing education credits and appropriate exams. The ABA online training was designed specifically to be cost affordable and flexible. This is why they aim to constantly update the information and learning experienced which is now able to be accessed at any time, from any place.

Annual Percentage Rate (APR)

The annual percentage rate, or APR, is the actual interest rate that a loan charges each year. This single percentage number is truthfully used to represent the literal annual expense of using money over the life span of a given loan. Annual percentage rate not only covers interest charged, but can also be comprised of extra costs or fees that are attached to a given loan transaction.

Credit cards and loans commonly offer differing explanations for transaction fees, the structure of their interest rates, and any late fees that are assessed. The annual percentage rate provides an easy to understand formula for expressing to borrowers the real and actual percentage number of fees and interest so that they can measure these up against the rates that other possible lenders will charge them.

Annual percentage rate can include many different elements besides interest. With a nominal APR, it simply involves the rate of a given payment period multiplied out to the exact numbers of payment periods existing in a year. The effective APR is often referred to as the mathematically true rate of interest for a given year. Effective APR's are commonly the fees charged plus the rate of compound interest.

On a home mortgage, effective annual percentage rates could factor in Private Mortgage Insurance, discount points, and even processing costs. Some hidden fees do not make their ways into an effective APR number. Because of this, you should always read the fine print surrounding an APR and the costs associated with a mortgage or loan. As an example of how an effective APR can be deceptive with mortgages, the one time fees that are charged in the front of a mortgage are commonly assumed to be divided over a loan's long repayment period. If you only utilize the loan for a short time frame, then the APR number will be thrown off by this. An effective APR on a mortgage might look lower than it actually is when the loan will be paid off significantly earlier than the term of the loan.

The government created the concept of annual percentage rate to stop loan companies and credit cards issuers from deceiving consumers with fancy expressions of interest charges and fees. The law requires that all loan issuers and credit card companies have to demonstrate this annual percentage rate to all customers. This is so the consumers will obtain a fair comprehension of the true rates that are associated with their particular transactions. While credit card companies are in fact permitted to promote their monthly basis of interest rates, they still have to clearly show the actual annual percentage rate to their customers in advance of a contract or agreement being signed by the consumer.

Annual percentage rate is sometimes confused with annual percentage yield. This can be vastly different from the APR. Annual percentage yield includes calculations of compounded interest in its numbers.

Annual Percentage Yield (APY)

APY describes the amount of compound interest which individuals or businesses will earn in a given year (or longer time period). Investments in money market accounts, savings accounts, and CD Certificates of Deposit all pay out such interest. It is the annual percentage yield that demonstrates precisely the amount in interest individuals will receive. This is helpful for people or businesses trying to ascertain which investments and banks offer superior returns by comparing and contrasting their real yields. In general, higher Annual Percentage Yields are better to have (unless one is comparing interest on credit card debts).

This APY is practical to understand and measure simply because it considers compound interest and the miracle of compounding within any account. Simple interest rates do not do this. Compounding is simply earning interest on interest that has already accrued and been paid. It signifies that individuals are gaining a greater amount in interest than the corresponding interest rate literally indicates.

It is always a good idea to consider a real world example for clarification purposes. If Fred deposits $10,000 into a particular savings account that provides a two percent yearly interest rate, then at the end of that first year Fred will have $10,200. This assumes that the interest is paid one time per year. If the bank were to figure up and pay out the interest on a daily basis, it would increase the amount to $10,202. The extra $2 may seem small, but given a longer time frame of from 10 to 30 years, this amount can add up, particularly if larger deposits are involved.

APY should never be confused with APR. They have some similarities, but APR does not consider compounding. It is once again a simpler means of computing interest. Credit card loans are an area where it is important to understand the differences between annual percentage rate and annual percentage yield. When people carry a balance, they will be paying higher APY's then the APR the firm actually quotes. This is because interest is assessed monthly, which means that interest on the interest will be computed on each following month.

The key to obtaining a better APY on investments and savings accounts lies in getting as frequent a compounding period as possible. Quarterly compounding is better than annually, yet daily is the most superior form of compounding possible. This means that as individuals are looking to increase their APY's personally, it is important to have the money compounding as frequently as they can practically achieve.

When two CD Certificates of Deposit pay out the same rate, it is best to select that one which actually pays out both more frequently and also boasts the greater APY. With CD's, the interest payments become automatically reinvested. More frequent reinvestment is always better. This will help any individual or business to earn a greater amount of interest on the interest payments already earned and paid out.

Calculating the annual percentage yield is not an easy task. Business calculators as well as computer algorithms mostly do it for people nowadays. The simplest way to find the APY for a given account is to plug in the information including the initial deposit, compounding frequency period, interest rate, and amount of overall time for the period considered. These smart calculators will then tell you both the effective annual percentage yield as well as the ending balance on the hypothetical account at the end of the given time period.

Assumable Loan

An assumable loan is one that permits a home buyer to take over, or assume, a home seller's contract on their mortgage. This is not permitted by every mortgage lender in the place of a typical home purchase. Loans that do not have Due On Sale clauses, such as the majority of VA and FHA types of mortgages, can usually be assumed and are considered to be assumable loans.

Assumable home loans work in the following manner. A current home owner will simply transfer over his or her mortgage contract and obligations to a purchaser who is qualified to take over. In the past decades of the 1970's and 1980's, these types of mortgage note assumptions proved to be quite popular. Back then, they could be done without even having to obtain the mortgage lender's authorization. These days, the only types of mortgages that may be assumable loans without needing a lender's actual permission are those that are made by the FHA or VA.

Assumable loans provide opportunities for both buyers and sellers. It is often the case that a home buyer will not be able to secure a better rate for a new mortgage than that provided by an already existing mortgage. This could result from the negative credit history of the buyer in question or the conditions existing in the market place at the time. As existing interest rates rise, the appeal of non-existent lower rates on mortgages commonly pushes prospective home buyers to look out for assumable loans. Such a home buyer who secures an assumable loan then has the responsibility for the mortgage that the home seller previously carried.

The existing rates of the mortgage carry over for the buyer as if the person had made the original contract themselves. This assumable loan process also saves the buyer a number of the settlement costs that are incurred in making a new mortgage. This can be a substantial cost savings benefit.

Sellers similarly benefit from assumable loans. It is not uncommon for sellers to wish to be involved in the savings that buyers realize in the process of transferring over an assumable loan. Because of this, the two parties commonly share in the savings.

As an example, when the sale price of the home in question is greater than the amount owed on the mortgage itself, then the buyer will often have to put down a significant down payment, which goes straight to the home seller in this case. Otherwise, the buyer might have to get another mortgage to come up with the difference in amounts. A seller's principal benefit in participating in such an assumable loan transfer lies in having a good chance of getting a better price for the home.

Bad Bank

A Bad Bank refers to a special bank which a government agency typically establishes in order to purchase the failing loans from one or more banks that possess a large number of non-performing assets. They purchase these at the market price in order to not wreck the bank. Through the action of transferring such toxic assets from the institution's balance sheet over to the new bad bank, such damaged banks are able to free up their balance sheet from the toxic assets that they would eventually be writing down otherwise.

Bondholders and shareholders alike will likely lose money off of such a solution, not the bank depositors. These banks which devolve into insolvency from such actions can be liquidated, nationalized by the government authorities, or recapitalized and kept going on life support (hoping that their situation will improve with time).

There are countless examples of bad banks. In 1988, Mellon Bank created its own bad bank which it named Grant Street National Bank. The 2008 global financial crisis renewed the old interest in this solution for dealing with the assets of bad banks. The managers of many of the world's largest banks started thinking seriously about segregating out the toxic assets into these bad banks.

It was the then Chairman Ben Bernanke of the Federal Reserve Banking System who put forward the idea to set up a government administered and backed bad bank following the recession created by the subprime mortgage crisis. He wanted to clean up the balance sheets of the commercial banks which were suffering from devastating levels of poorly performing assets so that they could start over with their lending. Another competing strategy they contemplated was issuing a guaranteed form of insurance plan that could allow the banks to maintain their toxic assets on the books. At the same time it would pass the risks from the banks on to the taxpayers.

Banks can easily build up a massive portfolio position of financial instruments and debts that can suddenly grow in risk. This makes it far harder for the banks in question to raise additional fresh capital by selling more bonds. In such scenarios, the bank may decide it is a good idea to separate out their bad assets and good assets with the bad banks concept. This goal lies in permitting the investors to contemplate the financial health of the bank with more certainty. The bad bank could be set up in order to help deal with a worsening financial situation, or alternatively by a government agency as part of their official government response to the various financial problems in a range of financial institutions throughout the financial sector.

Besides removing these debilitating assets off of the balance sheet of the parent bank, the bad bank will allow them to have special management teams to work on the problems of the badly performing debts. This concept helps the banks to do what they do best, which is to concentrate their efforts on the primary business model of lending. Meanwhile, the bad bank itself will be able to concentrate on delivering the optimal value which it can from the remaining high risk assets.

Thanks to the global financial crisis which raged from 2007 through 2010, a number of nations established their own bad banks. The Emergency Economic Stabilization Act of 2008 suggested a bad bank to deal with the subprime mortgage crisis across the United States. Over in Europe, Ireland set up its own bad bank the National Asset Management Agency in 2009 to deal with the financial crisis as it spread in Ireland.

Bad Debt

Bad debts are those accounts receivable that simply can not be collected. Once businesses make the determination that they are not likely to be able to collect on such sums, then they actually write these off as complete losses for the company. A debt is not typically deemed to be un-collectable until every effort within reason has been made to collect on the debt that is owed. This status is not typically reached on a debt until the person or firm owing the debt has filed for bankruptcy. Another reason for a debt to be declared a bad debt would be when the costs of continuing to collect on the debt are greater than is the amount of the debt in question.

Such bad debts commonly show up on a company income statement as an expense. This actually reduces the company's net income. At this point, bad debts have been completely written off via crediting the account of the debtor. This cancels out any remaining balance on the debtor's account. Such bad debts prove to be money that has been totally lost by a firm. Because of this, these kinds of bad debts are referred to as expenses for a business.

Companies attempt to estimate their expenses in the form of bad debts using records from similar past time frames. They look to figure out how many bad debts will show up in the current time frame based on what happened before so that they can attempt to estimate their actual earnings. The majority of corporations come up with an allowance for bad debts, as they understand that a percentage of their debtors will never repay them completely. Banks and credit card companies are especially concerned with bad debt allowances, since much of their entire business model revolves around the issuing of credit and repayment of debts from businesses and individuals.

The real difficulty with bad debts lies in determining if and when they are actually dead. When a debtor disappears, the collateral is destroyed, a lawsuit statute of limitations expires, bankruptcy is discharged, or significant pattern of a debtor abandoning debts is present, then a debt is finally determined to be bad debt. These can be subjective measurements in some cases.

Income tax laws contain a different definition for bad debts. These debts can be deducted against regular income on a 1040 C Form. These personal debts are also able to be deducted against short term types of capital gains. Debts that are owed for services which have been rendered to a person or business are not considered taxing purpose bad debts. This is because no income is present for such unpaid services that can be taxed.

Where individuals are concerned, bad debt can refer to credit card debt or any other form of high interest debt. These kinds of debts take away money from the individual in interest payments every month, creating a negative cash flow. Good debt for an individual would be debt that is used to properly leverage investments. Such leveraged investments that create positive cash flow prove to be the most desirable forms of debt.

Bailout

Bailouts prove to be the action of handing money or other capital to a company, individual, or nation that will likely go down without help. This is done in an effort to keep the entity from financial insolvency, bankruptcy, or total failure. Sometimes bankruptcies are pursued to permit an organization to fail without panic, so that fear and systemic failure does not become endemic, taking down other similar entities along the way.

Various different groups might qualify for urgent bailouts. Countries like Greece have been prime examples in the year 2010. Companies such as major banks and insurance outfits have been deemed too big to fail in the several years preceding 2010, during the height of the financial crisis and resulting Great Recession. Other industries have qualified as well, including car manufacturers, airlines, and vital transportation industries.

A good example of companies that receive preferential bailout treatment lies in the transportation industry. The Untied States government believes that transportation proves to be the underlying core of the nation's economic versatility, necessary to support the country's geopolitical power.

Because of this, the Federal Government works to safeguard the largest companies involved in transportation from failing with low interest rate loans and subsidies, which are a form of bailout. Oil companies, airlines, railroads, and trucking companies could all be considered to be a critical part of this industry. Such firms are considered to be too big and important to fail because their services prove to be nationally and constantly necessary to support the country's economy and thereby its eventual security.

Bailouts that are done in an emergency fashion typically prove to be full of controversy. In 2008 in the United States, intense and angry debates erupted regarding the failing banking and car manufacturing businesses. The camp standing against such bailouts looked at them as a means of passing the expensive bill for the failures over to the taxpayers.

Leaders of this group savagely denounced any monetary bailouts of the big three car makers and large banks, which they said all needed to be broken up as punishment for mismanagement. They criticized a new moral hazard that was being created by guaranteeing safety nets to other businesses. They similarly did not like the big central bureaucracy that arises from government agencies selecting the size and disposition of the bailouts. Finally, government bailouts of these groups were attacked as a form of corporate welfare that continues the cycle of more corporate irresponsibility.

The other camp argued that these bailouts were necessary evils, since the state of the American economy did not prove to be solid enough to suffer the failure of either the major banks or the car makers. With the car makers, fully three million jobs stood on the line. The banking industry had the argument of systemic failure of the financial system backing it up. No one on the side of the bailouts pretended to like having to engage in them, but they were said to be necessary nonetheless. In the end, such bailouts were issued to both major industries totaling in the trillions of dollars.

Balloon Loan

A balloon loan is a kind of loan that does not divide its payments up evenly throughout the life of the loan. These kinds of loans are not fully amortized over the loan's term. As a result of this, one time balloon payments are mandatory at the end of the loan's time frame in order to pay off the loan's remaining principal balance.

Balloon loans have their advantages. They are often appealing to you if you are a short term borrower. This is because balloon loans commonly come with an interest rate that is lower than the interest rate of a longer term loan. These lower interest rates provide a benefit of extremely low interest payments. This leads to not only lower payments throughout the loan, but also incredibly low outlays of capital in the life span of the loan. Because the majority of the loan repayment is put off until the loan payment period's conclusion, a borrower gains great flexibility in using the capital that is freed up for the term of the loan.

The downsides to these balloon loans only surface when the borrower lacks discipline or falls victim to higher interest rates later on. If a borrower does not possess focused and consistent discipline in getting ready for the large last payment, then the individual may run into trouble at the end of the loan. This is because substantial payments along the way are not being collected. Besides this, if a borrower will be forced to engage in refinancing towards the end, then the borrower may suffer from a higher interest rate on the balloon payment that is rolled forward.

Some balloon loans also include a higher interest rate reset feature later in the life of the loan. This further exposes a borrower to the risk of higher interest rates. This is common with five year types of balloon mortgages. When a reset of the interest rate feature is present at the conclusion of the five year period, then the interest rate will be adjusted to the current rates. The amortization schedule will then be recalculated dependent on a final term of the loan. Balloon options that do not include these reset options, and many that do reset, generally encourage the loan holder to sell the property in advance of the conclusion of the original term of the loan. Otherwise, many borrowers will simply choose to refinance the loan before this point arrives.

The reasons that you might choose to get a balloon loan are several. A person who does not plan to hold onto a house or property for a long period of time would benefit from such a loan arrangement. This individual would plan to resell the house in advance of the loan expiration. Another reason for taking a balloon loan is in a refinancing. Finally, if a person anticipates a significant cash settlement or lump sum award, then they might take on a balloon loan. Commercial property owners often like balloon loans for the purchase of commercial properties as well.

Balloon loans are sometimes called balloon notes or bullet loans.

Banco Santander

Banco Santander is the largest Spanish banking group in the world. This giant financial institution boasts over 121 million customers among its various divisions. Founded in 1856, it maintains a staff of over 193,000 employees. For 2015, the group boasted a nearly six billion euros profit and a market capitalization of over 65.5 billion euros.

Banco Santander and the entire Santander Group is successful because it has a geographically diverse range in its top ten national markets. The group commands significant market shares in each of these countries. They are Spain, Germany, Portugal, Poland, Great Britain, Brazil, Mexico, Argentina, Chile, and the United States. The bank also controls important market shares in Puerto Rico and Uruguay. Its consumer finance business gives it a major reach into a number of other countries in Europe. It has exposure to China from both its consume finance and wholesale businesses.

Banco Santander operates a number of global divisions for business and consumer banking customers. These include Commercial Banking, Global Wholesale Banking, Santander Asset Management, Santander Private Banking, Santander Insurance, and Santander Cards. These groups all work together to help the Spanish financial services conglomerate satisfy its customer needs throughout the globe.

Retail banking and business customers receive financial services and products from Banco Santander's commercial banking division. They also employ their extensive commercial networks and their online services to locally distribute their wide range of services and products to customers of all kinds. This way the global business divisions are able to reach out to the group's over 100 million customers.

The Global Wholesale Banking division provides the group's extensive services and products to large corporations, institutions, and customers with particular needs. These groups require value added products and specially personalized service.

Santander Asset Management delivers investments and savings products on a global scale. These are distributed effectively via the Banco Santander commercial branch networks. In order to provide for the diverse needs of its customer base, the SAM incorporates a large range of investment products. These include pension plans, investment funds, and portfolio options. Money which is placed into these vehicles the group invests in a wide range of locations and assets types.

Banco Santander Private Banking focuses specifically on the customers who are high income throughout the globe. It delivers both asset management and personal financial advice to these individuals. This division runs from locations in Spain, Italy, the United Kingdom, and Latin America. It also supports private domestic banking operations throughout the nations of Latin America and Portugal. This sub group works with locally based commercial banks to jointly manage these special operations.

Santander Insurance is a large and impressive division. It delivers insurance protection and savings vehicles in 20 different countries to its more than 17 million customers. The group employs multi channel distribution networks to provide segmented insurance. This model is global in nature but local in its customer appeal and commercial network reach. It focuses on superior service, quality, and efficiency while working with low risk profile customers whenever possible.

Banco Santander Credit Cards is another global and significant division. The business provides payment processing services to a variety of businesses. It handles both credit and debit cards. As such the credit card division manages fully 110 million different cards throughout 16 nations. This important division comprises 11% of all the gross margin for the group. It utilizes a cutting edge and constantly changing technology and platform to standardize the risk and provide effective training and management for its employees and business customers.

Bank for International Settlements (BIS)

The Bank for International Settlements proves to be the oldest entity in the world for international financial organization. Central banks of the world established this bank on May 17 of 1930. Today 60 different central banks are members of this bank of central banks. Their economies represent 95% of all the combined Gross Domestic Product of the globe.

This Bank for International Settlements is also known by its acronym the BIS. It has an elegant mission. The goals of this organization are to help out the member central banks as they seek out financial and monetary stability, to serve as the bank for central banks, and to promote international financial cooperation in achieving stability. World headquarters for the BIS are located in Basel, Switzerland. The group also maintains two other important representative regional offices. These are in Hong Kong the Special Administrative Region of China for Asia-Pacific and in Mexico City for the Americas.

The two regional representative offices are hubs for the various BIS activities. They work to encourage cooperation between the region's central banks, supervisory authorities, and the BIS itself. This is why these offices promote data and information exchange, help to set up seminars and meetings, and provide information on the economic and financial research for the Americas and Asia.

Another important role of the Bank for International Settlements lies in its banking services. These two regional offices assist with delivering such services to the Americas and Asia-Pacific regions. Officers routinely visit the member central banks' reserve managers as part of this mission. In its Asian office it maintains a treasury dealing room for the region that offers daily trading functions for regional central banks.

The BIS set up its regional Representative Office of the Americas back in November of 2002 in Mexico City. The goal was to increase the Americas regional activities of the bank in better coordination with the headquarters office in Switzerland. They also established the Consultative Council for the Americas back in May of 2008. This advising committee helps the board of directors for the BIS to better understand the issues in the Americas region.

Members of this council include central bank governors from the Americas' region member central banks. This includes the U.S., Peru, Mexico, Colombia, Chile, Canada, Brazil, and Argentina.

The bank founded its increasingly important regional Asian office on July 11 of 1998 in Hong Kong as the Representative Office for Asia and the Pacific. It acts as an area forum for economic and monetary research that is useful for the central banks and provides the regional central banks with the settlement and exchange banking services.

Improving cooperation among the various member central banks in the Asian region is another important function. This office also maintains the Asian Consultative Council. The group is comprised of central bank governors from the Asia-Pacific region member central banks. Its members include Thailand, Singapore, the Philippines, New Zealand, Malaysia, Korea, Japan, Indonesia, India, Hong Kong, China, and Australia.

The Bank for International Settlements is different from other banks in the world in several important aspects. All of its customers are either international organizations or central banks. They do not open accounts for international companies or private individuals. The BIS does not offer any financial or advisory services to any investors or corporations. It also does not take in deposits from or make loans to parties that are not central banks or international organizations. The bank does make some of its research available at no cost to companies and members of the public.

Bank of England

The Bank of England is the prestigious and incredibly old central bank for the United Kingdom. The country founded this model central bank in 1694 to promote the good of the individuals in the U.K. through maintaining both monetary as well as financial stability. The bank is often affectionately referred to as the "Old Lady" of Threadneedle Street.

The bank of England carries out the first part of its mission of maintaining monetary stability quite literally. Not only does it bear responsibility for keeping up the public's confidence in the national bank notes. It also literally designs, makes, and issues into circulation these quality and durable bank notes with state of the art security features. These help insure the pound sterling notes are resistant against counterfeiting efforts and are simple to check.

This role extends to safeguarding the value of the notes through time. It enables businesses and consumers to save, plan, invest, and spend their pound notes confidently. The Bank carries out this crucial role of keeping up the confidence in the notes via its monetary stability goal.

They do this by ensuring stable, low prices throughout the broad spectrum of goods and services sold around the United Kingdom. The government has defined stable prices as those which include an inflation rate of two percent year on year as demonstrated by the Consumer Prices Index. The decisions to meet this objective of inflation targeting are made in the Bank of England's Monetary Policy Committee, the MPC.

The financial crisis of 2008 demonstrated that price stability by itself will not guarantee all-around economic stability. The second mandate of the bank is to ensure financial stability. This means public confidence and belief in the important financial markets, institutions, infrastructures, and total system. Since the financial crisis, the Bank gained a few critical additional responsibilities to help it provide financial stability to the U.K.

The first of these new powers is the Bank of England's PRA Prudential Regulation Authority. This allows it to encourage financial soundness and safety of the many crucial financial firms in this global banking center. The

PRA supervises and now regulates around 1,700 different banks, credit unions, building societies, insurance companies, and major investment companies.

The second new authority is the Bank of England FPC Financial Policy Committee. This is intended to enhance and safeguard the stability of the British financial system in total. They strive to ameliorate or remove altogether the risks to the overall system. This task centers on stopping financial crises in the future, or at the least lessening their severity and frequencies.

Besides these important roles, the Bank of England has a few other tasks to foster financial stability. They provide the services of market maker and lender of last resort when there is financial stress in the system. They monitor and regulate the important clearing, payment, and settlement systems in Britain. They also labor to calmly wind down any financial institutions which are failing.

Some might feel that the many responsibilities of the bank are too vast and wide ranging. The Bank of England is confident in the advantages of doing them all under the roof of one institution. The various responsibilities and tasks need a common set of analyses, information, and skills to complete.

Many of the competing objectives have common interconnections between them. These need rapid, capable, and efficient management and decision making regarding any of the conflicting trade-offs. This makes it the ultimate task of the bank to carry out each of these roles by laboring with capable coordination. It helps the Bank of England to maximize the effectiveness of its various policies to carry out their single mission of promoting the good of the people of the U.K.

Bank of Japan

The Bank of Japan is the name of the central bank in Japan. The Bank of Japan Act established this entity. Unlike a number of central banks, Japan's central bank is neither a private corporation nor a government agency.

The bank has several key objectives. These are to create and issue the country's banknotes, to handle monetary and currency control, and to guarantee the normal settlement of funds between banks and financial institutions. They do this to help maintain the financial system's stability in Japan.

The Bank of Japan Act gives the central bank its mandate for monetary and currency control. It is intended to help them achieve stability of prices so that the economy is able to develop normally. In January 2013, the bank began to interpret this price stability to be an inflation target of two percent. This means that they are looking for a change in the year over year consumer price index by a plus two percent increase. While they are committed to reaching this level of inflation as soon as they can, the bank has not yet succeeded.

Price stability is important to the Bank of Japan because they feel it is critical as a basis for the economic activity of the country. They state that as prices change significantly, it is difficult for companies and consumers to make the right investment and consumption choices. Unstable prices are also negative for fair income distribution.

To make the decisions on its monetary policy, the Bank of Japan holds eight Monetary Policy Meetings (MPMs) each year. Here the policy board considers the financial and economic situation in Japan and then chooses what money market operations they should pursue. All decisions are made by the majority vote of the nine members on the Policy Board.

The board is comprised of the Governor, two Deputy Governors, and six remaining members. Following each MPM, the bank releases to the public an assessment of prices and economic activity. They also divulge the monetary policy of the bank for that point and for the near future. This comes out with their guideline for money market operations.

The guideline that they decide on and release at the MPMs determines how many funds they will allow in the money market using their money market operations. The bank engages in funds-supplying operations by making loans to the country's financial institutions. These are backed up by the collateral the banks submit to the central bank. Opposite transactions called funds-absorbing operations occur as the Bank of Japan issues and sells government debt in the form of bills.

In the Financial Crisis of 2008, the central bank chose three areas in which to expand monetary policy to help stabilize the economy and encourage economic expansion. They began by reducing their policy interest rate. They next took appropriate measures to make sure that Japanese markets had financial stability. As part of this effort, the Bank of Japan restarted purchasing bank stocks. It also engaged in offering additional loans to banks at subordinated interest rates.

Finally, the bank took various steps to facilitate struggling corporate financing. They created and designated special funds and operations to encourage lending to corporations in Japan. They also expanded the variety of collateral they would accept for corporate debt. For a year, they even purchased company's commercial paper and corporate bonds in an effort to help companies find the financing they needed for normal operations.

The bank has also engaged in quantitative easing, creating money and using it to buy assets of banks and companies that needed support. They continue to pursue these policies in an effort to encourage growth and inflation in their economy.

Bank Run

A bank run is an event that happens when a bank or financial institution's customers choose to withdraw all of their deposits at the same time. This happens because of fears of the solvency of a particular bank. The effect is like a snowball. The more individuals who pull out their funds the greater the default probability becomes. This in turn leads still other customers to pull out their deposits. Severe bank run cases can create a scenario where the reserves of the bank are insufficient to meet all withdrawal demands.

Bank runs like these are not usually a result of actual insolvency of a financial institution. Rather they occur because of panic. Such fear can still evolve into a self fulfilling prophecy as a greater number of clients request their money. What starts as rumor and panic can transform into an actual ugly insolvency scenario. This means the fear of a default can actually cause a default in banking circles.

Banks run into these troubling situations sometimes because they generally only hold a tiny percentage of their actual deposits at hand. When withdrawal demands rise, it forces banks to boost their cash reserves. A common method for doing this is to sell assets, often at fire sale prices because they need funds immediately. The losses banks book for selling off assets at greatly reduced prices can lead them to actual insolvency. A bank run can become a full scale bank panic when a number of banks experience such runs on them all at once.

The best known example of a bank run occurred surrounding the infamous stock market crash in 1929. This led to numerous runs on financial institutions throughout the United States and finally to the Great Depression. The cascade of runs on the banks in the end of 1929 and the beginning of 1930 became like dominos falling. One bank's failure created fear and caused the panic of customers at neighboring banks that motivated them to take out their deposits as well. A failing bank in Nashville at the time created a number of bank runs throughout the Southeastern U.S.

Still other runs on banks occurred in the Great Depression because of the rumors begun by individual clients of the banks. The Bank of United States told a New York customer in December of 1930 he should not sell a certain stock he held. He departed from the branch and told other customers and individuals that the bank could not or would not sell his stock shares. Clients of the bank thought this meant the bank was insolvent. Thousands of them then lined up and withdrew more than $2 million out of the bank in only hours.

The developed nations' governments enacted a serious of steps to decrease the possibilities for future date bank runs as a result of the chaos in the 1930s. The most effective centered on minimum bank reserve requirements. These dictated what percent of aggregate deposits banks had to keep readily available in cash.

In 1933, the American Congress also created the FDIC Federal Deposit Insurance Corporation. They established it as a direct result of the numerous bank failures. The government agency has since then insured deposits in banks to a maximum account amount. It works to keep up public confidence and banking stability within the financial system of the United States.

Bank Stress Tests

Bank stress tests are special analyses that a government authority or company runs to determine the strength of a bank to resist difficult economic times. They conduct such tests using economic conditions that are unfavorable to learn if the banks possess sufficient capital to survive the effects of negative financial environments. In the United States, the law requires that banks which claim at least $50 billion worth of assets must perform their own internal stress tests. Their risk management department is responsible for overseeing these. The Federal Reserve conducts these stress tests on such banks as well.

The idea behind these bank stress tests is to look at several critical risks which can afflict the banks and banking system. They are supposed to evaluate the financial condition of the bank being tested in one or more crisis scenarios with regards to liquidity risk, market risk, and credit risk. The tests simulate fictitious potential crises using a number of different factors that the International Monetary Fund and Federal Reserve determine.

This mostly came about after the worldwide financial crisis and Great Recession of 2007-2009. As many banks had failed or nearly collapsed, government and international bodies became more concerned about checking on the financial strength of banks in potential crisis scenarios.

These bank stress tests were effectively set up and used on a widespread basis after this worst collapse since the Great Depression of the 1930s. The financial crisis had left in its wake a number of financial institutions, investment banks, and commercial banks that had insufficient capital. The stress tests were established to deal with this threat before it became severely problematic again.

There are two main types of bank stress tests that exist. The Federal Reserve runs its own yearly oversight stress tests of the U.S. banks that have at least $50 billion in assets on their balance sheets. The primary purpose of such a stress test is to learn if the banks possess sufficient capital to weather the storm of challenging economic conditions.

The company operated stress tests are done twice a year by law. They must be strictly reported according to the deadlines set by the Fed. Results must be turned in to the Federal Reserve board by no later than January 5th and July 5th.

In either of the stress tests, the banks receive a typical set of circumstances to evaluate their performance. It might be a 30% free fall in the prices of housing, a 5% to 10% decline in the stock market, and a 10% or higher unemployment rate. The banks must then take their future nine quarters of financial forecasts to ascertain if their capital levels are sufficient to endure the hypothetical crisis.

These bank stress tests have broader repercussions. Banks must make public their results by publishing them after they undergo the tests. The pubic and investors then learn how the bank in question would survive in a significant crisis situation. Laws and regulations passed since the financial crisis require that companies which are unable to pass the stress tests must cut their share buyback programs and dividend payments so that they can preserve the capital they have.

There are cases where banks receive a conditional passing grade on a stress test. This result states that the bank nearly failed its test. It puts them at risk of not being allowed to engage in more capital distributions going forward. Conditional passing means that a bank has to turn in a plan of action to address the capital shortfall.

These failures cause a bank to look bad to not only investors but the banking public. There have been a number of banks that failed such stress tests. Foreign banks like Germany's Deutsche Bank and Spain's Santander have failed to pass such tests on a number of occasions.

Barclays

Barclays is a British based banking giant that calls its twin home markets both the United Kingdom and the United States. The bank is well known as a transatlantic consumer, investment, and corporate bank that provide financial services and products through investment, corporate, personal banking, wealth management, and credit cards. The banking group's goal is to concentrate on its core strengths in investment banking, consumer banking, and corporate banking from its two anchors in the financial capitals of the globe - London and New York City.

Barclays is the oldest of the major international global banks. Its history stretches back over 325 years to 1690 where it began on Lombard Street in London. Since then the bank has pioneered numerous first in banking achievements such as the first ATM machine in the globe to industry leading cell phone payment services.

The bank today operates in more than 40 countries and territories and maintains over 130,000 employees around the globe. It operates in such key international markets as the United States, Brazil, Canada, and Mexico in the Americas; Australia, India, China, Hong Kong, Indonesia, Malaysia, South Korea, Taiwan and Singapore in Asia Pacific; Egypt, Israel, Nigeria, South Africa, Kenya, Tanzania, and the UAE in Africa and the Middle East; and France, Germany, Italy, the Netherlands, Russia, Spain, Sweden, and Switzerland in Continental Europe.

The banking giant operates as two well defined and differentiated businesses. These are Barclays UK and Barclays Corporate & International. The bank's UK division caters to both consumers and small to medium sized businesses. This franchise has substantial scale throughout the United Kingdom. It is made up of their UK retail banking operations, the UK wealth offering, the UK consumer credit card business, and their corporate banking for smaller businesses.

This division counts 22 million individuals as retail customers and another one million business clients. This makes Barclays a leading financial products and services provider within the United Kingdom as well as the world. The bank will ring fence this division from its other operations by

2019 in an effort to protect traditional banking assets from other riskier endeavors of the investment bank.

Under Barclays UK, personal banking offers checking and savings accounts; personal, car, and credit card loans; travel, home, and life insurance; and mortgages. The UK credit cards business focus on the Barclay Card brand. Its wealth, entrepreneurs, and business banking business covers such offerings as private banking, wealth advisory, and wealth investment services.

Barclays Corporate & International division focuses on all of the rest of the bank's operations and offerings throughout the world. This diversified transatlantic banking division comprises their U.K. market leading corporate banking, world class investment bank, growing and powerful U.S. and global credit card businesses, international wealth services, and world leading merchant payments processing systems through Barclaycard merchant and corporate banking. The division boasts impressive size and scale in consumer lending and wholesale banking. It offers tremendous growth potential for the future, core strength in critical markets, and solid balance of revenue streams.

The bank's Corporate & International Division focuses on three key businesses. Its Corporate and Investment Bank provides big business banking, access to market securities and debt issue, and business research for its corporate clients. Consumer Cards and Payments concentrate on the proprietary Barclay Card credit card offering and merchant processing in the United States and overseas.

Barclaycard and Wealth International handles over 40 different credit card branding relationships, providing credit card services for travel, entertainment, educational, financial, and retail institutions. It also provides the wealth management services to the bank's many international individual and institutional clients.

Barings Bank Collapse

The Barings Bank collapse is a tale of tragedy involving greed, poor banking oversight, and a complete failure of internal checks and balances that ruined the oldest bank in London and banker to the Queen. It took only several weeks for Nick Leeson the Singapore trading head of the bank to amass hundreds of millions of pounds in losses which he camouflaged as profits before fleeing from the law. After the family led management uncovered how severe the losses were, the bank went into bankruptcy protection until the Dutch banking giant ING acquired it for only a single pound.

Barings had originally been founded by brothers John, Charles, and Francis Baring on Christmas of 1762. The company started out as a merchant firm but quickly began to finance other merchants as a true bank. The bank gained fame over the years for financing many historic events. It helped the British government pay for the Revolutionary War in America and then the Napoleonic Wars in France. The bank financed the Louisiana Purchase for America in 1803 so that the fledgling country could double the size of U.S. for $15 million. In 1806, Barings moved to its Bishopsgate office in London which remained its headquarters for nearly 200 years until the Barings Bank collapse.

The banker to Queen Elizabeth had grown its commercial activities successfully for centuries. It floated the renowned Guinness brewery in 1886 and expanded its commercial endeavors after barely surviving collapse through a Bank of England bailout because of an Argentina near debt default. The bank eventually bought a Japanese based securities firm in 1984. In 1991 it obtained a 40 percent stake in Dillon Read the U.S. investment bank.

The negative turning point for the bank came after they put Nick Leeson in charge of Barings Futures Singapore (BFS) in 1992. He had come over from Morgan Stanley three years before as a banker in the back office. His unit's function centered on only trading futures contracts for customers on the Nikkei 225 and 10 year Japanese bonds. The mistake came in putting Leeson in charge of both the transaction settlement operations and the trading floor. At the time, James Bax the head of Barings' Asia lamented that the structure they were setting up would lead to both a loss of a huge amount of money and customer goodwill.

Barings Bank collapse was brought on by the BFS group starting to trade with its own account. Leeson was attempting to gain from arbitrage spreads between Singapore and Japanese exchanges. The London management and chairman Peter Baring believed that this was extremely profitable and basically risk free trading. The problems arose from Leeson establishing a secret account called 88888 where he began to make enormous bets on Japanese markets.

At first he appeared to make the company huge amounts of money, including 10 million pounds in 1993 that represented 10% of all the bank's annual profits. In 1995, the secret account was uncovered, along with losses of 827 million pounds he had wracked up in the name of Barings in only a matter of weeks. Leeson had left a note that said "I'm sorry" in the Singapore office and gone on the run.

Once he was captured and extradited back to Asia, Singapore charged him with fraud and forgery. They sentenced him to jail where he spent four years. Leeson later emerged from prison and sold his story as an autobiography Rogue Trader and the rights to the movie of the same title.

As a result of the Barings Bank collapse, the Bank of England lost banking oversight powers that were given to the newly organized Financial Services Authority. This organization later received criticism for ineffectively overseeing the banks under its charge and making the 2008 financial crisis significantly worse. The name Barings ceased to exist except in an asset management arm that an American life insurance group purchased. The bank's collapse ended the longest running and most famous banking dynasty in the world.

Blanket Loans

Blanket loans are those which cover multiple properties or parcels of land. They handle the costs for or can be secured by more than a single piece of real estate. These are most typically employed by commercial land developers or investors. For individual consumers, they can be utilized as a type of bridge between new and old properties and mortgages. For these consumers, such a blanket loan will make it possible to pay for both mortgages until the owner reaches the point of selling the old property.

The feature that makes these mortgages most useful for developers is their release clause. These permit the borrowers to sell a single or even several pieces of real estate without the need of being forced to refinance the mortgage. This makes them significantly different from traditional mortgages. Normal mortgages make borrowers completely pay down their loan balance before they can sell the property which secures them.

For developers of residential properties, they find these blanket loans particularly helpful. They employ them to pay for large tracts of land on which they will build. When it is time for the loan to fund, it becomes secured by the full piece of property. The developer is allowed to subdivide his property and sell it in individual lots. For part of the security to be released, the developer must utilize some of the sale proceeds to pay down part of the loan.

This is helpful when builders are constructing subdivisions. Such a developer could put the blanket loan to use to buy the consecutive pieces of land while they are available. The developer would then be able to subdivide the total land into specific lots for building houses. With each home that he finishes and sells, the property becomes detached from the blanket loan without the financing having to be disrupted on the remainder of the development project.

Consumers also find these types of blanket loans helpful in making it possible to transition from the sale of their current home to the building or buying of the new house. This makes much more sense than having two concurrent mortgages or obtaining a more costly short term bridge loan. It can also help them so that they do not have to sell the property early and move into a rental while they look for a property to purchase.

These kinds of blanket loans are often governed by a contingency clause. These clauses detail that the newly purchased house and its mortgage will not close until the person is able to sell the existing home. The problem with such a contingency clause is that they have limited time frames on them. They may force a borrower into selling the home in a panic in order to meet the clause expiration date. This can lead to a lower selling price or disadvantageous terms on the sale.

Blanket loans get around such a dilemma by providing the borrowers with an extended period of time in the clause to sell their old house. Sometimes they are arranged as interest payment only loans for a full 12 months before amortizing starts. This gives the seller a sufficient time period to sell the house for a good price and reduces the overall burden of the mortgage at the same time.

The main downside to blanket loans for individuals is that they are significantly harder to find since the real estate crash and Great Recession of 2009. Their advantages include both flexibility and efficiency in financing. For an individual consumer, this means a single mortgage payment rather than two. Developers do not have to worry about constantly refinancing their property debt as they sell off parts of the property. Should a developer default on his loan, the bank simply assumes control of all remaining property which secures the loan.

BNP Paribas

BNP Paribas is the largest French-based bank in the world. It has strong roots in the banking history of Europe. Today it remains one of the leading banks on the continent and Euro zone as well as an important international banking group. The group claims 189,000 employees around the world, of which the overwhelming majority of 146,610 are based in Europe.

It also has an extensive international network of branches and employees. The bank maintains 19,845 employees in America; 12,180 workers in Asia; 9,860 staff members in Africa; and 580 employees in the Middle East, as of 2015. BNP Paribas locations can be found in 75 different countries and territories around the world. For 2015, it boasted 42.9 billion euros of revenue and 6.7 billion euros of net profit.

The bank organizes itself along two main business lines. These are Retail Banking and Services (RBS) and the Corporate Institutional Banking (CIB) divisions. The Retail Banking & Services division covers its retail banking activities and specialized financial products and services in both France and the rest of the world. The company subdivides this into Domestic Markets and International Financial Services.

The group's Domestic Markets is comprised of the company's four retail banking networks found in the euro zone, as well as three specific lines of business. The retail bank networks are FRB French Retail Banking located in France, BNP Paribas Fortis in Belgium, BNL in Italy, and BGL BNP Paribas found in Luxembourg. Its three specific business lines are Arval the long term corporate leasing program, its Leasing Solutions that provide financing and rental services, and its Personal Investors that offer online brokerage services and savings vehicles.

Corporate clients also can access the business of Cash Management and Factoring. High Net Worth Individuals have the company's Wealth Management business as their private banking franchise within the domestic markets of the group. As of 2015, the Domestic Markets subdivision boasts over 15 million individual customers located in 27 countries. The bank also counts almost 1 million clients comprised of professional individuals, small businesses, and corporate entities. To service these numerous accounts, they devote the efforts of 68,000 employees in these over two dozen countries.

International Financial Services of the group handles the company's diversified business activities operating in over 60 countries. The group's Personal Finance provides credit to people residing in 30 countries. They deliver products and services via such major brands as Findomestic, Cofinoga, and Cetelem.

The IFS division also operates several other businesses. International Retail Banking covers the retail bank operations in another 15 non-euro zone nations like TEB in Turkey and Bank of the West in the U.S. BNP Paribas Cardif offers savings and insurance for assets, projects, and individuals living in 36 countries.

IFS rounds out its business lines with three specific asset management and private banking operations. These include the group's Wealth Management for private banking, their Investment Partners for asset management, and their BNP Paribas Real Estate for international real estate services. All of the International Financial Services businesses and lines together employ over 80,000 staff residing in over 60 countries.

The group's Corporate & Institutional Banking (CIB) prides itself on being a leading worldwide provider of financial products and services to its institutional and corporate clients around the globe. They group counts 13,000 of these clients in 57 countries throughout Europe/Middle East/Africa, the America, and Asia Pacific. To support them it maintains nearly 30,000 staff.

The company delivers specialized services that help their clients through treasury, financing, securities services, capital markets, and financial advisory offerings. It proves to be a world-renowned leader throughout numerous disciplines. As such, CIB has vast expertise in derivatives, risk management, structured financing, and other areas. The CIB division serves as a bridge between the two types of clients it counts by helping its corporate clients to obtain financing while offering investment possibilities to its institutional investors.

Bridge Loan

A bridge loan is a temporary short term loan whose purpose is to help a home owner to afford to buy a new house before they are able to sell their present house. They might do this to avoid having to move into a rental in between houses. The home buyer's existing house secure these loans. The money that comes from these loans is utilized to purchase the house into which the buyers are moving.

A bridge loan can be more popular in real estate markets which favor the buyer, or a buyer's market. The home owner may find it easier to buy a new house than to sell his or her existing one in these cases. This means that the buyers will have to come up with the down payment through either these types of loans or by using a home equity loan. Home equity loans can be less costly than bridge loans are.

A bridge loan will offer some borrowers greater advantages. Besides this, a great number of lenders will refuse to make a home equity loan on a house that is already up for sale. The best thing is to compare the advantages of the two different kinds of loan in order to decide which works best for a given buyer's unique scenario before he or she puts in an offer on another house.

Bridge loans do not always involve credit score minimums and set debt to income ratios. It depends on the lender and the underwriting process that is involved. Instead approvals are more often granted based on whether such underwriting makes sense to the loan officer and lender. There would be stricter guidelines on the part of the loan that pertains to the new house and its long term mortgage.

There are lenders who will make conforming loans and not consider the bridge loans' payments when qualifying the borrower for the new mortgage. In other cases the borrowers become qualified to purchase the new house by combining the present loan payment with the additional mortgage payment on the new house.

A great number of lenders will qualify the borrowers on two payments for a variety of reasons. They understand that the majority of buyers already have a current first mortgage on the home which they own. Banks also know that buyers would probably close on the new house they are buying before they sell their present home. Most importantly, banks are aware that home buyers in this scenario will own two different houses, even if for a short time frame. Qualifying on a bridge loan based on two payments requires a greater income or a lower payment on one of the houses.

With conforming loans, banks and lenders can find more room to work with a greater debt to income ratio. They can do this by using one of the automated mortgage underwriting programs with Freddie Mae or Fannie Mac. In general with jumbo loans, the restrictions are greater. The majority of lenders will limit the borrower to a maximum of 50% debt to income ratio.

British Bankers Association (BBA)

The British Bankers Association turns out to be the members' representative for the biggest international banking cluster in the world. This main trade association for the British banking sector boasts over 200 member banks headquartered in both the U.K. and more than 50 other countries that run operations in over 180 jurisdictions around the globe. As such fully 80% of all the systemically critical banks on earth carry membership with the BBA. This is the voice of UK banking.

The BBA claims the greatest and most comprehensive policy resources for those banks operating in the UK. They represent membership not only to the government of the U.K., but also throughout Europe and globally. Besides this impressive membership roster, their network also is comprised of more than 80 of the foremost professional and financial services organizations in the world.

The BBA's members collectively manage over £7 trillion (British pounds) of British bank assets. The members employ almost half a million people throughout the country. Their contributions to the British economy every year are more than £60 billion. Members loan in excess of £150 billion out to business based in the U.K.

The British Bankers Association works to encourage both initiatives and policies that promote the interests of not only banks but also the overall public. They have three principal priorities in their work. The first is to help out customers. This includes both businesses and consumers. The second is to encourage growth. By this they intend to support Britain as the world's global financial center. Finally they are interested in improving standards in the industry on both an ethical and professional level.

The BBA works with two strategic aims in mind. The first is to encourage a superior and improving banking sector for the overall U.K. They do this by working alongside banks and other beneficiaries to increase trust in the banking industry, by raising standards, by encouraging growth, and by assisting customers. They promise to facilitate public approval and overall awareness of the important position banks play in the economy. They are also aspiring to build appreciation for the advantages of hosting an internationally critical banking sector.

Chief among their public relations tasks are to encourage acknowledgement of the substantial improvements the sector has gone through since the global financial crisis. The BBA's goal is to be understood as an agent of positive change that makes a better banking industry by its non members and members alike. They strive to be a trusted partner of both banking regulators and the government. They also take the initiative to impact international and national debates on banking issues.

Their second strategic aim is to be the banking industry's trade association that is world class. They are the principal trade association for the foremost sector of the British economy as well as the main trade group for the foremost banking cluster in the world. This is why they aim to be best in class in their operations.

Before September in 2012, the BBA both compiled and published the LIBOR London Interbank Offered Rate, the most important interest rate in the world. They lost their role in managing the rate after the Barclays scandal erupted that showed the bank had been consistently manipulating the rate for a number of years. As lobby organization for the rate submitting banks, the Bank of England decided the BBA's conflict of interest was too great.

Nowadays the BBA puts on training and events throughout Britain. These include training classes, briefings, and forums besides their annual industry dinners and conferences. They also publish a monthly report that covers figures on high street banking. This is used in their Annual Abstract of Banking Statistics that they produce every August. BBA furthermore runs the GOLD Global Operational Loss Database for members. This serves as a helpful tool in helping to manage risk from operations.

Bundesbank

The central bank of Germany is the Deutsche Bundesbank. The Federal Republic of Germany established it as the German central bank in 1957. The bank headquarters reside in Frankfurt in the state of Main. The bank maintains regional offices throughout nine cities in the country. These regional offices have a total of 35 different branches.

This bank is different from many central banks in its many locations and interactions with the public. The Bundesbank has a presence in every major region of Germany. Every regional office has responsibility for either one federal state or sometimes several of them.

The Bundesbank Executive Board makes the decisions for the central bank. The President of the bank, Vice President, and other members comprise this critical body.

The Bundesbank carries out a number or roles. It provides the German economy with bank notes. The bank is also the regulator for supervising the German banks. Besides traditional central banking roles like these, it also provides information to the public in the form of economic education through its around 40 locations in the country. About 2,600 staff work in the regional offices. Another approximately 2,600 employees serve in the branches of the bank.

Bundesbank branches and regional locations have different roles. The regional offices prove to be the on-site financial institution supervisors. Each of the regional offices is responsible to oversee the financial services and banks that operate in their one or more regions. These supervisors have to consider and evaluate reports and notifications that the banks must submit in turn routinely. Among these is their statement of annual accounts.

The supervisors from the regional offices of the central bank also have regular meetings with these financial institutions' senior management teams. Inspectors from the regional office determine if the liquidity and capital on hand are sufficient according to the laws. They also decide if the banks are meeting the minimum risk handling requirements.

Assessing credit is another critical role that the regional office staff carry out with the individual banks. They provide the banks with money in exchange for collateral the central bank accepts as eligible. Regional offices make sure that the balance sheets are healthy.

Economic education comes from the regional offices as well. Experts from the central bank give updates in plain language on important issues like monetary policy, cash, and financial markets. They do this at events held in each region, like the "Bundesbank Forum." Any member of the public is allowed to attend. Regional offices also provide seminars to students and teacher on developments in monetary policy.

Branches of the central bank are where matters related to cash are handled in the country. These branches issue the new banknotes and coins into circulation by delivering them to the major customers such as grocery stores and financial institutions. The branches are responsible for checking deposited coins and banknotes to make sure they are authentic and of high quality. They replace damaged ones for any customer who brings them to the branch.

In order for a customer to exchange a bank note, he or she must have minimally 50% of the note in hand. If they do not, customers must offer conclusive proof that the missing part of the note was destroyed.

Germany's central bank does not set interest rates or conduct monetary policy on its own. As a member of the euro zone, the country has ceded control of this important function to the European Central Bank. The German central bank is an important member of the ECB and plays a major role in influencing the overall policy of the euro zone wide central bank.

Capital Adequacy Ratio

The Capital Adequacy Ratio refers to a metric for sizing up the capital of a given bank. It is usually written out in terms of a percentage of the risk weighted credit exposures of a bank. This formula is also referred to as CRAR or capital to risk weighted assets ratio. It is commonly employed to help ensure that the money from depositors is safeguarded while promoting the efficiency and stability of the globe's various financial systems.

There are two different types of capital which this ratio measures. The first is Tier One Capital, able to absorb significant losses without causing a bank to stop trading. Tier Two Capital instead refers to those losses which will be sufficient to see through a bank wind down which actually offers less protection to the bank depositors. The official expression of CAR takes the form of Tier One Capital plus Tier Two Capital divided by the amount or Risk Weighted Assets.

Government regulators have determined that such minimum capital adequacy ratios are crucial in order to be sure that the various banks maintain a large enough cushion to suffer a reasonable sum in losses before the y fall into insolvency, having lost the funds of their depositors. By reducing the risks of banks sinking into insolvency, the Capital Adequacy Ratios make certain that the financial system of the nation are both providing stability and efficiency. When even one good-sized bank becomes officially insolvent, this shatters the financial system confidence potentially in a move that upsets the whole financial market system of the nation in which it occurs.

When such an insolvent bank is being wound down, the depositors' funds receive the highest possible priority as compared to the capital of the bank. This means that depositors only have their savings at risk if the losses which the bank experiences are higher than the level of capital which it claims on its balance sheet. In other words, the larger the Capital Adequacy Ratio of the bank proves to be, the greater the amount of protection exists for the monies deposited by the bank depositors.

The Tier One Capital turns out to be that money which is constantly available and readily liquid in order to offset any losses which the bank suffers without having to cease operations. Ordinary share capital is considered to be a fine example for such Tier One Capital.

The Tier Two Capital by contrast is the amount which cushions depositors from losses when the bank winds down. It offers a significantly lower amount of protection to both the depositors and especially to the creditors. If the bank were to suffer the devastating loss of all of its Tier One Capital, this Tier Two Capital would be the one the bank fell back on subsequently.

Actually measuring the banks' credit exposure requires making necessary adjustments to the asset values declared on the balance sheet of the lender. Every one of the loans the bank made will be weighted according to its degrees of risk. Loans which were made to the government or one of its agencies weight at zero percent. Those made to individuals receive a weighting of 100 percent for maximum potential risk.

There are also off-balance sheet agreements, foreign exchange guarantees and contracts that pose credit risks to the banks. These will be converted over to their credit equivalent amounts before being risk weighted according to the same design of the on-balance sheet credit kinds of exposures. Both on-balance and off-balance sheet credit exposures will finally be combined in order to come up with the final risk weighted credit exposures.

The United States sets its own minimum Capital Adequacy Ratio depending on the tier which the regulators assign to the individual bank in question. They do not allow the Tier One Capital for the bank as divided by its total risk weighted exposure to drop below four percent. The total capital requires that the full risk weighted credit exposure remains higher than eight percent.

Cash Savings Account

A cash savings account is a place that you can park your cash and gain interest on it. Effective short term savings accounts are ones that permit you to meet your needs in four important areas. The access to the funds is critical.

Cash savings accounts should allow you to withdraw funds from the account whenever you need. This should be accomplished through convenient methods like ATM cards or online means. Funds in all types of cash savings accounts are insured by the FDIC, or Federal Deposit Insurance Corporation, to $100,000 for all people and $250,000 for retiree accounts.

Interest is another area of concern for cash savings accounts. This pertains to the rate that the bank or institution will give you for holding your money. Larger amounts generally attract superior rates.

Penalties should not have to be endured for withdrawing cash from cash savings accounts either. Certificates of Deposits and other instruments feature such penalties, but cash savings accounts should not. These terms of withdrawal should be clearly specified in any cash savings account.

Finally, service is an issue to be considered with cash savings accounts. You might wish to have customer service in a bank branch included. Otherwise, do it yourself online accounts can be established.

There are several types of cash savings accounts from which you can choose. One is a checking account that includes interest. This might be called a money market account. Such money market accounts include check writing privileges and check based access to funds. These can be held at banks or brokerage houses, which are gaining in popularity at banks' expense. Some privileges besides check writing include higher money market rates of interest and ATM card and machine access to funds. Downsides to these types of accounts include sometimes high minimum balances and possible fees.

Standard savings accounts are another option with cash savings accounts.

These were once called passbook accounts. The interest rates provided by these accounts are lower than inflation, which proves to be their major downside. Their major advantage lies in the extremely low account minimums and fees charged to have them.

High yield bank accounts are a third type of cash savings accounts. Providing versatility of adding or withdrawing funds without penalties, they also offer the liquidity of not tying up your money for long periods of time. Nowadays, there are high yield bank accounts that provide interest rates that prove to be comparable to Certificates of Deposits, without showcasing these investments' restrictions on taking out money. The highest rates available on high yield bank accounts come from banks that are online only versions of the traditional lending institutions.

They accomplish this by not offering branches and in person customer service benefits. This means that unless such an online high yield account includes an ATM card, the only way to withdraw the funds is through electronic transfers to other brokerage, savings, or checking accounts, which can result in delays of as much as two to five full days. Without such an ATM card, it can be inconvenient to access cash stored in these accounts in a hurry or emergency situation. High yield accounts sometimes offer shorter term teaser interest rates, so individuals should investigate the product's prior six month history of interest rates to learn what their consistent rates turn out to be.

Central Bank

Central banks are national monetary authorities or reserve banks that are given the unique privilege and responsibility of loaning a government its currency. Central banks have many of the same characteristics that traditional banks do, such as charging set rates of interest on loans that they make to borrowers like the government of the country that they represent, or alternatively to commercial banks in dire need and as a last resort.

Central banks are different from regular banks in a variety of interest ways. Chief among these is their monopoly of creating the nation's currency. They also have the power to loan such currency out to their government as fully legal tender. These banks are the only ones that will lend to commercial banks in difficult times of need, too.

The main role of a central bank is to issue and oversee a country's supply of money. Besides this, they also engage in a number of more vigorous activities including setting and monitoring the interest rates of subsidized loans and helping out the banking sector in periods of financial difficulties or even crisis. Some central banks additionally supervise the commercial banking sector and individual banks in order to make certain that they do not engage in corrupt behavior or rash decision making and practices.

Not all countries possess central banks that are independent of the other branches of government's meddling and interference. Most of the wealthy countries of the world do have this type of central bank in a system that stops politicians from intervening in monetary policy. The European Central Bank, Bank of England, and Federal Reserve System of the United States are all good examples of independent central banks. Central banks can be privately held or publicly owned. In the U.S., the Federal Reserve proves to be a unique combination of private and public components.

Central banks are involved in many important functions. These include carrying out monetary policy and fixing the nation's interest rates. They also control their country's whole money supply. They act as both banker for the government and for all of a country's banks in difficult times. Central banks similarly handle the nation's gold reserves and foreign exchange reserves.

They may adjust these by buying or selling more gold, or by balancing the amount and kinds of currencies that they hold at any time. Many central banks supervise their banking industries as well, though not all perform this function. Central banks also help to deal with and combat inflation and manage a country's currency exchange rate by modifying the nation's official interest rates and utilizing similar policies to ensure that the desired outcomes of low inflation and stable currency exchange rates are in fact achieved.

Certificate of Deposit (CD)

A Certificate of Deposit refers to a kind of savings vehicle which generally provides greater returns for money invested than the typical savings accounts do. There is very little risk in such an account. They also come without monthly fees. Besides this, these CDs prove to be significantly different from the age old savings accounts for several reasons.

Such a Certificate of Deposit stands for a time deposit. While an individual who has a savings account is freely able to make additional deposits or withdraw available funds relatively at will, this is not the case with CDs. Holders of CDs consent to tying up their money for a minimum length of time. Banks calls this the term length. Such term lengths might be only a few days. They could also extend up to ten years out. Standard CD's run from typically three months to five years.

In general, the longer the term length proves to be, the better the rate of interest the Certificate of Deposit will pay. The longer the term length is, the greater amount of time an individual ties up the money in the account at the bank too. It makes sense that the bank rewards customers for committing to a longer amount of time with a larger CD rate than they pay on comparable savings accounts.

Banks generally quote these CD rates using the APY annual percentage yield. This rate takes into account the compounding periods on how often the CD pays interest which can then earn still more interest on it. The banks have the choice of compounding periods based on annually, quarterly, monthly, and daily compounding. The closer a CD compounds to a daily rate, the higher the APY will actually prove to be.

There are penalties involved with drawing the money out of the certificate of deposit before its final maturity date. While every bank is different, most banks will levy a penalty of from three to six months in accrued interest for breaking the time deposit early. This is why financial professionals will counsel against taking money out of a CD early unless it is desperately important to access the funds.

The U.S. FDIC Federal Deposit Insurance Corporation backs the CDs at the overwhelming majority of commercial banks in the country. These Certificates of Deposit are government guaranteed in amounts of up to $250,000. With the credit union CDs, these certificates become insured by the NCUA National Credit Union Administration for the same maximum amounts. Credit unions which are state-chartered will often utilize private insurance for their CDs. Not any of these forms of insurance cover the penalties for taking out the funds ahead of maturity. Such coverage comes automatically and does not have to be applied for in order for the time deposit to be insured.

There are several different varieties of Certificates of Deposit available. Variable rate CDs are those whose interest rate is connected to the prime interest rate, market indices, Treasury bills rates, or another underlying benchmark. They help depositors to gain from any future point interest rate increases. Callable CDs often include a better rate of interest than a traditional CD. The bank can unilaterally reduce the maturity term period on demand though.

No or low penalty CDs pay lower interest rates but allow investors to more easily obtain their money back from the time deposit without expensive penalties. They often require holders to keep a certain minimum balance in the CD. IRA CDs are traditional certificates of deposit which are contained within an IRA Individual Retirement Account. There are tax advantages and deferrals on taxes of interest payments with these. Finally, Jumbo CDs pay greater rates of interest in exchange for extremely high minimum balances of typically $100,000 and higher.

Citigroup

By number of countries and territories in which it operates as well as raw numbers of customers, Citigroup is the largest global bank. The United States based banking giant offers a substantial variety of financial products and services to its 100 million individual, corporate, institutional, and government customers around the world. The bank maintains a presence in more than 100 countries and territories throughout the globe. It operates in two primary groups of the Global Consumer Bank and the Institutional Clients Group.

Citigroup's Global Consumer Bank offers services throughout the most rapidly expanding cities in 24 different countries around the world. This group boasts over 100 million individual customers. Within the Global Consumer Bank (GCB), Citi runs four geographically based business lines in their four regions of North America, Latin America, Asia, and Europe/Middle East/Africa.

These are Retail Banking, Commercial Banking, Retail Services, and Branded Credit Cards. The Citi GCB boasts over a century of well-respected market leadership and brand recognition throughout areas such as the United States, Mexico, and Asia. It is focused on expanding its high credit profiled customer base utilizing its global abilities and reach.

The Institutional Clients Group operates in over 100 countries. It is here that Citigroup is able to assist multinational corporations in expanding, hiring, providing services, and delivering products. Citi proudly offers finance capabilities and support to not only companies, but also governments at every level. It assists them not only in funding their daily operations, but also in creating sustainable transportation, housing, infrastructure, schools, and other key public works and services.

Institutional investors are able to maximize the depth of product offerings and global footprint to reach into both local and international markets. Citigroup boasts an impressive history of financing among the most transforming projects in the world during the last two centuries. They remain devoted to supporting expansion and creative innovation around the world today with cash management, lending, and advisory services.

The Citigroup ICG maintains trading floors in over 80 nations, as well as custody and clearing networks in more than 60 countries and has connections via 400 different clearing systems. This means that Citi proudly controls among the biggest global financial facilities and infrastructure platforms. These help it to facilitate the movement of a daily average of more than $3 trillion in global monetary flows.

The ICG Group if Citigroup operates six primary businesses. Citi's Capital Markets Origination business concentrates on raising capital for their institutional clients. This includes cross border issues, transactions, and exchanges.

The Citigroup Corporate and Investment Banking business delivers complete relationship coverage and service utilizing product, sector, and nation expertise to provide their worldwide abilities to clients in whichever market they wish to have a competitive presence. They organize these teams by country and industry. Every team is comprised of the two parts. Strategic Coverage Officers provides for merger and acquisition and equity financing activities. Corporate Bankers work with the Global Subsidiaries Group and Citi Capital Markets in order to help provide finance and banking services to local, national, regional, and global customers.

Citi's Markets and Securities Services business delivers world-leading financial services and products to its thousands of institutions, investors, corporations, and government clients. It covers an impressive array of asset classes, sectors, currencies, and products. Among these products are commodities, equities, futures, credit, emerging markets, foreign exchange, G10 rates, prime finance, municipals, and securitized markets.

The Citigroup Global Private Bank business is a world leader. They have 800 private bankers residing in 16 countries at 51 individual offices who provide dependable advice to members of the most successful families and influential private individuals on earth.

Finally, the Citigroup Treasury and Trade Solutions, or TTS, business delivers trade finance and seamless cash management services to Citi's wide range of financial institutions, multinational corporations, and public sector outfits throughout the world. These services include receivables, payments, investment services, liquidity management services, commercial card programs, working capital solutions, and trade finance.

Clearing House

A Clearing House refers to a financial intermediary that exists between sellers and buyers of financial instruments such as stocks, bonds, futures, options, and mutual funds. At the same time, it is also an agency which operates in tandem with a futures exchange. In this capacity, they handle clearing trades, settling trading accounts, collecting and maintaining monies for margin accounts, reporting trades, and regulating delivery of the relevant financial instruments. These clearing houses serve as third parties for all options and futures contracts. They are also simultaneously buyers for each seller who is a clearing member and sellers for every buyer who is a clearing member.

Another way of looking at this is that the clearing houses take on the opposite side of every trade transacted. As two investors consent to a financial transaction and its terms, the clearing house will work in the critical capacity as middle man for the two participating third parties. This involves selling and buying securities. The ultimate reason of existence for clearing houses lies in boosting the efficiency of markets and increasing the financial stability of the relevant markets.

Futures markets are most closely connected to clearing houses. The reason for this is that their financial instruments prove to be exceedingly complex. They must therefore have a stable financial intermediary backing them up. Every futures exchange maintains its own proprietary clearing house. This forces every exchange member to clear its trades via the clearing house by no later than the end of every trading session. They will have to deposit a given amount of margin money with the clearing house based on the maintained margin requirements so that they can cover any deficit member balance.

It always helps to consider a real world clear example to illuminate a challenging concept such as this one. If Godfrey's Futures, a member broker, alerts the clearing house of the commodity and futures exchange at trading day end that it net bought 30,000 bushels of May soybeans for its customer accounts, then it will subsequently be required to deposit the margin cover of six cents or each individual net bushel position. This would amount to $1,800 in total deposit to be on hand with the clearing house in question. Since every member will have to clear out all trades via the house and so has to keep enough funds to cover their debit balances, it is ultimately the clearing house that carries the responsibility to all member broker dealers to fulfill the contracts according to the appropriate terms.

Within the United States today, there exist two separate most important clearing houses. These are the NASDAQ and the NYSE New York Stock Exchange. At the NYSE, they facilitate all mutual funds, bonds, exchange traded funds, stocks, and derivatives trading and contracts. They serve as the middle man on every side of an auction trade which allows for investors and brokers to purchase and sell off securities to other third parties and customers. They do this by matching up the highest bid price with the lowest ask price.

The NYSE actually maintains an expansive physical trading floor in pursuit of this important mission and purpose. On the other hand, the NASDAQ also has to do the same functions, yet it does not have the advantage of a physical trading floor on which to do it. All NASDAQ trades they match up entirely electronically for their various broker dealers and investor customers.

Collateralized Debt Obligations (CDO)

Collateralized Debt Obligations are one of the financial weapons of mass destruction that helped to derail the global financial system in the financial crisis of 2007-2010. They are literally securities that are supposed to be of investment grade. The backing of collateralized debt obligations proves to be pools of loans, bonds, and similar assets. These investments are rated by the main ratings agencies of Moody's, Standard and Poors, and Fitch rating companies.

The actual value of collateralized debt obligations comes from their asset backing. These asset backed securities' payments and values both derive from their portfolios of associated assets that are fixed income types of instruments. CDO's securities are divided into different classes of risk that are called tranches.

The senior most tranches are deemed to be the most secure forms of securities. Since principal and interest payments are given out according to the most senior securities first, the junior level tranches pay the higher coupon payments and interest rates to help reward investors who are willing to take on the greater levels of default risk that they assume.

The original CDO was only offered in 1987 by bankers for Imperial Savings Association that failed and became folded in to the Resolution Trust Corporation in 1990. This should have been a warning about collateralized debt obligations, but their popularity only grew apace during the following ten years. CDO's rapidly became the fastest expanding part of the synthetic asset backed securities market. There are several reasons for why this proved to be the case. The main one revolved around the returns of two to three percentage points greater than corporate bonds that possessed identical credit ratings.

CDO's also appealed to a larger number of investors and asset managers from investment trusts, unit trusts, and mutual funds, to insurance companies, investment banks, and private banks. Structured investment vehicles also made use of them to defray risk. CDO's popularity also had to do with the high profit margins that they made for their creators and sellers.

A number of different investors and economists have raised their voices against collateralized debt obligations, derivatives in general, and other asset backed securities. This includes both former IMF Head Economist Raghuram Rajan and legendary billionaire investor Warren Buffet. They have claimed that such instruments only increase and spread around the uncertainty and risk that surrounds these underlying assets' values to a larger and wider pool of owners instead of lessening the risk via diversification.

Though the majority of the investment world remained skeptical of their criticism, the credit crisis in 2007 and 2008 proved that these dissenters had merit to their views. It is now understood that the major credit rating agencies did not sufficiently take into account the massive risks that were associated with the CDO's and ABS's, such as a nationwide housing value collapse.

Because the value of collateralized debt obligations are forced to be valued according to mark to market accounting, where their values are immediately updated to the market value, they have declined dramatically in value on the banks' and others owners' balance sheets as their actual value on the market has plummeted.

Collateralized Mortgage Obligation (CMO)

Collateralized mortgage obligations are investments that contain home mortgages. These mortgages underlie the securities themselves. These CMO yields and results derive from the home mortgage loans' performance on which they are based. This is true with other mortgage backed securities as well.

Lenders sell these loans to an intermediary firm. Such an intermediary pools these loans together and issues certificates based on them. Investors are able to buy these certificates to earn the principal and interest payments from the mortgages. The payments these homeowners make go through the intermediary firm before finally reaching the investors who bought them.

The performance of collateralized mortgage obligations depends on the track record of the mortgage payers. What makes them different from other types of mortgage backed securities is that it is not only a single loan on which they are based. Rather they are categorized by groups of loans according to the payment period for the mortgages within the pool itself.

Issuers set up CMOs this way to try to reduce the effects of a mortgage being prepaid. This can often be a problem for investments based on only a single mortgage as owners refinance their loans and pay off the initial one on which the investment was based. With the CMOs, the risk of home owners defaulting is spread across a number of different mortgages and shared by many investors.

Tranches are the different categories within the mortgage pools on which the collateralized mortgage obligations are based. The tranches are often divided according to the mortgage repayment schedules of the loans. For each tranche, the issuer creates bonds with different interest rates and maturity dates. These CMO bonds can come with maturity dates of twenty, ten, five, and two years. The bondholders of each individual tranche receive the coupon or interest payments out of the mortgage pool. Principal payments accrue initially to those bonds in the first tranche which mature soonest.

The bonds on collateralized mortgage obligations turn out to be highly rated. This is especially the case when they are backed by GSE government mortgages and similar types of high grade loans. This means that the risk of default is low compared with other mortgage backed securities.

There are three types of groups who issue these CMOs. The FHLMC Federal Home Loan Mortgage Corporation issues many of them. Other GSE Government Sponsored Enterprises like Ginnie Mae provide them as well. There are also private companies which issue these CMOs. Many investors consider the ones issued by the government agencies to be less risky, but this is not necessarily the case. The government is not required to bail out the GSEs and their CMOs.

There are investors who choose to hold their CMO bonds until they mature. Others will re-sell or buy them using the secondary market. The prices for these investments on this market go up and down based on any changes in the interest rates.

The other most common type of mortgage backed securities besides these CMOs are pass through securities. Pass throughs are usually based on a single or few mortgages set up like a trust that collects and passes through the interest and principal repayments.

Commercial Banks

Commercial banks are those financial institutions which offer a wide range of financial services to a variety of clients. Chief among these services are issuing loans and receiving deposits. The customers of such commercial financial institutions are able to avail themselves of a broad range of investment products that such banks offer. Included in these are certificates of deposit and savings accounts. Such banks issue a wide variety of loans which range from car loans and business loans to home equity loans and mortgages.

Banks which are commercial in nature deliver a range of financial products like checking accounts, savings accounts, and certificates of deposit. Customers of banks prefer these kinds of financial products since they are guaranteed by the FDIC Federal Deposit Insurance Corporation within the U.S.

In consideration for their funds' deposit, the commercial banks provide interest to their clients against their deposits. This is how these institutions realize profit--- they utilize the deposits of their customers to make loans that bring in higher interest rates than the ones they offer to their depositors. This spread from the amount the banks are paying out to the ones it is gathering back in becomes the net interest income of the commercial banks.

Such financial institutions do not all offer the same exact loan products to their various customers. They may specialize in several types or only a single kind of loan. These commercial banks are able to provide mortgages to purchase homes and home equity loans. In these cases, the houses provide the collateral to underlie the loans. Such financial institutions also provide auto loans with the vehicles as the loan collateral. The institutions similarly deliver personal loans, credit cards, and lines of credit to well-qualified borrowers.

Besides the interest such banks earn for their loans on the books, they can also create income through levying fees on their customers for banking services. This is common on products including checking and savings accounts, credit cards, and especially mortgage applications and originations.

There has been an evolution within the universe of commercial banks over the last two decades. Institutions that originally began as traditionally physical "brick and mortar" outlets complete with bank tellers, ATM's, bank vaults, and safe deposit boxes are still dominant. Yet a new and powerful challenger has arisen. This is the story of the commercial bank without physical branch locations.

Such virtual banks, or online only banks, lack physical branches. They force customers to do all of their transactions either over the Internet or by phone banking. The trade off for this accommodation is that these financial institutions deliver higher interest rates for accounts, deposits, and investments as their overheads are substantially lower. They also tend to charge significantly smaller and fewer fees. They can do this since they lack all of the associated costs which come with property taxes, rents, utilities, and additional staff salaries and benefits.

It is important to realize that the activities of commercial banking are vastly different than those of their colleagues in investment banking. With investment banking, the institutions engage in a number of stock and financial markets-related businesses. Among these are financial markets underwriting, performing tasks as intermediaries between the investors of and issuers of securities, fostering and participating in mergers and acquisitions and various kinds of corporate restructurings, and performing services as primary broker on behalf of institutional clients.

Other commercial banks boast investment banking divisions. This means that they are both involved in commercial banking and investment banking all at once. These include such well-known and enormous American financial institutions as JPMorgan Chase and Citibank and the multinational giant British banks like HSBC and Barclays. Other operations including Ally focus exclusively on the commercial banking segment of the industry.

Corporate Banking

Corporate Banking refers to the banking services for businesses. It relates specifically to those accounts that apply to corporate clients. The United States initially employed the term to separate it from the branch of banking activity known as investment banking following the congressionally passed Glass-Steagall Act of 1933. This act separated out the two different activities for more than half a century.

In the 1990s, Congress repealed this act and once again allowed for investment banking and corporate banking to be combined jointly under a single roof. Most banks jumped at the chance to become involved in both activities once again. Where the majority of banks are concerned, this banking for corporate customers proves to be a mainstay profit center. At the same time, this largest originator of customer loans also turns out to be the continuous source of routine write offs for loans that have not repaid. In fact, combing investment and retail banking again led to the root causes of the Global Financial Crisis.

The divisions of banks which handle corporate banking commonly help a large variety of customers. This might range from international multinational conglomerates with billions in revenues and offices around the world on down to medium-sized regional businesses that boast several million in income to small family run companies in only a single city. These commercial banks provide a significant range of services and products to companies and corporations, as well as other smaller financial institutions.

Treasury and cash management operations are a first key service. Corporations utilize these services to convert currency and manage their daily cash and working capital. There are also credit products and loans, often the largest segment of the corporate banking world. It is also among the greatest single sources of both risk and profit for the corporate banks. There will also be commercial real estate services offered involving portfolio evaluation, real asset analysis, equity and debt structuring.

Besides this, many such banks will provide trade finance such as bill collecting, letters of credit, and factoring. Equipment lending is another important arena as the commercial banks will structure specifically tailored loans as well as leases for a wide variety of different types of equipment which companies may need for various industries. Finally, employer services deliver group retirement plans and payroll services. They offer these through special subsidiaries of the bank.

The commercial banks will also offer to cross-provide a range of useful services through their investment banking divisions. These include securities underwriting and asset management.

Commercial banks prove to be crucially important to both national and global economies. Commercial institutions provide the loans which help businesses to expand and hire additional staff members. It is the fuel that allows the economy to grow larger. In the wake of the Global Financial Crisis of 2007 to 2009, banks suddenly stopped lending money to companies and corporations alike.

It led to an almost complete freeze in the worldwide lending and banking activities necessary to keep companies operating. This meant that the recession which ensued proved to be the most devastating and deep one since the Great Depression of the 1930s and early 1940s. The global economy suffered the total shock of a near-death experience. It woke up the global regulators and forced them to renew their regulatory focus on the biggest international banks which have since been considered to be "too big to fail" thanks to their critical importance to the global financial system.

The largest commercial banks in the United States (as of 2017) are JPMorgan Chase, Bank of America, Citigroup, Wells Fargo, and U.S. Bancorp. This contrasts with the largest American banks overall which include Bank of America, Wells Fargo, JPMorgan Chase, Citigroup, and U.S. Bancorp.

Credit Agricole

Credit Agricole calls itself the foremost financial partner in the French economy. This is not idle boasting as they have a number of impressive accolades to their credit. It is rated the second largest bank in France and third largest banking group in Europe by assets. What makes it different from other global banks is that it proves to be a cooperative and mutual organization rather than a standard commercial bank.

The Credit Agricole group counts 140,000 employees working under the leadership of 31,500 directors in its regional and local banks. The bank serves 52 million individual and business customers and has 8.2 million mutual share holders. There are also 1.1 million traditional individual share holders.

By some measures, this banking group is the most important bank on the continent. It turns out to be the foremost retail bank in Europe by branch numbers and the largest manager of European assets. The group is the leading bank assurer in the continent and the third biggest player in the world of project financing.

The group operates under the universal retail bank model. The individual retail banks cooperate together under a unique arrangement. Their regional banks are independent banks in which the corporate Credit Agricole owns 25% stakes. They work together on the common business lines. Besides retail banking, these include real estate, insurance, asset management, payments, consume finance, leasing and factoring, and investment and corporate banking. The group is listed on the stock exchange Euronext in Paris.

The group provides finance and technical assistance for not only customer projects found in France, but also throughout the world. Credit Agricole has locations in more than 37 countries and territories around the globe. The bank corporation operates with a central body, a central bank, and an entity which handles the group's strategic development. The entity provides coordination to the numerous business lines in France and internationally. They ensure that the bank runs smoothly and cohesively despite the independent nature of the regional banks.

The banking group operates in three lines of business. These are French and international retail banking, specialized business lines, and corporate & investment banking.

Credit Agricole has 2,512 local banks that are the basis of the banking group. These local banks own the majority of the capital of the Regional Banks. The other 25% is owned by the corporation. There are over 6.9 million members who own the local banks. The group's 39 regional banks provide services to farmers, individuals, corporations, businesses, and local governments. In daily banking services, this group is the leading French bank.

The regional banks provide a wide range of services. This includes investments, savings, loans, life insurance, property/casualty insurance, and payment instruments. They boast 20 million customers and hold the rank of number one in practically every local market in France. These regional banks also own the majority stake position in the Credit Agricole corporation as a whole. Regional banks obtain information, express opinions, and engage in dialogue with each other through the FNCA Fédération Nationale du Crédit Agricole.

Credit Agricole's main rivals in France include BNP Paribas, Societe Generale, and Group BPCE. These other competing banks are more traditional commercial banks that are not majority owned by their members as cooperatives or mutual organizations. This has not helped any of them to become larger by assets except for BNP Paribas.

Credit Bureaus

Credit bureaus are agencies that collect financial information. They go by different names in various countries around the world. In the United Kingdom they are known as credit reference agencies. In Australia, the bureaus are called credit reporting bodies. India knows their credit agencies as credit information companies.

Within the United States, these organizations are called consumer reporting agencies. Whatever name they go by, they all serve the same function. The bureaus gather information from banks and other financial sources to deliver consumer credit information about individual consumers.

The U.S. consumer reporting agencies are governed by the Fair Credit Reporting Act. Other laws that regulate the activities of the bureaus are the Fair and Accurate Credit Transactions Act, the Fair Credit Billing Act, the Fair Credit Reporting Act, and Regulation B. These acts attempt to safeguard consumers against unfair practices and mistakes made by the data providers and the credit reporting agencies themselves.

The U.S. has two separate government organizations who oversee the credit bureaus and their data suppliers. These are the FTC and the OCC. Primary oversight of the credit reporting agencies as they deal with consumers belongs to the Federal Trade Commission. The banks are monitored for all of the information that they provide the reporting agencies by the Office of the Controller of the Currency. This government agency supervises, regulates, and charters all of the national banks and any information they turn over to the consumer credit reporting agencies.

Three main credit reporting bureaus dominate nearly all credit reporting in the U.S. These are Experian, Equifax, and TransUnion. None of these three agencies are owned by government entities. All of them exist as companies seeking to make a profit and are traded publically. They are carefully monitored for fairness by the government provided oversight organizations.

The consumer reporting agencies operate through a vast network with the credit card issuing companies, banks, and other financial entities with which individuals have accounts. All of these ties ensure that credit account information and histories show up on the credit reports of one, two, or even all of the bureaus.

The credit bureaus compile all of this information into a consumer credit report. They each then utilize proprietary trade secret formulas to determine every individual's FICO credit score. Each of the three bureaus formulates its own score that is different from that of its competitors. They also come up with educational credit score numbers which are often vastly different from the official scores.

Consumers do not have to settle for educational credit scores. They have the rights to see what is on their credit reports. Each and every year, individuals are able to obtain an official credit report from each of the three credit bureaus. This can be done by going to the government mandated website AnnualCreditReport.com.

Besides this, consumers are allowed to go to the websites of the three main consumer reporting agencies and order credit reports and scores from them directly. The only way to get the official credit score is to pay for and order it from the credit bureaus themselves. These are not provided in the annual free reports. Experian and Equifax offer all three credit reports in a single convenient to view document.

Sometimes the credit bureaus will make mistakes with individuals' credit reports. When this happens, it is important to get in touch with the credit bureau itself in order to dispute any information that is inaccurate. These organizations also should be contacted directly if there is concern about fraud so that they can place a security alert or fraud alert on the person's credit report.

Credit Derivatives

Credit derivatives refer to bilateral contracts which are privately held. These contracts permit the holders to manage their credit risk exposure. Such derivatives turn out to be financial assets. Examples of the better-known ones in the derivatives universe are swaps, forward contracts, and options. The price of these is necessarily based upon the credit risk of economic entities like governments, companies, or private investors. This means that banks which are worried about one of their customers not being capable of repaying their loan are able to purchase protection against such a potential loss in default. They do this by keeping the loan on their books at the same time as they transfer the credit risk off to a third party more commonly referred to as the "counter party."

Such credit derivatives are only one of numerous different kinds of financial instruments available to investors and financial institutions today. With these derivatives, they are merely instruments whose existence derives from underlying financial instruments. The value which underlies them comes from a stock or other asset.

Two different principal forms of derivatives exist. These are calls and puts. Calls provide the right but not obligation to purchase a stock for a pre-set price called the strike price. Puts deliver the right but not obligation to sell particular stocks for pre-arranged strike prices. With either calls or puts, investors are obtaining insurance in case a stock price rises or falls. This makes every form of derivative product an insurance vehicle and particularly these credit derivative examples.

Numerous credit derivatives exist on the markets today. Among these are CDO Collateralized Debt Obligations, CDS Credit Default Swamps, credit default swap options, total return swaps, and credit spread forwards. Banks are allowed to utilize these complicated instruments in order to completely take away their default risk from even an entire loan portfolio. The financial institutions or banks pay a premium, or upfront fee, for this accommodation.

Considering a concrete example helps to make the credit derivatives concept clearer. Plants R Us borrows $200,000 off of a bank with a ten year repayment term. Because Plants R Us shows a poor credit history, they are forced to buy the bank a credit derivative in order to be able to receive the loan. The bank accepts this product which will permit them to transfer all of the default risk to a third counter party. This means that the counter party would be forced to deliver all unpaid interest and principal on the loan in the event that Plants R Us defaults on the said loan. For this guarantee, Plants R Us pays an annual fee to the counter party for their assumed risk. Should the Plants R Us not default on the loan, then the counterparty firm keeps the entire fee. This makes it a win-win-win situation for all three parties. The bank is protected against a default by Plants R Us, which gets to have its loan. The counter party collects the yearly fee. All parties gain and benefit from the arrangement.

Credit derivatives' values vary widely depending on several factors. These include the borrower's credit quality as well as the counter party's credit quality. The biggest concern comes down to the credit quality of the third party - counter party. If the counter party defaults or is otherwise unable to honor their commitments specified in the derivatives contract, then the financial institution will not get its payment for the loan principal and interest. The counter party would naturally no longer receive its annual premium payments any longer either. This is why the quality of credit for the counter party is so much more critical than is the credit quality of the borrower (Plants R Us in the example).

Credit Score

Credit Score refers to a number generated by the credit bureaus to represent the creditworthiness of an individual. The credit bureaus possess literally from hundreds to thousands of distinct lines worth of information on each person with a credit profile. This makes it extremely difficult for lending institutions to go through it all. Since they lack the man hours to carefully peruse each applicant's credit reports personally, the majority of financial institutions which lend money employ these credit scores rather than tediously read through credit reports on applicants.

These Credit Scores are actually numbers that a computer program generates after crawling through an individual's credit report. Such programs seek out certain fundamentals, patterns, and so-called warning flags in any credit report and history. They then generate a credit score based on what they find. Lenders love these scores since they can be basically interpreted by a consistent set of comparative rules.

Consider the following examples. Lending institutions might automatically approve any application that comes with an associated 720 credit score or higher. Those profiles with 650 to 720 would likely be approved but with a greater interest rate. Applications with credit scores below 650 might simply be rejected. The computer is consistent and fair using these standards, so no one is treated in a discriminatory way relative to any other applicant.

Federal laws require that each individual be granted a free credit report annually from every one of the big three credit bureaus Experian, Trans Union, and Equifax. This does not mean that anyone is required to hand out free credit scores. In fact there is no such thing as a truly free credit score offer. There are scores provided in exchange for signing up for trial membership services in things like credit monitoring services. In general though, individuals pay for their credit scores from each of the major credit bureaus.

The particulars of a Credit Score are interesting. It is always a three digit formatted number that ranges from 300 to 850. These become created using one of a variety of mathematical algorithms that work off of both the individuals' credit profiles and their credit report's particular information.

This score is crafted with the intention of predicting risk to the lenders, not to benefit the person it covers. It is particularly concerned with the chances of an individual going delinquent on any credit obligations within the next 24 months after the score has been issued.

It is a common misnomer among many individuals that there is only one credit scoring model in the country. There are countless models that exist. It is only the FICO credit score that matters in nearly all cases though. This is because fully 90 percent of financial institutions within the United States rely on FICO credit scores in making their decisions on to whom they will extend credit and at what interest rate.

The higher the FICO score these algorithms generate, the lower the risk is to the various lenders. What makes matters more confusing is that there is not only one FICO credit score in existence for every adult American. Each of the three major bureaus generates its own particular score. Since 2009, consumers are only able to view two of their credit scores, those from both Trans Union and Equifax. This is because Experian chose to terminate its myFICO.com arrangements in 2009. Experian does not share their proprietary credit scores with consumers any longer.

Five different significant categories make up the FICO Credit Score. These are payment history (35 percent of the total component), Amounts owed (30 percent), length of credit history (15 percent), types of credit used (10 percent), and new credit inquiries and accounts opened (10 percent).

Credit Suisse

Credit Suisse is a leading global Swiss-based banking giant whose history stretches back to 1856. Their global reach is supported by operations in more than 50 different countries. This banking group maintains over 48,000 employees who hail from more than 150 different countries around the globe. Their broad international reach allows the bank to create a well-balanced revenue stream geographically and helps them to engage in significant opportunities for growth throughout the globe.

Credit Suisse serves its international clientele in three divisions which are regionally focused. These are the Swiss Universal Bank, the International Wealth Management, and the Asia Pacific divisions. The three principle divisions receive support from Global Markets and Investment Banking & Capital Markets support divisions.

The Swiss Universal Bank focuses on the home country market of Switzerland. Here Credit Suisse delivers a significant variety of financial products and services to corporate, private, and institutional clients residing generally in Switzerland. The Private Banking business here is one of the leading brands in the country.

More than 1.6 million individuals or entities count themselves as customers of this business of the bank. This includes not only regular retail clients, but also affluent and ultra high net worth individuals (HNWI). Included in this division is their Bank-now consumer finance business. This division also provides top of the line service, technology, and platform support for asset managers throughout Switzerland. The bank within Switzerland is comprised of 184 branches and 1,570 relationship managers. Included in this is their affiliate bank Neue Aargauer Bank.

The Swiss Universal Bank division also has the Corporate and Institutional Banking business. It provides best in class services and advice to over 100,000 corporations, businesses, financial institutions, and commodity traders. Included in this business is their Swiss investment banking business. This division comprises 48 different locations and 490 relationship managers.

The second Credit Suisse division is the bank's International Wealth Management. Here they take care of international institutional, corporate, and private clients by offering them expert advice and a wide variety of financial products and services. The Private Banking business helps wealthy individual clients and outside asset managers throughout Europe, Africa, the Middle East, and Latin America.

The bank maintains 46 locations and 1,200 relationship managers. Besides their own products, they also represent a number of third party services and products. The Asset Management business provides investment products and services worldwide to governments, pension funds, endowments, foundations, individuals, and corporations. This business concentrates on both traditional as well as alternative asset allocations and strategies.

The third Credit Suisse division is the group's Asia Pacific group. Here they focus on providing financial services and products to their high net worth and ultra high net worth individual clients, as well as corporate, entrepreneur, and institutional customers. The group offers its clients integrated access and support to the wider financial markets, specific financing solutions, and numerous products.

Within this division, the Private Banking business offers tailored products and services that include digital access to the private banking services. They maintain 13 locations throughout 7 countries and 590 relationship managers within them. The Investment Banking business in this division advises their important clients on merger and acquisition deals, on takeover defense strategies and divestitures. Also on corporate restructuring and sales, and offers debt and equity underwriting services to institutions and individual and business clients.

Besides this, the Investment Banking business covers trading and sales of both equities and fixed income instruments and offers a variety of derivatives, equity and debt securities, and opportunities for financing for its sovereign, corporate, and institutional customers.

Credit Suisse's core strengths remain its leading worldwide reputation and presence as a wealth manger, its impressive market share in home country Switzerland, and its particular skills and abilities in investment banking.

Credit Union

A credit union represents a financial cooperative. Members own these financial institutions. It is these members who both start and run them so that they can reduce costs for financial services and share profits with each other.

There are a variety of sizes of these institutions. A credit union might be a small operation that volunteers run. It could also be a substantial outfit with thousands of members or more. The idea is the same in either case. The business model has members pooling their savings within the credit union so that they can make loans to other members and receive financial benefits. Such benefits include lower interest rates on loans and higher savings rates.

Credit unions are similar to building societies in Britain, Australia, and other countries. Many of the building societies that allow members to invest their money to help members buy or build houses were started in the 1800's. Halifax in the United Kingdom is the largest in the world with 18 million members.

It is easy to become a member of a credit union, especially when individuals are invited. Once they deposit initial funds into the account at the institution, they become part owners of the organization. This allows them to share in the profits that it makes. They also gain the rights to vote for the board of directors of the credit union and in other important decisions.

Many credit unions get started because a large corporation or other organization wants to offer these benefits to their employers or their members. In cases like these, profits can be invested in community services, membership interests, or projects that benefit the members. Credit unions are considered not for profit. This is because they are helping the community or their members out rather than making a profit for the organization itself.

When credit unions began in America, the membership had limitations to those who held a common bond with others in the group. They might have to live in the same town or work in the industry of the other members. Credit unions have since loosened up the rules for becoming a member. Banks have been frustrated by this development that permits many people to participate in a rival organization which does not have to pay taxes.

There are some risks to belonging to this type of organization. If the union is unable to cover its expenses beyond the services, they could possibly fail. Should the organization not possess enough cash flow, it will be unable to run the operations smoothly enough to take care of the members. At this point, it would be closed.

The benefits of belonging to such an organization are significant. The friendliness and feeling of community is greater than from an average bank. The unions also give benefits that a bank will not, like less expensive loans, better rates for credit, and other financial services without fees or with lower costs. Other unions provide the membership with significant advantages like free insurance coverage or reduced cost and free education.

The building societies of Europe predated credit unions in America. The first ones in the U.S. appeared in the 1900s. St. Mary's Bank Credit Union of Manchester, New Hampshire became the first such organization in America. They are now found all over the globe. Some of them in the U.S. now run under the regulations of the Federal government instead of state regulations.

Creditor

Creditors are those financial institutions or individuals who extend credit to a business or other individual. They carry this out by providing financing which they expect will be paid back at a set time in the future. There is another type of creditor as well. This is a company which delivers services or supplies to a person or other business yet does not insist on immediate payment. Since the customer actually does owe the company money for the goods or services provided in advance of payment, that company becomes their creditor de facto.

Within the universe of a creditor there are real and personal categories of them. Finance companies and banks represent real creditor situations. This is because they possess official and legally binding contracts which they sign with the borrower. In this action, they bind assets of the borrower as collateral against the loan in many cases. Typical collateral would be the underlying asset for which the borrower is obtaining credit in the first place. This is often a car, a house, or some other piece of Real Estate. A personal creditor is a family member of friend choosing to loan out money to their loved one or friend.

Real creditors do not loan out money out of the goodness of their hearts. Instead, they intend to earn profits by charging the borrowers interest for these loans. Looking at an example helps to clarify the concept. A creditor might loan out $10,000 to a borrower at a six percent rate of interest. The lending institution will realize earnings in the form of loan interest.

For this accommodation, the creditor is taking on some amount of risk that the borrowing business or individual might potentially default on the loan. This is why the majority of those extending credit will price the interest rate which they charge the borrower based on the business or persons' prior credit history and creditworthiness. It becomes important to borrowers of especially large amounts of money to have high credit quality so that they are able to obtain a more advantageous interest rate and save money on the interest payments.

The rates of interest on mortgages depend heavily on a host of different variables. Some of these are the nature of the lender, the credit history of the borrower, and the amount of the upfront down payment. Still, it is usually the creditworthiness that overwhelmingly determines the final interest rate which becomes applied to a loan such as a mortgage. This is because those borrowers who boast fantastic credit histories and scores come across as low risk for the creditor in question. It is why they enjoy the lowest of interest rates. As lower credit score-carrying borrowers prove to be considerably riskier for the creditors, they manage their risk by requiring a greater rate of interest in compensation.

There are cases where a creditor will not obtain repayment. In such cases, they do have several options. Banks and official real credit issuing entities are allowed to repossess the underlying collateral. This would mean they have the ability to seize either the car or home which secured the loan. Where unsecured debts are concerned, it is more difficult to collect. They might sue the borrower for the unpaid debts in these cases. Courts could choose to issue orders attempting to force the borrower to pay them back. They might do this by seizing assets in their bank accounts or by garnishing their wages with their employers.

Sometimes the borrowers will choose to file for bankruptcy. In these cases, the courts will be the ones to alert the creditor to the situation. There are cases where any non- necessary assets can be liquidated so that debts can be paid back. The order of priority will make unsecured creditors last in the receiving line.

Custodial Account

A Custodial Account refers to a particular type of savings account. These can be accessed via a mutual fund company, financial institution, or brokerage firm. With these accounts, an adult controls and manages the funds or assets on behalf of a minor who is less than 18 years old. State laws govern the rules that affect these special accounts. Minors may not perform transactions in such an account without first obtaining mandatory approval of the custodian. Such an account might also be one of the retirement accounts which a custodian handles for any and all employees in a firm who are eligible to have one of these.

With a Custodial Account, it is typically the guardian or parent of the minor in question who has oversight on the account. Such investments contained in these forms of accounts are limited to mutual funds or similar products that regulated investment companies offer their clients. Every company that administers such a Custodial Account will have its own particular rules on the interest rate levels and account balance minimums they maintain.

What is interesting is that any person is allowed to contribute into a Custodial Account. The minors will not have access to any choices made by the account or money in it without their guardian's consent until they attain the legal age of adult hood. At this point, the ownership of the account transfers over from the custodian(s) and on to the minor. The minor would then gain full decision-making powers over how and when to utilize this money.

Two different kinds of Custodial Accounts exist in the United States. These are the UGMA Uniform Gift to Minors Act administered accounts and the UTMA Uniform Transfers to Minors Act ones. With the UGMA, parents and other are able to provide assets to their minor children in the forms of cash, savings bonds, life insurance, annuities, or stocks. The UTMA permit parents to postpone any distributions from the account. Each state has its own age limits which can be established by the parents or guardians.

There are a number of advantages to these two types of Custodial Accounts. Withdrawal penalties, contribution limits, and income restrictions do not apply to either of them. When a single contribution in excess of

$14,000 goes into the account, this does become treated as a "gift," and the IRS will naturally then levy a gift tax on the total. Custodians also have the ability to transfer the account balance over to a 529 plan. In order to do this, the custodian first will be required to close out any investments inside the account which are not cash.

There are a few disadvantages for the minors to having one of these accounts. The government and university/college systems recognize such accounts as assets. This means that they will often decrease the ability of the minor to obtain financial aid in the college or university admissions process. This is why financial planners will often suggest that such an account should not be opened for any minor who might hope to qualify to receive financial aid packages.

Taxes will also apply to withdrawals from these accounts. Every state has its own ruling on the matter regarding whether they will be taxed at the rate of the minor or the parents' income tax bracket. Some of the unearned income becomes tax free. The rest will become fully taxable at either the child's or guardian's federal tax rate. There will also be capital gains taxes assessed on any earnings from liquidated assets in these Custodial Accounts.

Any gifts presented to such an account can not be rescinded later. The beneficiary of the account also can not be changed subsequently. The parents are required by law to file the child's tax returns when they have such an account until the minor becomes old enough to transfer over the ownership of the account. Once the minor attains the age of 18, then all dividends and earnings within the account will become subject to the minor's applicable tax rate.

Custodian Bank

A custodian bank is a special financial institution that carries the responsibility for protecting the financial assets of individuals or companies. These institutions can also be called simply custodians. Such outfits serve as a third party check that protects the assets they are guarding against the fund managers and any illegal activities they may pursue.

Congress established these custodian banks with the Investment Company Act of 1940 in order to protect investors. Thanks to this particular legislation, investment companies must adhere to specific stringent listing requirements and must be registered with the Securities and Exchange Commission.

The custodian bank performs a number of activities in their primary function of watching over the financial assets of businesses and individuals. They settle sales and purchases of bonds and equities and physically protect the certificates of these assets. These institutions also gather information about and income from such assets. When the assets are stocks this means dividends. When the instruments are bonds, they collect the interest from the coupons. The custodians also disperse information they gather, pertaining to yearly general meetings and shareholder voting. They handle any foreign exchange transfers as necessary and manage all cash transactions. Finally, custodians deliver routine reports on their various activities to the customers.

Custodians banks provide reports on every trade or deal which they transact on behalf of the clients. They must be consistently delivered. Along with these reports they furnish information on the companies whose assets they hold besides information on general meetings. When a custodian is holding foreign shares or bonds, they will also have to change currencies as necessary. This is the case when the fund manager buys or sells foreign currency assets. It is also necessary when companies pay out dividends or bonds receive interest with these overseas financial instruments. Custodian banks are a critical component of the modern investment environment. Without them to carry out these functions, all of the important financial record keeping and housekeeping items would be neglected.

Not all custodian banks are national operations in the United States. A number of the major international financial institutions offer these services around the globe. These are called global custodians. Such international outfits use their own branches in the various countries in which they operate to manage the accounts and assets for their customers. In other cases, they may employ other custodians to assist them with these services. In these types of situations, the customer assets will be held by pension funds.

There are also local custodian banks whose job is to handle the ADR American Depository Receipts. These stock certificates are from foreign based companies that wish to offer their securities to the American stock markets. There are a number of international and large national American banks that participate as these local custodians. Among them are BNP Paribas, PFPC (a subsidiary of PNC Financial Services Group), Brown Brothers Harriman and Company, Kaupthing Bank, Citigroup, Northern Trust, Credit Suisse, RBC Dexia, Societe Generale, State Street Corp., German Bank AG, Goldman Sachs, HSBC, The Bank of New York Mellon, UBS AG, Union Bank of California, JPMorgan Chase Bank, and TD Bank NV.

Debasing the Currency

Debasing the currency refers to the all too common historical process of lowering a currency's actual value. In the past, this phrase commonly came to be associated with commodity money made principally from either silver or gold. Should the sum total of silver, gold, nickel, or copper be reduced, then the physical money is called debased. Even venerable institutions like the Roman Empire, with a thousand year history of growth and stability, have stooped to such debasing of the currency.

Reasons that a government chooses to debase the currency in this way center around the financial benefits that the government is able to reap. These are done at the citizenry's expense though. Governments that lowered the quantity of gold and silver in their coinage found that they could quietly mint more coins from a given fixed quantity of metal on hand.

The downside to this for the general population centers on the inflation that this in turn causes. Such inflation is yet another benefit for the currency debasing government that then finds that it can pay off government debt or repudiate government bonds easier. The populace's purchasing power is significantly reduced as a result of this, along with their then lowered standard of living.

Debasing a currency lowers the value of the currency in question. Given enough time and abuse by the governing authorities, this debasing can even lead to a collapse in the existing currency that causes a newer currency or coinage to be created and launched for the nation or state.

In present day times, debasing the currency is accomplished in more subtle means. Since currencies these days are made of only paper, involving no metal, debasing the currency simply involves printing additional paper dollars. With the advent of electronic banking, even this printing press operation is no longer required. The government simply creates money on a computer screen, literally conjuring it out of thin air.

They are able to accomplish this in one of two ways. One way that they do this is via the Federal Reserve, which buys treasury securities by simply crediting the receivers' bank accounts with electronically created money.

The Federal Reserve then has tangible assets in Treasury bills that is it able to trade or sell when it wishes.

Another way that this creation of money that debases the currency is able to be performed is through the Fractional Reserve Banking System. Since the Federal Reserve only requires banks to keep a ten percent reserve ratio of deposits on hand, these banks when they are credited funds from the Federal Reserve are able to loan this new money out in multiples that are equivalent to the leverage created by this ten percent only reserve ratio. In both of these ways, the Federal Reserve is able to create more money quietly and at will. This is how modern day debasing of the currency is effectively accomplished.

Debit Card

Debit cards are plastic cards that function like a check and are easily utilized like a credit card. Debit cards are commonly one of two types, either branded Visa or Master Card. When you use such a debit card to pay for a purchase, then this amount is deducted immediately from your checking account. Both convenience and security features are included in the use of a debit card.

Debit cards provide tremendous convenience in their ease of use. No longer do you have to make sure that you are carrying enough money on you, or to take the time to write out a physical check while the long line waits impatiently behind you. Besides this ease of use, debit cards are accepted at literally millions of places around the country and the world.

Nowadays, they can be used for almost any purchase, such as lunches or dinners at restaurants, monthly bill payments, merchandise in retail stores, groceries, prescriptions, gas, online purchases, over the phone orders, and even fast food.

Debit cards' spending is easy to keep track of as well. The majority of such transactions are both deducted and posted to a checking account in twenty-four hours or less. This allows for you to conveniently monitor your constantly updated transaction record and balance either over the phone or the bank or card issuer's website. Besides this, debit cards also offer statements, much like credit cards, that outline all purchases made, with details on the name of the merchant, date, location, and amount of transaction.

Debit cards offer another benefit in their security provisions. These cards include free fraud monitoring that helps to find and stop activity that is suspicious with your debit card. They also come with policies of zero liability that protect you from charges that you did not make or authorize. Fraudulently taken out funds are guaranteed to be returned to your account. The vast majority of debit cards also come with the security feature of three digit security codes that allow you to confirm your identity for both phone and Internet orders and purchases.

Debit cards allow two ways for completing in person transactions. One of these is through swiping the card and then signing the receipt issued by the merchant representative. The other is via using a pad with your PIN, or personal identification code, after the card is swiped.

A final benefit that you gain from a debit card is that most of them provide rewards that are earned simply by utilizing them. These are earned in one of two ways. With Visa Debit cards, you are able to receive discounts from some merchants who provide these special price breaks for the holders of Visa cards.

Other debit cards provide extras rewards programs. These rewards programs pay you back with some type of reward for every purchase that you make. These can be cash rebates or more commonly awards that are earned through the collection of such points.

Debt Coverage Ratio (DCR)

Debt coverage ratio has different meanings dependent on what entity is using it. In the world of corporate finance, it is the amount of cash flow that a company has to service its current debts. This ratio utilizes the net operating income divided by the debt payments due in a year or less. This includes principal, interest, lease payments, and the sinking fund.

It has a different meaning with governments and individuals. For finances of a national government, debt coverage ratio refers to the export earnings required for the country to make its yearly principal and interest payments with the external debts of the nation. With individual finance, banks and their loan officers utilize this ratio to decide on income property loans.

Debt coverage ratios must be higher than one in order for the government, company, or individual to prove enough income to satisfy its present debt obligations. With a DCR under 1, it lacks the means to do so. This ratio is determined by dividing Net Operating Income by the Total Debt Service.

The net operating income turns out to be the revenue of a company less its operating expenses. This does not cover interest payments or taxes. The NOI can also equate to the EBIT Earnings Before Interest and Tax. Investors and lenders which are evaluating the creditworthiness of corporations and companies should use criteria that is consistent when they figure out the DCR.

Total debt service is the term that concerns the present debt obligations. This will include principal, interest, lease payments, and sinking fund all owed in the next year. Balance sheets also include both the long term debt current portion and the short term debt.

When a debt coverage ratio is lower than one, it says that the entity cash flow is negative. With a DCR of .90, the company would only possess sufficient NOI to handle 90% of their yearly debt payments. With personal finance this would mean that the borrower had to access some outside funds each month in order to cover the payments. Lenders usually discourage loans with negative cash flow. They may permit them when the borrower can show a strong outside income.

Lenders almost always consider the debt coverage ratio of borrowers before they extend loans to them. They do not want to loan money to entities with lower than one. Such groups will have to draw on sources outside of their traditional income or borrow more in order to make their debt payments. When the DCR is dangerously close to one, then the borrower is considered to be vulnerable to a slowdown in income. Only a minor setback to its cash flow would mean it would not be able to service the debts. Some lenders will actually insist that the borrowers keep minimum levels of debt coverage ratios while they have a loan balance. In these cases, borrowers whose ratios decline below this minimum level are in technical default.

Lenders can be more lenient on debt coverage ratios when the economy is booming. An expanding economy means that credit is available more easily. This often causes lenders to work with companies and individuals on their lower ratios. The problem is that borrowers which are under qualified can impact the stability of the economy.

In the 2008 financial crisis, subprime borrowers received credit in the form of mortgages without proper consideration of their finances. As such borrowers defaulted in large numbers, the lenders that had made loans to them failed. The largest savings and loan institution Washington Mutual turned out to be the most egregious example of this scenario.

Debt Deflation

Debt Deflation refers to the scenario where the loan collateral (or any other type of debt) sees a decrease in value. This is generally a negative end result. It often causes the loan issuer to insist on a restructure of the loan agreement. In other cases, they may be able to demand that the loan itself be completely restructured. Other phrases that describe this concept are collateral deflation and worst deflation.

Mortgages are a great example of this to consider. They are a traditional type of secured debt. If an individual takes out a mortgage to buy a house with, then the house itself proves to be the securing underlying collateral on this mortgage loan. This means that if the buyer later subsequently defaults on the payments which he or she make to the bank each month, then the bank would begin the tedious process to repossesses the house. A problem arises when the value of the house diminishes in value at the same time that the buyer is still caught up in the process of making the payments owed to the bank. This would create a potentially devastating debt deflation downward spiral and uncomfortable situation. In severe cases, this can be enough to cause a home owner to completely despair and simply walk away from the house and its associated mortgage come what may.

This actually happened back in the Subprime Mortgage Meltdown, Great Recession, and Global Financial Crisis of 2007-2009. So many homes had been purchased in the boom period of the early 2000's that when prices began to plunge on a breath taking national and regional scale, many buyers found themselves severely underwater on their mortgage loan collateral. The houses in many cases became worth significantly less than the principal balance on the loan which purchased them. Defaults went through the proverbial roof as many buyers realized that they had no realistic hope of seeing the value of the house rise back up.

It helps to look at an example of the despair this subprime mortgage crisis meltdown caused countless Americans, many of whom had been irresponsible, it is true. If a person had purchased a $300,000 priced house with a mortgage for $270,000 before 2006 peak pricing in the national housing market, then he or she might have sat helplessly by as the value of this same house subsequently plummeted by even 25 percent. It would meant that the $300,000 dream home was then only worth $225,000. Now in order for the house to again be worth just what the buyer owed on it, it would have to rise back up to the $270,000 mortgage total balance amount. This meant that the value had to increase by $45,000, or a staggering 20 percent, just to get back to even on the mortgage balance amount owed. In order for the house to be worth the actual $300,000 the buyer had originally paid out, it would have to rise by an even steeper $75,000, representing a whopping 33.3 percent. This would take years once the market actually bottomed out, itself a hopeless-looking procedure that require literally years before rock bottom was finally hit.

Nationally, home values that began to crash and burn in 2007 did not start to slowly crawl back up until 2011 to 2012, four to five long years later. A decade after the original crash period began many of the homes that lost 25 percent (or even far more in many cases and in overinflated-valued regions around the country) have still not recovered or just barely recovered.

It helps to explain why so many people quickly despaired and chose to default on their mortgages and to simply give the house back to the bank lender and then to walk away free and clear. Ironically in many cases, their shattered credit history and associated credit rating would actually recover faster than the value of their severely underwater home and mortgage finally did.

Debt Service

Debt service refers to the cash that is necessary to be paid over a certain period of time in order to repay both principal and interest on a given debt. For individuals, monthly mortgage payments, or credit card bill payments, prove to be good examples of personal debt service. For businesses, payments on lines of credit, business loans, or coupon payments of bonds represent samples of corporate debt service.

Where businesses or personal debt service is concerned, this is used to calculate the DSCR, or debt service coverage ratio. This ratio is that of the cash that is on hand for servicing the debt's principal, interest, and lease payments. This measurement is a much utilized benchmark that helps to determine a company or an individual's capability of generating sufficient money to cover the payments on their debt. With a higher debt service coverage ratio, loans are easier to get for both companies and people.

The commercial banking industry also employs this phrase. Here, it can refer to the minimally acceptable ratio that a given lender will accept. This might turn out to be a condition of making the entity such a loan in the end. When this type of a condition is part of the loan covenant, then violating the debt service coverage ratio can sometimes be considered an action of default.

Debt service coverage ratios are similarly used in the world of corporate finance. Here, they describe the sum of available cash flow that is usable for covering yearly principal and interest payments on any and all debts. This includes payments for sinking funds.

Commercial real estate finance similarly utilizes debt service and debt service coverage ratios as the main means of discovering if a given property is capable of maintaining its level of debt using only its own cash flow. In the past ten or so years, banks would look for a minimum debt service coverage ratio of minimally 1.2. Banks that proved to be more aggressive were willing to work with lower ratios.

This practice led to greater risk in the system that helped to bring on the financial meltdown and resulting crisis that stretched from 2007 to 2010.

When an entity has more than a ratio of one debt service coverage ratio, it is theoretically capable of covering its debt requirements with cash flow. Similarly, if this ratio is less than one, then the statistics claim that an insufficient amount of cash flow exists to meet the required loan payments.

Deficit Financing

Deficit Financing refers to a particular emphasis in money management. In this unique angle on financing, companies or governments happily spend a greater amount of money than they take in over the comparable period. This is also called a budget deficit strategy. In fact governments on most levels, small businesses to corporations, and individuals with their household budgets all attempt to engage in this form of financing whenever they can. If it is used carefully and constructively, such a means of financing can create conditions which improve the financial condition of the entity along with the creation of debt that comes alongside it. Such debt might or might not ever be repaid.

Governments take the lead role in such Deficit Financing. Among the more commonplace examples of this is attempting to stimulate the national economy to end recessions. To do this, governments will borrow resources and use the funds to purchase things. This will directly boost the demand for output from businesses sectors, who will in turn hire workers to keep pace with growing government demand. It lowers unemployment and provides salaries to employees who will also increase their spending apace.

This creates a money multiplier effect within the economy. As the marketplace strengthens, consumer confidence will also typically rise, helping still other consumers to save less out of fear and purchase more out of increasing optimism about economic prospects. This leads to a greater quantity of goods and services being purchased by the consumer sector. When properly followed, such a deficit spending plan will actually increase the economic prosperity of a given national economy throughout a period from several months to even a few years in length.

Deficit Financing in the science of economics is not merely restricted to the government though. All sizes and types of businesses may attempt to spend more money than they can practically afford upfront in an effort to generate plenty of funds down the road to pay back the investment when it comes due.

Consider a concrete example. A manufacturing company might elect to buy new factory plants or machinery. They realize that the updated equipment and greater production line space will allow them to produce more goods in a shorter time frame and at a more advantageous cost per unit produced. Given enough time, such advantages of using the strategy will allow them to pay down the upfront debt and maintain a surplus to corporate cash flow and retained earnings.

Consumers similarly attempt to do this with their money management tools. Deficit financing for them means that the individuals will buy things now to improve their house in an effort to boost the value of their real estate. The debt would be then paid back and the owner would keep the higher fair market value home. When the homeowner sells the house, he or she will realize a greater price than before the improvements were made using the Deficit Financing. In the meanwhile, the occupants of the home have the pleasure of enjoying the upgraded facilities, appliances, and amenities that have improved the home value over the long run.

Economic theory and development has held with the idea of Deficit Financing for a long time now. John Maynard Keynes is credited with coming up with the full articulation of the idea in economics. Many economists since him have appreciated the strategy, its advantages, and the dangers if it is not carefully orchestrated. Deficit financing and spending is not necessarily the best means of righting a poor and deteriorating financial situation for an economy, business balance sheet, or household budget. Yet responsibly deploying it may boost the financial status of the country, business, and quality of life of the individuals involved.

Denomination

Denomination refers to a means of classifying the face value for financial instruments. This would involve currency coins and bank notes along with bonds and other kinds of fixed income investments. It can also refer to base currencies for which financial assets will be quoted in ultimately. Governments and companies find it useful to classify the types of acceptable forms of payments which can be used to complete a given transaction.

Such denominations represent the units of value which will most typically be assigned to represent a literal currency. This will include notes and coins used as currency, along with financial instruments that have preset values, like with bonds issued by sovereign governments. Such a value will commonly be referred to by its face value. This value is clearly denoted on the face (front side) of the financial instrument in question.

This becomes important where ATM automated teller machines are concerned. Those currency notes that ATMs dispense to customers will only come out in a set type of denomination. This could be $20s, $50s, and $100 bills. Where trade is concerned, European-based exporters could invoice their customers in American dollars. The transaction would then end up being a United States' dollar denominated transaction. The majority of commodities like gold and diamonds are quoted in dollars still. Yet by 2011, other commodities like crude oil could also be quoted in a rival reserve currency like the euro, the pound, the Japanese Yen, or even the Chinese Yuan.

Bonds also come with face value denominations. These represent the value of the bond which will be paid back on maturity date. Investors can buy bonds in a range of denominations. The issuers will sell these bonds for lower than the face value. It is this difference from maturity value to sales price that serves as the total interest which would be earned on the investment by the purchaser or holder of the bond on maturity date.

Where stocks are concerned, stocks also have a par value and a denomination. Yet this value is commonly vastly different from the securities' actual market value as determined by supply and demand on the stock market exchanges. Par values in fact refer to minimum values for the given security. The majority of stock issuers choose to set out a one cent par value per share in order to make sure that they do not end up guaranteeing a stock value which is higher than the actual market value.

Collectible currencies also carry denominations. These would often boast higher retail market values than their face value. It is always useful to consider a clear cut example of a difficult concept. American quarters which the mints struck from the years of 1932 to 1964 held 90 percent silver content. The face value was a mere tepid 25 cents. Yet the market value for such coins based on their generous silver content is significantly higher both when they were issued and still to this day.

This is because this melt value also enjoys a complimentary rarity and collectible value alongside it. Because the difference in the values between the denomination and the melt values were so high, the U.S. Mint finally accepted the recommendation to alter the materials which comprised these quarters to a far cheaper nickel-copper alloy starting in 1965.

The United States currency is presently denominated in a range of dollar amounts. These include the $100, $50, $20, $10, $5, $2, and $1 bills. As of 2017, the Federal Reserve System and Department of the Treasury have no intentions to alter the denominations which have been in use since at least the end of the Second World War.

Depository Bank

A Depository Bank refers to a facility like an office, building, or even warehouse that acts as a depository for safeguarding and storage purposes. This might be a bank, a vault, an organization, or even a financial institution which inventories and helps with the act of trading securities. The term also pertains to any depository institution which takes in financial deposits from their clients.

These depository institutions deliver financial services to both business and personal customers. These do not have to be cash-based only. They could be stocks and bonds certificates. The institution will inventory the securities. They often keep them in an electronic format called book-entry form. They might also hold physical paper certificates or dematerialized virtually-based certificates as well.

Depository banks carry the primary function in this regard of transferring stock shares ownership from the seller of an investment to the buyer as the trade becomes executed. They also assist with reducing paperwork needed to execute trades. They also increase the speed at which the transfer process will be completed. These depositories also get rid of any risk in maintaining physical format securities and keeping them from loss, theft, damage, fraud, or delay in actual delivery.

There are other depository services these institutions carry out for their clients. These include savings and checking accounts and also transferring funds electronically via debit cards and online banking. They also handle electronically submitted payments as part of these services. Customers surrender their cash to these banks and financial institutions under the core belief that the firm will simply hold on to them and then return them as the customer requests the money back upon demand.
In reality, the banks cheerfully take the clients' money and then pay them interest on this money slowly over time. As they hold the customers' money, they loan it out to other businesses and individuals as business loans and mortgages. They do this with the goal and hope of generating a higher amount of interest on the money than the amount which they pay out to their customers as interest.

In the field of depository institutions are three different types. These are commercial banks, savings institutions, and credit unions. All of them count on deposits from their clients in order to obtain their primary sources of funding. The Federal Deposit Insurance Corporation insures these consumer accounts up to a limit of $250,000 per account in case of bank failure.

Commercial banks prove to be for profit enterprises that represent the biggest of the depository institutions. These often times mega-banks provide a vast array of services to businesses and consumers in the form of commercial and consumer lending, checking and savings accounts, certificates of deposit, investment products, and credit cards. Their goals in accepting inbound deposits are to offer them back out to still other clients in the form of real estate loans, commercial loans, and mortgage loans.

With savings institutions, these are also for profit ventures called savings and loan institutions. They concentrate their efforts mostly on consumer mortgage lending although they do also provide commercial loans and consumer credit cards. The customers deposit their money in an account. This purchases shares within the firm. In one fiscal year, savings institutions might approve 710 real estate loans, 250,000 personal and automobile loans, and 75,000 mortgage loans. They then collect interest on all of these various loans, a portion of which pays the interest on their clients' deposits.

Credit Unions are quite different from the above two previous types. They are not for profit groups which instead concentrate their efforts on customer service. The customers bring in their deposits to the account. This is much like purchasing shares within the credit union in question. The earnings of the credit union become distributed back to the customers as dividends on a regular basis.

Deutsche Bank

Deutsche Bank is the leading German bank in the world. It commands a substantial market share in Germany, a strong place in European banking, and an important presence in both the Asia Pacific and Americas regions.

The group has grown from its founding in Berlin, Germany in 1870 to encompass strong operating bases in all of the major developed and emerging markets. This gives them a solid prospect for business expansion in the world's rapidly growing markets, comprising Lain America, Central and Eastern Europe, and the Asia Pacific regions. Their important position in Europe provides the bank with a solid foundation from which to benefit not only from the resilient economic conditions in native market Germany, but also from rebounding strong corporate activity levels throughout the euro zone.

From Deutsche Bank's first international foray into Asia in 1872 on, the bank has always looked abroad for opportunities to expand. This has carried it into more than 70 nations around the world today. Of its 2,790 total branches, 1,827 are located in Germany and another 963 are found in other countries and markets beyond the bank's home base. With the ongoing theme of continuous globalization in the international economy dominating, this puts the banking group in a strong position. It has more than adequate diversification throughout different regions of the world and significant revenue streams coming in from all the major areas around the globe.

Deutsche Bank offers practical banking solutions and services to private individuals, medium and small businesses, corporations, institutional investors, and governments. They operate a number of businesses specifically focused on the needs of these client bases.

The Corporate Finance Business group takes responsibility for M&A merger and acquisition activities. This includes equity and debt issues, advisory services, and coverage of capital markets for medium to large corporations. They deliver this complete range of financial services and products to the business clients via industry- and regional- specific teams. A subdivision of this is the CIB Corporate & Investment Banking business. It combines the expertise of Deutsche Bank's corporate finance, commercial banking, and transaction banking under the direction of a single unified leadership team. It is made up of both the Corporate Finance and Global Transaction Banking businesses.

The Deutsche Bank Private & Business Clients Corporate business offers in branch financial and banking services to self employed entrepreneurs, private clients, and medium to small businesses on an international scale.

The bank's Wealth Management business provides high quality and extremely personalized services to the ultra high and high net worth families and individuals along with certain institutions. These particular clients receive a complete package of wealth management services, philanthropic activity advisory services, and inheritance planning advice.

The Asset Management business at Deutsche Bank delivers investment and mutual fund services and products to its retail clients around the world. The bank brands this franchise as the DWS Investments group. It also provides institutional clients of the bank like insurance companies and pension funds with a wide variety of services and products that range from traditional to alternative investments. Among these products and services are the DWS Funds, Deutsch Insurance Asset Management, DB Advisors Institutional Asset Management, and RREEF Real Estate Investment Management.

Deutsche Bank also operates a large and important Asia Pacific division of the bank. The company's history in Asia traces back to the first branches they opened in Shanghai, China and Yokohama, Japan which it founded in 1872. Nowadays the operation is quite a bit larger. The group maintains office presences in 16 national markets and employs 16,000 staff in Asia Pacific. The bank's Asia Pacific division headquarters are located in Singapore.

Dodd-Frank Act

The Dodd-Frank Act is fully entitled the Dodd-Frank Wall Street Reform and Consumer Protection Act. This enormous law served to reform the financial world following the financial crisis and Great Recession that began in 2008. President Obama's administration passed it through congress in 2010.

This Dodd-Frank Act legislation is literally thousands of pages long and contains numerous provisions. The regulations of this Dodd-Frank Act law are set for implementation over the course of a number of years. They were meant to reduce the obvious risks for failure in the American financial system. In order to oversee and carry out the numerous parts of the act it addresses, the controversial legislation created a range of new government agencies.

The first of these new agencies is the Financial Stability Oversight Council and Orderly Liquidation Authority. This group is tasked with overseeing major financial firms whose continued financial stability is necessary for the proper and continuous functioning of the U.S. economy.

These companies were negatively referred to as "too big to fail." The agency also handles necessary restructurings or liquidations of such firms in an orderly fashion should they become too unstable. They are charged with preventing these firms from being propped up with tax dollars. This council has great authority. They can even break apart banks which they deem in their judgment to be so big that they pose a risk to the banking system. It may also order higher reserve requirements for such banks. Another new group the Federal Insurance Office is similarly tasked with identifying and overseeing insurance companies which are too important to fail.

The CFPB Consumer Financial Protection Bureau was created to stop predatory forms of mortgage lending by the lenders. They are also responsible for increasing the simplicity of mortgage terms so that consumers can understand what they are signing before they complete the contracts. The group stops mortgage brokers from obtaining larger commissions when they close loans that have higher interest rates and fees.

It states that originators of mortgages may not direct possible borrowers to loans which provide the largest payouts to the loan originators. This group also governs various other kinds of lending to consumers. Their domain includes debt and credit cards and consumer complaints. They insist that lenders provide information in a manner that is simplest for consumers to comprehend. Credit card application simplified terms are an example of their work.

One potent rule that emerged from this Dodd-Frank Act legislation proved to be the so-called Volcker Rule. Named for the former Federal Reserve Chairman Paul Volcker, the rule was intended to reduce the amount of speculative trading, while simultaneously banning proprietary trading, by banking institutions. Banks have complained that these changes in the business model will make it more difficult to stay profitable.

The rule addresses regulating the derivatives like the infamous credit default swaps that majorly contributed to the financial meltdown in 2008. This rule also limits the ability of financial companies to utilize derivatives. The goal is to stop the systemically critical institutions from building up enormous risks that could ruin the banking system and overall economy.

The Dodd-Frank Act further created the new SEC Office of Credit Ratings. This group received the job of watching the credit agencies to ensure that the credit ratings they provide for various entities prove to be both dependable and reliable. Credit rating companies received a lot of blame for the financial crisis for falsely dispensing investment ratings that were misleading and overly positive.

Critics of the Dodd-Frank Act legislation claim the law will hamper economic growth and lead to higher unemployment in the future. Fans of the act insist that over time it will reduce the chances of the economy suffering from another 2008 styled crisis all the while safeguarding consumers from the abuses that eventually led to the crisis.

Electronic Funds Transfer (EFT)

EFT is the usual acronym for Electronic Funds Transfer. This program refers to the all-electronic money transfer processed out of one bank account and into another. This could be done within a single bank or over a number of different and often intermediary financial institutions. Computer systems handle these transactions entirely unaided by the intervention of human bank personnel. There are actually many different names for EFTs. Within the United States, they are often called e-checks or even electronic checks.

The phrase relates to a wide range of varying payment systems. Some of these are bank debit card or other credit card payments which a cardholding customer initiates voluntarily at a store or merchant, direct debit payments in which the firm directly debits the bank account of the consuming customers in payment for their services or goods, and payer initiated direct deposit. Other examples of this EFTs include wire transfers done utilizing the SWIFT banking international network, private currency transactions that deal with electronic money storage, and online banking electronic bill pay services that are often delivered via Electronic Funds Transfer or alternatively by using paper based checks.

Government agencies within the United States have also taken to utilizing Electronic Funds Transfers in recent years. The federal government touts them as an efficient and often practical means of collecting money and similarly paying it out electronically without having to engage in the time consuming and wasteful process of resorting to relying on paper based checks, purchasing and obtaining stamps, and generally considerable processing and mailing time lags. They encourage government agencies to adopt this payment technology if they have not already.

As the Federal Government has recently noted, EFT payments are secure, safe, and efficient. They are also less costly to utilize than any form of paper check collection or payment process. As a clear and concrete example, it helps to consider a real world case. The federal government calculates that it requires a full $1.03 in order to make a payment via a check. This represents over a dollar for a single payment transaction. Naturally this cost adds up considerably when agencies are engaging in millions of individual payments per month. Compare these costs with the government expenses for running payments via electronic formats. Every time the government enters and initiates an electronic funds transfer, it only pays the equivalent of .105 dollars (or slightly more than a single dime) per individual transaction.

In order to participate in either the government's version of EFT or any bank's version of electronic funds transfer, individuals must first sign up for the payment platform. Nowadays, all federal benefits have been switched over to and must be paid out electronically, which makes this more critical and timely to do now than ever before. For any person who receives any kind of these benefits, including SSI Supplemental Security Income, Social Security payments, civil service retirement payments, Veteran's benefits, railroad retirement payments, or military federal retirement, all benefits must be received by electronic funds transfer in order to be processed and paid out each month.

There are still other benefits which both the federal government and other private parties pay utilizing Electronic Funds Transfers. The Federal government calls its various benefit payment programs either Direct Express or Go Direct. Private parties and banks utilize a range of different labels and names for these various privately run programs.

Equity of Redemption

Equity of redemption refers to a property owner's legal rights. This term represents the right of a home owner to reclaim his or her property which a mortgage loan secures. Such a right pertains to the period before the bank or lender has foreclosed on the home when the home owner is in default on the mortgage payments that include principle and interest.

As a home owner gets behind on his or her monthly mortgage payments, the lender has the right to accelerate the loan. They will generally not do this until they have attempted to work with the owner to help them get caught up on the mortgage. It is everyone's best interest for the home owner to remain in the home. Banks often lose money on houses which they sell through foreclosure.

Accelerating the loan means that the bank demands payment in full. It is still possible that the lender may be willing to let the behind home owner catch up on the mortgage payments which are in arrears at this point. Otherwise, if the owner does not meet this demand or make full payment, then foreclosure on the property begins in earnest.

In order to meet this order for full payment, home owners are permitted to find an alternative source of funds to pay off the original mortgage principle, interest, and late fees. If they are able to secure such a funding source, then the equity of redemption gives them the rights to keep the house. The problem for most home owners is that if they are in financial trouble and can not pay their mortgage, then they probably will be unable to secure another loan with which to pay off the first one.

This equity of redemption right only lasts until the home has been foreclosed upon and sold. The equity of redemption is also considered to be a valuable interest in the property and a legal estate in and of itself. This means that the home owner can sell or even transfer away this right to another individual or a company.

Equity of redemption should never be mixed up with the statutory right of redemption. The right of redemption is a separate legal right that is not universal throughout the United States. Some of the states allow for this separate right of redemption which gives home owners significantly greater maneuvering room and legal avenues.

In fact a right of redemption means that for an amount of time determined by state law, the owner is able to redeem his or her house and property simply by paying all principle, interest, costs, and fees. This right is for the period after foreclosure or seizure for unpaid taxes has already occurred. By paying the amounts demanded, the right of redemption means that the owner is able to reclaim his or her home, even if it has already been sold.

How long the statutory right of redemption period lasts depends on the state in question. This amount of time could be for several months. In other states and scenarios, it could stretch on for several years after the foreclosure has been completed. Investors who buy houses in states with this legal right must be aware of the repercussions.

Those who buy seized or foreclosed upon houses could run into a situation where the original owner comes up with the money to pay off the entire original obligation on the house. In this case, the original owner would receive back his or her home. The investor would be left to work out compensation for the lost property with the lender from whom they had purchased it.

European Central Bank (ECB)

The European Central Bank is responsible for the European Union's monetary system and for maintaining the euro currency. The EU created this central bank of European central banks in June of 1998. It works alongside the various national banks of the EU member states to come up with unified monetary policy. This policy is intended to help achieve price stability throughout the countries in the EU.

The ECB became responsible for the EU's monetary police on January 1 of 1999. This was the point in time when the euro currency became adopted by the various EU nations. This landmark event was the culmination of 20 years of steps towards a currency union.

In 1979, eight of the EU nations created the EMS European Monetary System. It effectively fixed the exchange rates between the eight participating nations. By 2002, the ECB had become more entrenched. Twelve EU nations signed on to a common monetary policy and formed the European Economic and Monetary Union that year.

The European Central Bank is independent of political groups in the various institutions of the EU such as the European Commission, European Parliament, and European Council. It handles all EU monetary issues and policies. Maintaining price stability is the first goal of the central bank. It also sets the important interest rates for the Eurozone and area.

Besides creating monetary policy for the Eurozone block, the ECB also engages in foreign exchange, holds reserve currencies, and authorizes euro bank note issues. Euro currency is actually created, printed, and maintained by the European System of Central Banks, also known as the ESCB.

The ECB has become involved in some controversial activities which were beyond the scope of its original role. It has further expanded its mandate in recent years by buying up bonds of financial companies like banks and also sovereign countries whose bonds are not finding enough interested subscribers at competitive low rates.

They have been practicing this quantitative easing and injecting money into euro area economies in an effort to encourage growth and to increase financial liquidity in the banking system. Keeping the interest rates down on sovereign national bonds also improves the budgets and balance sheets of the euro area countries which are struggling. The result of these activities has led to negative real interest rates in Europe.

Individual EU countries collect their own taxes. They also determine their own national budgets. The ECB has nothing to do with these activities. National governments work together at the EU level to come up with uniform rules on public finances. This helps them to cooperate better on policies for employment, growth, and financial stability.

The financial crisis that broke out around the globe in 2008 hit some European countries especially hard. It created a need for the ECB to work closely with the European Commission and the national governments of the EU and Eurozone members in a series of coordinated, sustained actions.

These groups are continuing to strive together to promote employment and growth, keep credit flowing to consumers and businesses at affordable prices, safeguard savings, and to guarantee inter-European financial stability. This has led to the accusation of critics of the European institutions that they only work effective when there are crises, as in a management by crisis style.

Despite these ongoing and best efforts of the ECB and other European institutions, severe imbalances and problems remain in several Eurozone countries. As of 2016, unemployment in Spain still sat at over 25% and Greece teetered on the brink of yet another recession and potential insolvency.

European Debt Crisis

The European Debt Crisis refers to the ongoing European sovereign government struggle to repay various national debts the countries ran up over the past several decades. There were five of the peripheral EU states in particular that were unable to create sufficient economic growth in order to make possible their repaying of the national bondholders as they promised to originally.

These countries included especially Greece, Portugal, and Ireland, but also enmeshed were Spain and Italy to one degree or another. Though only these five nations showed signs of potential default during the crisis peak in the years 2010 to 2011, the crisis had broad and dangerous consequences that impacted not only the rest of the European Union, but also the world in general. The governor of the Bank of England called this the "most serious financial crisis at least since the 1930s, if not ever," back in October of 2011.

The European Debt Crisis did not suddenly appear overnight, but was years and even decades in the making. Slower growth from the time of the American based financial crisis and Great Recession from 2007 to 2009 demonstrated that many spending policies in Europe and the world at large were truly unsustainable any more. Greece became the poster child for the effects of reckless overspending in the following years. The Greeks had spent with great largesse for seemingly endless years and avoided painful but urgently needed financial and fiscal reforms. They were the first to feel the negative effects of weaker ongoing growth as it so happened.

As growth slows down, tax revenues also decrease apace. This means that greater budget deficits become impossible to sustain. The Greeks had been hiding the amounts of their large and increasing national deficits for years, but by the end of 2009, it was no longer possible to keep them from world markets and the enraged Greek populace any longer. The Greek debts had become so vast that they substantially exceeded the entire economy of the smaller nation.

Investors in their sovereign debt naturally retaliated by insisting on larger yields on their Greek national bonds. The unfortunate side effect of this action was that the interest payments on the Greek debt also skyrocketed, causing their debt burden to become so onerous that they could not manage it any longer. The EU and European Central Bank had to come riding to the rescue of the Greek government and economy in consequence. This did not stop investors and markets from pushing up the yields of bonds in other similarly indebted nations throughout Europe, where they expected similar crises and potential collapse as had already tragically occurred in Greece.

The vicious cycle of higher demand yields leading to greater borrowing costs for the nations in crisis led to greater fiscal strain which caused investors to require still higher interest yields on the troubled European sovereign bonds. This gradual erosion of investor confidence did not stay focused on Greece, but impacted the other shaky economies of Portugal, Ireland, Cyprus, Spain, and even G7 trillion-plus dollar economy Italy. This became known as financial crisis contagion. Portugal, Ireland, Cyprus, and Spain were forced to seek out bailouts either for their embattled sovereign government finances, their national primary banks, or in the cases of Portugal and Ireland, both.

The problems were exacerbated by the fact that the European Union moved so slowly to address the severe problems. This is because their actions required the approval of all 28 countries in the economic and political union. Bailouts were offered to the troubled governments via the European Stabilization Mechanism or ESM. The European Central Bank acted in a substitute capacity by cutting interest rates and providing unlimited loans to European national banks which were in trouble in exchange for assets (which were highly questionable at best) as collateral.

The problems of the European Debt Crisis are far from over fully five long years later. Italy's banks have not yet addressed their over $360 billion in bad loans to this day. Their third largest and oldest bank Monte Dei Paschi Di Sienna has 28 billion Euros in bad debts it has been trying unsuccessfully to offload as it sought out 5 billion Euros in fresh capital from skeptical investors. Greece is on its third consecutive bailout program from the EU so far in only five years. Portugal, Ireland, and Cyprus have all emerged successfully from their bailout and bank recapitalization programs, while Spain is on the right track and making measurable and material progress in escaping from theirs.

European Investment Bank (EIB)

The European Investment Bank proves to be the bank of the European Union. As such it is the one and only bank which is both representing the EU member states' interests and also owned by the same member countries. This EIB works hand in glove with the other institutions of the European Union in order to carry out the common EU policies.

This European Investment Bank turns out to be the biggest multilateral lender and borrower on the planet. It delivers finance via loans and joint ventures as well as expertise to support projects of sustainable investments. While over 90 percent of the bank's projects remain in Europe, they are still a substantially large investor throughout the globe.

The European Investment Bank betters the quality of life for individuals within and without the continent of Europe by offering expertise and finance on projects which encourage SME's (small to medium enterprises), infrastructure, innovation, and climate action. Their enormous and far flung enterprises in areas of lending, blending, and advisory services work for the good of EU residents and citizens, along with residents of numerous countries which are not a part of the European Union.

Lending is the overwhelming center of activity for the European Investment Bank. By far the greatest share of the bank's financing occurs via loans. They do also provide microfinance, guarantees, and equity investment, among other types of financing. The bank is able to harness their vast financial resources in order to borrow money on the world markets at extremely competitive rates. They then deliver these cost savings to those projects which they deem to be economically practical and which foster the objectives of EU policy.

Lending accounts for nearly 90 percent of all their financial commitments. The European Investment Bank actually lends money to clients of all sizes and purposes in order to encourage jobs and sustainable growth. The support of this well-regarded institution tends to attract other investors to the projects. Such projects must be over 25 million Euros in order to qualify for a loan. They also facilitate intermediated loans through local area banks.

With their venture capital program, they assist fund managers to invest capital in growth area SME's and high technology companies. Microfinance they offer for both fund and equity investments as well.

Blending is the tool whereby the European Investment Bank helps to release funding from other financial sources by collaborating on a project. This support especially comes out of the EU budget. When blended along with loans, it helps to ensure a fully financed package of investment in a given project.

The EIB offers structured finance to give support to high priority projects. Guarantees ensure that a good project will be able to bring in sufficient new investment from other partners. Project bonds help to unlock funding for infrastructure projects. The InnovFin initiative delivers innovators EU based finance. The bank also partners with donors in trust funds. They support transport infrastructure and the JEREMIE project which delivers financial engineering and flexible finance to SME enterprises.

Other blending programs include ESIF Financial Instruments, the JESSICA program which supports urban development, the Private Finance for Energy Efficiency (PF4EE) program, and the Mutual Reliance Initiative offering efficient partnerships for development and growth.
Blending programs also include the Natural Capital Financing Facility to combine the bank's financing with that of the European Commission as part of the LIFE Program to assist climate and environmental actions. An interesting last blending program proves to be the Risk Capital Facility for the Southern Neighborhood. This gives access to debt and equity financing for SMEs found throughout the Mediterranean regions. Its goal is to foster growth which is inclusive, job creation in the private sector, and development in the private sector.

Advising services provide technical assistance and expertise in the form of project and administrative management capabilities. This helps to bring in other investment. Both pubic authorities and private companies are able to rely on the technical and financial experience of the European Investment Advisory Hub to make sure the entity obtains the best people needed for a given project.

European Monetary System (EMS)

In 1979 a few European nations linked their currencies together in an arrangement and system to stabilize exchange rates called the European Monetary System. This system endured until the EMU European Economic and Monetary Union succeeded it.

As an important institution within the European Union, the EMU established the euro. The origin of the EMS lay in an effort to reduce significant changes in exchange rates between the European nations and to reign in inflation. It led to the creation of the European Central Bank in June of 1998 and the euro in January of 1999.

After the failure of the defunct Bretton Woods Agreement in 1972, the Europeans wanted to create a new exchange rate system of their own to help encourage political and economic unity throughout the EU. They came up with the EMS in 1979 as a means of moving towards the common currency of the future.

The EMS eventually formed its successor the European Currency Unit. With the ECU, exchange rates could be formulated by methods that were official. In the first year of the EMS, currency values proved to be uneven. Adjustments had to be made to lower weaker currencies while increasing the stronger currency values. In 1986 they came up with a more stable system of altering national interest rates instead.

Crisis broke out in the EMS in the early years of the 1990s. Germany's reunification created political and economic conditions that made the exchange rate bands less workable. Britain withdrew permanently from EMS in 1992. They became more independent from the central EU this way and banded together with Denmark and Sweden in refusing to become members of the eurozone.

This did not stop other nations within the EU from continuing to push for closer economic integration and a common currency. They formed the European Monetary Institute in 1994 to set up an orderly transition to the ECB that arose in 1998. The main tasks of the new ECB were to come up with one interest rate and monetary policy by laboring alongside the national central banks.

The ECB was not given the role originally of lending money to governments in financial crises or increasing employment rates like the majority of central banks. This would later cause delays and problems in bailing out struggling countries in the financial crisis that began in earnest in 2008.

The end of 1998 saw the majority of nations in the EU cut their interest rates at the same time to encourage economic growth while preparing to implement the Euro currency. This is when they established the EMU to succeed the EMS as the primary economic policy mechanism in the European Union. The adoption and subsequent circulation of the euro by the eurozone countries proved to be a significant step towards the aimed for European political unity. The EMU has helped member nations attempt to work toward lower inflation, less public spending, and lesser government debts.

Hidden weaknesses in the European Monetary System became obvious during the global financial crisis of 2008 and the following years. Member nations like Greece, Portugal, Spain, Ireland, and Cyprus ran up high deficits that later erupted in the European sovereign debt crisis.

Because these countries did not have national currencies to devalue, they could not increase their exports. The EMU forbade them from spending additional money and running higher deficits to help increase employment. EMS policies had expressly forbidden eurozone bailouts to any countries whose economies were in trouble.

After months of arguments from the larger economy members such as Germany and France, the EMU at last came up with bailout policies that allowed aid to be dispensed to peripheral members who were struggling. They set up the European Stability Mechanism as a permanent pool of money to help out economies of struggling EU member states in 2012. This allowed a few of the countries in trouble like Spain, Portugal, and Ireland to make some progress on recoveries.

European Monetary Union (EMU)

The European Monetary Union is also known by its long-time acronym of EMU. The full name of this is the European Economic and Monetary Union. This refers to the succeeding protocol to the original EMS European Monetary System. It means the combining of European Union member nations into a frame work for a centralized economic policy set and system. The most visible and greatest representation of this union is the euro currency, which has become the national currency for more than half the EU member states.

It was via a three-staged process that the EMU succeeded the EMS. The final third phase included the adopting of the euro currency which replaced the long-time national currencies such as the franc, peso, and mark. It was successfully concluded by all of the original EU members besides Denmark and the United Kingdom. Both of these countries received opts-outs from taking on the euro in place of their beloved sovereign national currencies.

The real history of such an economic and monetary union began with the French Foreign Minister Robert Schuman's speech, which became known as the Schuman Declaration on May 9th of 1950. He reasoned that the one sure way to ensure the peace lasted in Europe that had suffered from devastating world wars two times in only thirty years was to craft Europe into one single economic polity. It was his landmark speech that gave rise to the Treaty of Paris in 1951. This actually forged the ECSC European Coal and Steel Community betwixt signatories Germany, Italy, France, Belgium. Luxembourg, and the Netherlands.

This original treaty strengthened through the subsequent Treaties of Rome that led to the creation of the EEC European Economic Community. Next came the Treaty of Paris that lasted through 2002. In the 1960s and 1970s, the politicians across Europe adopted the Werner Plan, yet later economic disruptions including the Saudi oil embargo and break down of the Bretton Woods agreement meant that they could not merge economically any further at this point.

The Maastrict Treaty of 1992 created a literal timeline to establish the European Monetary Union. By 1998, they had successfully formed the ECB

European Central Bank which established conversion rates that were fixed between all of the member state currencies. This led to the rise of the euro single currency that started physically circulating in 2002.

Yet there were hidden flaw in the EMU design. Greece became the first severe example of these. It was revealed by 2009 that Greece had been intentionally under reporting the amount of its severe budget deficits it ran since they started using the Euro in 2001. As a result, the nation experienced what amounts to the most serious economic crisis in modern history. The proud country had no choice but to agree to two painful bailout and austerity packages from the EU and ECB in only five years. Continued bailouts remained essential to Greece being able to repay its massive debts to its many creditors.

The unemployment rate in Greece rose to as high as 25 percent (in general) and 50 percent (for people less than 25 years old). The county's government was forced to instill capital controls to prevent monetary flight and also launch a bank holiday to limit the amounts of euros which depositors could withdraw from the banking system in any given day. The only way out of their still ongoing crisis would be to leave the EMU and return to their ancient currency the Drachma. This would allow them to severely devalue their currency and increase the competitiveness of their exports abroad.

European Sovereign Debt Crisis

The European sovereign debt crisis threatened to overthrow financial institutions, sovereign countries' bonds, and even the Euro currency at several points. This crisis erupted in 2008 when Iceland saw its entire banking system collapse.

From here it spread to other peripheral European nations including Greece, Portugal, and Ireland throughout the subsequent year 2009. A number of peripheral EU countries like Spain and their financial institutions faced default as government debt and sovereign bond yields rose dangerously. The ensuing crisis in debt created a cascading confidence crisis for European economies, businesses, and consumers.

In the end it took financial backstop guarantees from European Union countries and the IMF International Monetary Fund to bring the crisis under control. EU member states became concerned that financial contagion would spread enough that even the Euro itself might collapse.

While the crisis raged, a few of the Eurozone countries suffered from repeated agency downgrading of their sovereign debt. Greece in particular experienced a debt rating of junk status at the low point of its crisis. Bailouts were issued to a number of the countries on the EU periphery, including Greece, Spain, Portugal, Cyprus, and Ireland. These loan deals involved austerity measures that were intended to reduce the growing public debts of the countries.

The sovereign debt crisis in Europe reached its climax in 2009-2010. At this point, nations ranging from Greece, Ireland, and Spain to Portugal and Cyprus could no longer pay their debt payments, refinance government debts, or save their struggling banks without recourse to third party help.

At this point, these countries turned to international financial institutions such as the International Monetary Fund, the European Central Bank, and the EFSF European Financial Stability Facility to provide financial assistance. The Eurozone 17 member countries created the EFSF itself in 2010 to combat the problems created by the sovereign debt crisis.

Other situations combined to contribute to this long lasting sovereign debt crisis. The financial crisis of 2007 and 2008, ensuing Great Recession of 2008 to 2012, and several nations' real estate crises all worked together to exacerbate the situation. A few EU members had also violated their government budget deficit limits and created a more serious crisis of confidence.

In 2009 Greece revealed that its prior government had intentionally under-stated its budget deficits. This violated policies of the European Union and led to fears that the Euro itself might collapse because of the ensuing financial contagion. Suspicions mounted that both the amounts of debt and financial positions of a variety of Eurozone countries were drastically and unsustainably overextended.

By 2010 this agitated level of fear of too much sovereign debt caused the lenders to insist on greater interest rates from the countries in the EZ that possessed both high deficit and debt amounts. This meant that such nations were struggling to finance their deficits because they suffered from a small level of economic growth.

Portugal and Ireland joined Greece in having their sovereign debt cut to humiliating junk levels by the major credit ratings agencies. Ireland had to obtain a bailout by November of 2010 while Portugal required one by May of 2011. Even Spain and also Cyprus needed help to save their ailing banking sectors by June of 2012.

In or by 2014 Ireland, Spain, and Portugal had made enough progress in financial reforms and undergone sufficient austerity to successfully complete their bailout programs. Most of their banks have been recapitalized and saved. Cyprus is also recovering well. As of 2016, Greece continues to struggle and limp along with additional aid payments from its Troika of lenders the EU, ECB, and IMF.

European Stability Mechanism (ESM)

The European Stability Mechanism is a significant part of the financial stability and safeguard mechanisms in the Euro Zone area. It replaced the EFSF European Financial Stability Facility in 2013. This original EFSF was never intended to be permanent. Instead it was designed as a temporary solution to financial problems within the EU.

The European Stability Mechanism that took over for it was better established to deliver financial help to those Eurozone member countries that found themselves either threatened by or actually experiencing financial difficulties.

These two financial facilities ran concurrently from October of 2012 through June of 2013. Beginning in July of 2013 the EFSF could no longer begin new programs for financial support or help. The program still exists to manage and collect repayments of debts that are outstanding.

Once all of the existing loans that the EFSF program made have been repaid and all funding instruments and guarantors have received full payment for their contributions, then the EFSF will cease to exist entirely. This makes the replacing ESM the only and ongoing internal means for delivering aid in response to new calls for financial assistance from Eurozone member nations.

The European Stability Mechanism proves to be the principal means of resolving crises for nations which participate in the Euro. It obtains its money by issuing debt obligations. This permits it to fund financial aid and loans to the member countries of the Euro area. The European Council actually created the ESM in December of 2010. Participating Euro member states came together and signed a treaty between the governments on February 2 of 2012. October 8 of 2012 was the day they inaugurated the new ESM.

This ESM has great flexibility in funding its distressed member states. As various conditions are met, it is able to deliver loans as part of a program for macroeconomic adjustment. The mechanism is also able to buy member countries' debt in either the secondary or primary markets.

It can help to recapitalize banks of member states by loaning the governments money for this purpose. It can also deliver credit lines as a means of providing financial help as a precaution. In worst case and last resort conditions, the facility is allowed to recapitalize banks and other financial institutions directly. This is limited to times when resolution funds and bail ins are not enough to make the bank financially viable again.

The resources of the ESM are considerable. It has a capital base that has been subscribed in the amount of €704.8 billion. Of this amount, €80.5 billion has been paid in to the facility. The remaining €624.3 billion is classified as callable capital when it is needed. The fund is able to loan out a maximum total of €500 billion.

The ESM is based in Luxembourg. It is governed by public international law as an intergovernmental organization. It has only government shareholders making up its ownership. These are the 19 member countries that make up the Euro area. In 2016, 153 staff members worked under the direction of Klaus Regling the managing director.

European countries which are in trouble have other outside recourses for help besides the ESM. The principal other provider of assistance is the International Monetary Fund. The EU has supported having its own ESM, along with the predecessors the EFSF and the European Financial Stabilization Mechanism because it feared the consequences of some of its member states' problems with debt. Not all of the EZ countries suffered from debt issues. One EZ country failing could have contagious effects and widespread repercussions on the other national economies' health.

Excess Reserves

Excess reserves represent a capital reserve which financial institutions such as banks hold. They keep more than what their overseeing regulators, internal control mechanisms, or creditors require. This is especially important for commercial banks. The reason is because the central banking authority within their jurisdiction sets their additional reserves by establishing a standard in reserve requirements. Such reserve ratios as these determine the least amounts of liquid deposits which the banks must hold in reserve. This could be cash or similar to cash instruments like Treasuries. When the banks hold more than the reserve ratio reserves require of them, it becomes excess reserves.

Financial companies may choose to hold excess reserves because it provides them with an additional safety measure. This comes in handy if there is plethora of cash withdrawals from the banks' customers or an unanticipated loan loss which the bank must book in the form of write downs. This additional cushion boosts the security in the banking system. It is particularly crucial when economic uncertainty hits. It is also possible to improve the credit rating of a financial company when it voluntarily increases the amounts of its extra reserves. The credit ratings agencies such as Standard & Poor's', Moody's, and Fitch Ratings all like to see higher reserves from financial institutions.

The United States' Federal Reserve is the central bank for the U.S. They possess a number of tools in their toolkit for monetary normalization. The first of these is the ability to establish the fed funds rate. Besides this, they can alter the interest rate which banks receive for their required reserves and excess reserves. Interest on reserves is known by its acronym IOR, while interest on excess reserves is called by the acronym IOER.

Before October 1st of 2008, the U.S. banks did not receive any interest on their reserves. It was actually the Financial Services Regulatory Relief Act of 2006 which permitted the Federal Reserve to give an interest rate and interest to banks in this the first American instance of it. The rule originally had been set to take effect for October 1st of 2011. Because of the outbreak of the Great Recession, the government made the decision to move up the implementation timetable with the Emergency Economic

Stabilization Act of 2008. This meant that for the first time ever, without warning, banks were required to keep excess reserves with the Federal Reserve.

By August of 2014, excess reserves had reached a record amount of $2.7 trillion because of the funds released by the quantitative easing program. The receipts from this program increased the reserves from $2.3 trillion as of the middle of June 2016. These QE funds came to the commercial banks from the Federal Reserve. They gave them out as reserves instead of cash. Yet the interest which the Fed doled out for the reserves became payable in cash. It also registered as an interest income to the banks that received it. This interest which the banks received in cash from the Federal Reserve would otherwise have accrued to the United States Treasury coffers.

From a historical perspective, this fed funds rate was the one for which banks would loan out money to each other. It is typically utilized as the benchmark rate for all loans based on variable rates as well. The two interest rates mentioned above, IOER and IOR, are each decided by the Federal Reserve. It is the FOMC Federal Open Market Committee which sets them. Because of these rules and laws, banks have both an incentive and an obligation to inventory excess reserves now. This is particularly the case when the market rates are under the fed funds rate. It also means that the interest rates payable on extra reserves now work as proxy for the future fed funds rate. It is only the Federal Reserve with the authority to alter this interest rate level.

Fannie Mae

Fannie Mae is the acronym for the FNMA Federal National Mortgage Association. This entity is a GSE Government Sponsored Enterprise along with brother organization Freddie Mac. It became a publicly traded company in 1968. This home lending giant proves to be the largest mortgage financing provider anywhere in the United States. As such, it funds significantly more mortgages than any competing company or entity. It ensures that homebuyers, homeowners, and renters around the U.S. all can obtain financing options which they can afford.

As the GSE became established in 1938, it has provided funding for the housing market of the country for over 75 years. Franklin D. Roosevelt's New Deal established the company in the midst of the Great Depression. This is why the mission of the company is to aid individuals in purchasing, renting, or refinancing a home whether economic times in the country are good or bad.

The company's explicit purpose is to boost the size of the secondary mortgage market. They do this when they securitize mortgages and package them into MBS mortgage backed securities. This process returns the mortgage loaned money to lenders who are then able to reinvest this money into additional lending. It also acts to grow the numbers of lending institutions who are issuing mortgages. This ensures that there are more than just savings and loan associations making local loans for housing.

The model worked well until between 2003 and 2004. At this point the subprime mortgages crisis started. It began when the mortgage market turned away from the GSEs like Freddie Mac and Fannie Mae and began to migrate rapidly to unregulated MBS Mortgage Backed Securities that major investment banks put together. This shift to private MBSs caused the GSEs to lose their control over and ability to monitor mortgages in the country.

Increased competition between the investment banks and the GSEs reduced the power and market share of the government mortgage backers further and boosted the mortgage lenders at their expense. This radical change in the way mortgages were overseen and made caused the underwriting standards for mortgages to dangerously decline. It turned out to be one of the major reasons for the ensuing mortgage and financial crises.

The situation became so severe at Fannie Mae by 2008 that the FHFA Federal Housing Finance Agency had to get directly involved. FHFA Director James Lockhart on September 7, 2008 placed both this organization and Freddie Mac under FHFA conservatorship. This proved to be among the most dramatic and far reaching government involvements in free enterprise financial markets for literally decades.

Among Lockhart's first actions, he fired both companies' boards of directors and CEOs. He then made the companies issue a new class of common stock warrants and senior preferred stock to Treasury for 79.9% of both GSEs. Those who had been holding either preferred or common stock in either entity before the conservatorship began saw the value of their shares massively decrease. All prior shares' dividends became suspended to try to hold up the mortgage backed securities' and company debt values. FHFA pledged that it had no intentions of liquidating the GSEs.

Since 2009, Fannie Mae has made great strides in its business of helping make housing work better for individuals and families. They have injected trillions of dollars into the mortgage markets in lending liquidity. This has gone a long way to helping the housing markets and overall economy to recover.

The company has also gone back to high quality eligibility and underwriting standards. In the first quarter of 2016, they have extended $115 billion in mortgage credit that has allowed for 210,000 homes to be purchased and 256,000 mortgages to be refinanced. They also financed the construction of 161,000 multifamily rental units.

Fed Funds Rate

Fed Funds Rate refers to the most key interest rate benchmark in the United States. Such a benchmark rate is the one which the banks charge one another in order to borrow money from each other overnight. The Federal Reserve similarly deploys this rate as a tool in order to meaningfully impact monetary policy within the country. This is not the only benchmark rate in America today, yet it has no rival for importance.

The way the Federal Reserve is able to influence banks with it is somewhat complicated. The commercial banks must maintain a minimum level of money either in cash funds or with their particular regional branch of the Federal Reserve on deposit. The idea behind this is that it allows banks to meet customer withdrawals from their current accounts, including both checking and savings.

Sensible banks hold more than this bare minimum. They keep an excess of the reserves that the regulations and rules pertaining to the banking universe require. These are appropriately referred to as excess reserves. It is such excess reserves that the Fed Funds Rate directly affects.

As the better prepared banks keep plenty of excess reserves available, they are able to overnight loan out to the less prepared banks so that they can end business day operations at their legally required minimum obligation. This unsecured overnight loan occurs at the Fed Funds Rate. It represents the effective rate that the lending bank will charge the borrowing bank.

In nearly all cases, this Fed Funds Rate proves to be the lowest practical interest rate in the nation. Since the financial crisis, it has remained at slightly higher than zero percent. The Federal Reserve began increasing it with their first rate hike in December of 2015, both slowly and gradually.

This rate matters for more reasons than just the price at which a lending bank will charge a borrowing bank to utilize its excess reserves. The reason is that the Federal Reserve is able to set their monetary policy with the rate. As an example, they might decide they need to cut the effective rate of unemployment in the U.S. This is one of their two reasons for existing (along with keeping inflation low). In order to increase employment opportunities, the Fed will push down the Fed Funds Rate through purchasing securities off of commercial banks. As bank reserves go up, the price for them declines. This is their means for pushing down the federal funds rate.

A lower Fed Funds Rate means that banks try to find better opportunities to engage their excess reserves. They might do this by loaning out the money to individuals who seek to purchase a house. They could also lend the cash to companies interested in expanding their business. Either of these actions will boost the economy in some meaningful way. A more active economy will create more jobs and drive down the unemployment rate.

Besides this, the banks also employ the Fed Funds Rate as their basing benchmark from which they determine their other key interest rates. Once the Federal Reserve boosted their federal funds rate target back in December of 2016 as an example, each of the main banks in the country instantly increased their prime loan lending rates. These represent those rates which they offer to their best customers who are extremely creditworthy. The best customers are usually the large and economically powerful MNC multinational corporations.

This means that the effective Fed Funds Rate is not simply the one that the banks are paying each other when they borrow excess reserves from one another. Instead, it has a dramatic and literal connection to the rate of interest any individual will pay for a car loan, home equity loan or line of credit, and mortgage. It also impacts the price that companies will pay to build and grow their business using bank loans.

Federal Deposit Insurance Corporation (FDIC)

The U.S. government started The Federal Deposit Insurance Corporation back in 1933. They created it because of the literally thousands of failed banks that went down in the 1920s and 1930s. The FDIC began insuring bank accounts at the beginning of 1934. Since then, no depositors have lost any insured bank account money despite a consistent number of banks failing every year.

The first role of the FDIC is to insure and to increase the public's confidence in the American banking system. They do this in several ways. The FDIC insures minimally $250,000 in bank and thrift accounts. They watch for and take action on any risks to the deposit insurance funds. They also stop the spread of any bank failures when one of the banks does fail.

The Federal Deposit Insurance Corporation only insures deposits. This means that it does not cover mutual funds, stocks, or any other investments that some banks offer to their customers. They offer a standard $250,000 amount for each depositor's account. This single limit amount does not apply to other types of account ownerships and accounts at other banks. To help individuals understand if the insurance provided is enough to cover their various kinds of account, the FDIC provides its Electronic Deposit Insurance Estimator.

Another important role of the FDIC lies in its supervisory position. The outfit oversees over 4,500 different savings and commercial banks to make sure that they are operationally safe and sound. This represents more than half of the banks. Those banks that are set up as state banks may choose to become a member of either the Federal Reserve System or the FDIC. Any banks that are not overseen by the Federal Reserve System are watched over by the FDIC.

Another job of the FDIC is to check on the various banks to make sure they abide by the government's consumer protection laws. These laws include The Fair Credit Reporting Act, the Fair Credit Billing Act, the Fair Debt Collection Practices Act, and the Truth in Lending Act.

Lastly, the FDIC checks banks to make sure the different institutions are abiding by their responsibilities under the Community Reinvestment Act. This law ensures that banks help the communities where they were started to achieve their needs for credit.

Despite all of these roles, the only one that members of the public really encounter on a personal basis is the FDIC protecting insured depositors. When a bank or thrift goes down, the FDIC immediately reacts to the situation. They come in fast with the group that chartered the bank to close it down. The charter group could be the Office of the Comptroller of the Currency or the state regulator.

The next step is for the FDIC to wind up the failed bank. In their preferred method, they sell both the loans and the deposits of the bank to another banking institution. Customers rarely feel the transition in the majority of the cases. This is the FDIC's goal, to make sure that people do not lose access to their accounts and money.

The FDIC carries out its several mandates through six regional branches. It has more than 7,000 staff members that help it to carry out these goals. The organization is based in its headquarters in the capital Washington, D.C. Besides these locations, they also have various field offices throughout the nation.

The leadership of the FDIC is supplied by the Federal Government. The President appoints the board which the Senate confirms. There are five members of their Board of Directors. No more than three of them may belong to one political party to ensure bipartisanship in the decisions.

Federal Funds

Federal Funds refers to the excess reserves which financial institutions such as commercial banks choose to deposit with their regional Federal Reserve Bank. These are also often called Fed Funds. Such funds may be lent out to other participants in the market who lack enough immediate cash on hand to cover their own mandatory minimum reserves and lending opportunities. Such loans are never secured and are offered at comparatively lower interest rates. This rate is known as the overnight rate or the Federal Funds rate. The name comes from the time period over which such loans are actually offered.

Such Fed Funds aid the commercial banks in their daily needs to attain their required reserves. These represent the sum of money which the banks must keep on hand with the regional Federal Reserve Bank. It is actually the total volume of a bank's customer deposits which determine the level of their particular reserve requirements. The Fed establishes either a range or alternatively a particular target rate for its fed funds rate. This is then adjusted from time to time according to monetary needs and economic conditions in the country.

Within the U.S., the market for fed funds operates on a parallel basis with the Eurodollar offshore deposit market. These Eurodollars trade on an overnight basis. Not surprisingly their interest rate proves to be nearly equal to that of the fed funds rate. Yet the transactions have to be actually booked from anywhere outside of the borders of the U.S. In fact many international banks will commonly employ their branches residing in Panama or the Caribbean (such as the Cayman Islands or Bermuda) to run such accounts. This is ironic, given that such transactions are typically executed from trading rooms located within the United States. Each of the two markets is wholesale and covers any transactions which range from at least two million dollars on up to in excess of a billion dollars.

The Federal Reserve carries on an important function using its Fed Funds. They deploy their famed open market operations in order to control the amount of money flowing through the national level economy and utilize adjustments to short term interest rates. This translates into the Fed selling and buying up a portion of the government bills and bonds it has previously issued out to commercial banks. Doing so actually decreases or increases the total money supply for the country. As a benevolent side effect, it then raises or lowers the shorter term time frame interest rates. It is actually the Federal Reserve Bank of New York (FRBNY) that physically carries out these open market operations.

As a point of fact, this federal funds rate is most similar to the shorter term time frame interest rates in the commercial markets. It means that their actions and the ensuing market reactions literally impact not only U.S. rates, but also LIBOR rates in London and Eurodollar rates. At the conclusion of every trading day, the Fed announces its daily effective fed funds rate. This proves to be the weighted average transaction rate for all tallied transactions throughout the business day.

There are a variety of participants in this enormous fed funds market. The key players prove to be the American- based commercial banks, American branches of the foreign
-based banks (like USB, Credit Suisse, HSBC, Barclays, RBS, RBC, Societe Generale, and BNP Paribas, to name just a few), government sponsored enterprises like Fannie Mae and Freddie Mac, savings and loan entities, agencies of the federal government, and securities companies.

Federal Open Market Committee

The Federal Open Market Committee is a group within the Federal Reserve, the central bank for the United States. This central bank is more commonly known as the Fed. They carry out actions of monetary policy. This impacts the cost and readily available quantity of money and credit. The Fed uses these tools to foster the country's economic goals. Thanks to the Federal Reserve Act of 1913, the Fed gained the authority to set the national monetary policy.

Under the mantle of the Federal Reserve are three different monetary policy tools. These are reserve requirements, the discount rate, and open market operations. It is the Federal Reserve System Board of Governors that carries out the task of setting the reserve requirements and the discount rate. The Federal Open Market Committee handles the Fed's open market operations.

With these three different tools, the Fed is able to influence the supply of and demand for balances that the financial institutions keep inside the Federal Reserve Banks. This is how it affects the federal funds rate. This is the interest rate that banks and other financial institutions are willing to loan money from their Federal Reserve accounts to other such institutions on an overnight basis.

When the federal funds rate changes, this sets off events which impact foreign exchange rates, other types of shorter term interest rates, longer term interest rates, and the quantity of money and credit in the economy. Eventually this affects a number of important economic indicators like economic output, employment, and the costs for goods and services.

Open market operations are the main tool that the Federal Reserve uses to carry out American monetary policy. Specifically they buy and sell government securities like Treasuries and T-Bills. They do this in the open market so that they can contract or expand the quantity of money that exists in the banking system. When they buy securities, it puts money into the banking system. This boosts growth in the economy. When they sell their securities, they withdraw money from the system. This shrinks the economy. Ultimately it is the federal funds rate the Federal Open Market

Committee is trying to adjust with these operations.

The Federal Open Market Committee is made up of twelve members in total. These are comprised of the Federal Reserve System Board of Governors' seven members, the Federal Reserve Bank of New York President, and four of the other eleven Presidents of the Reserve Banks. These other Reserve Bank Presidents rotate in and out serving one year terms. Rotating seats have a special order in which they are filled. There are four groups of Banks which each contribute a Bank President to the voting Federal Open Market Committee. The groups are Richmond, Philadelphia, and Boston; Chicago and Cleveland; Dallas, Atlanta, and St. Louis; and San Francisco, Kansas City, and Minneapolis.

Those Reserve Bank Presidents who are not voting members of the committee in a given year still attend all of the committee meetings, make their contributions to the economy and policy choices assessments, and take part in all discussions.

Every year the Federal Open Market Committee engages in eight routinely scheduled meetings. In these meetings, the committee does a number of important activities. It reviews national financial and economic conditions, considers the risks to maintainable economic growth and long term price stability, and decides on its monetary policy appropriate stance.

The FOMC legally is authorized to set its own internal organization. They have a tradition of electing the Board of Governors Chair to be the Chair of the FOMC and selecting the New York Federal Reserve Bank President to be the vice chair. The eight annual meetings occur in Washington D.C.

Federal Reserve

The Federal Reserve, also known as the Fed, or the Federal Reserve Board, proves to be the United States' central banking system. This central bank came about in 1913 as a result of Congress passing the Federal Reserve Act. Congress created the organization because of a number of serious financial panics that culminated in the severe panic of 1907.

With time, the Federal Reserve's roles and areas of responsibility have grown as the organization has expanded. Economic events such as the Great Depression have only served to encourage this.

The Federal Reserve today counts among its duties many responsibilities. Among these are regulating and overseeing the country's banks, managing the country's monetary policy and supply, assuring the financial systems' continuance and stability, and offering a variety of financial services to depositing banks, foreign central banks, and the United States government.

The Federal Reserve's structure is made up of a number of different components. Among these are the Federal Reserve Board of Governors, all of whom are appointed by the President. The Federal Open Market Committee, also known by its acronym of FOMC, sets the monetary policy, like the interest rates, for the nation. There are also Federal Reserve Banks, which are twelve regional institutions that are found in the biggest area cities around America. They offer physical currency to member banks when demand proves to be unusually high. Several councils that advise it are a part of The Federal Reserve, as are technically the member banks throughout the country.

The FOMC component of the Federal Reserve is actually comprised of all of these seven Board of Governors members along with the presidents of the twelve regional banks. Only five of these presidents are voting members at a time. Together, they review the state of the U.S. national economy in order to determine what fiscal policies need to be pursued. When the economic growth is slowing, or a recession is occurring, they cut the national interest rates. When inflation is appearing or the economy is overheating, they raise these interest rates.

The Federal Reserve proves to be a unique entity among the major central banks. This is because it divides up the various responsibilities into some public and some private parts of the institution. The Federal Reserve furthermore serves to create the currency used for the country, the U.S. dollar. The fact that it is both a public and private institution, with so many varied and vast powers, makes it one of a kind.

Because the U.S. dollar is still the reserve currency of the world, the Federal Reserve's powers are far greater than simply managing the U.S. economy. In actual practice, they also are the custodians and managers of the world's reserve currency. This gives them considerable power and influence throughout the entire world economy, since they are able to create not only dollars for the U.S. economy, but also for other central banks use in foreign countries. As a result of this, more than half of the physically printed U.S. dollars are found outside of the United States.

Federal Reserve Act of 1913

The Federal Reserve Act of 1913 created the Federal Reserve Bank. This proved to be the Act of Congress that set up the Federal Reserve System. This system became the Central Bank organization for the United States. As part of the act, the Federal Reserve acquired the powers to issue the nation's legal tender currency. President Woodrow Wilson actually signed this act, making it law in 1913.

The leadership of the country felt the need to create such a central bank for several reasons. The United States had operated without a central bank going back to the expiration of the Second Bank of the United States' charter. This meant that for about eighty years, the country had existed without any form of central bank.

In time, a number of financial panics had ensued without any central bank to intervene in them. The one that really galvanized congressional and public opinion for having a central bank proved to be the serious financial panic of 1907. As a result of these factors, a number of Americans decided that the nation required serious currency and banking reforms that could handle such panics by offering an available liquid assets' reserve. They also figured such an institution might be capable of managing a consistent expansion and contraction of credit and currency from time to time as appropriate.

The original Federal Reserve Act plan recommended an establishment of an unusual combined public and private entity system. They suggested that minimally eight and as many as twelve regional private Federal Reserve banks should be created. All of them were to have their own boards of directors, regional boundary lines, and branches. This new entity would be led by a Federal Reserve Board comprised of seven members and made up of public officials that the President appointed and the Senate would confirm. An advisory committee known as the Federal Advisory Committee would be created, along with a brand new U.S. currency that would alone be accepted nationally, the Federal Reserve Note. In the final version of the bill, twelve regional Federal Reserve Banks were actually created. The rest of the above provisions became law and subsequently a part of the newly created Federal Reserve System.

Another important decision that Congress settled on with the Federal Reserve Act revolved around the private banks throughout the U.S. Every nationally chartered bank had to join the Federal Reserve System as a part of this act. They were made to buy stock that could not be transferred in their own area's Federal Reserve Bank. It furthermore required that a set dollar total of reserves that did not pay interest had to be deposited to their own regional Federal Reserve Bank. Banks that are only state chartered have the choice, but not the obligation, of joining this system and being regulated by the Fed.

Finally, the act allowed the member banks to receive loans at a discounted rate from the discount windows of their own regional Federal Reserve Bank. They were promised a six percent yearly dividend on their Federal Reserve stock and provided with additional services. The act also gave the Federal Reserve Banks the authority to assume the role of U.S. government fiscal agents.

Federal Reserve Bank

Twelve different Federal Reserve Banks make up the Federal Reserve System that functions as the central bank for the U.S. Federal reserve banks are also utilized to sub-divide up the country into the twelve Federal Reserve Districts.

Every Federal Reserve Bank bears the responsibility for individually regulating the various commercial banks that are found in such a bank's geographical district. Ensuring the continuation of the financial system and all of the member banks is among the primary responsibilities of the Federal Reserve System.

Each Federal Reserve Bank also issues its own stock shares that can only be acquired by participating member banks. The banks are required to obtain these shares by law. While the shares may not be traded, pledged as a loan security, or sold, they do pay dividends that run as high as six percent each year.

American banks are required by law to keep certain fractional reserves of their actual deposits. These are mostly held by the regional Federal Reserve Banks. Although in years past, the Federal Reserve did not pay member banks interest on these funds kept on reserve, as of 2008 Congress passed the EESA that permits them to pay the participating banks interest.

The twelve Federal Reserve Banks and districts are found geographically spread out around the nation. They include the Federal Reserve Banks of Boston, New York, Philadelphia, Cleveland, Richmond, Atlanta, Chicago, St. Louis, Minneapolis, Kansas City, Dallas, and San Francisco.

The largest and still most important of the individual Federal Reserve Banks proves to be the Federal Reserve Bank of New York. Not only does this bank have the greatest asset base of all the twelve branches, valued at over a trillion dollars and representing four times the asset base of the next largest Federal Reserve Bank, but it also boasts the biggest gold depository on earth, valued at in excess of $25 billion. The gold kept in the New York Federal Reserve Bank vaults belongs to other nations who store it there for safe keeping. Saudi Arabia and Kuwait both keep their significant holdings here.

Among the various states that have Federal Reserve Banks headquartered there, a few of them contain more than one branch within their state. California, Missouri, and Tennessee are the ones that make this claim. Tennessee actually contains two branches from two different districts within its state boundaries. The only state that has two Federal Reserve Banks headquartered within it is Missouri. For the largest geographical areas covered by the districts, San Francisco is the largest, Kansas City is second biggest, and Minneapolis is the third largest.

Federal Reserve System

The Federal Reserve System is the United States' central banking system. It is made up of the Federal Open Market Committee, the Federal Reserve Board, 12 regional Federal Reserve Banks, and state and national member banks.

Seven members make up the Board of Governors. These the President appoints to 14 year terms upon approval by the Senate. The reason this system became established was to manage the movement of credit and money in the U.S. Congress set up this system in 1913. The U.S. had experienced a variety of central banks since 1791. The country needed a more stable banking system to help encourage a stronger economy.

Practically every bank in the U.S. participates in the Federal Reserve System. The program requires these institutions to keep a set amount of their assets deposited with their area Federal Reserve Bank. The Board of Governors determines how much these reserve requirements will be. The Board of Governors changes these required reserves in order to significantly influence the money supply that is circulating in the economy.

This Federal Reserve System provides a few different functions to the country. It is a bank for all the banks. A great number of interbank transactions go through this system. Banks may also borrow money from the Federal Reserve if they can not get credit from anywhere else. The system only gives them credit in emergencies or as it is unavailable on the open markets.

The Federal Reserve also functions like the bank of the government. The inbound and outbound payments of the tax system process via a checking account at the bank. The Fed further supplies the currency of the United States even though they do not produce it. They also purchase and sell government securities like Treasury Bills and Bonds.

Among the more important functions of this system is its purpose as a regulatory agency. They act as policeman to the banking sector to protect consumers' rights and to ensure smooth functions. They are also the main resource for banks and the public in times of financial crises or a panic surrounding the banks.

National banks have to be members of the system. In order to qualify, they are made to deposit the reserve requirements from their customer checking and savings accounts in their regional Federal Reserve bank. They must also keep mandatory reserve levels with this bank. Every nationally chartered bank has to be a member of the system. State chartered banks are also encouraged to join as members of the system.

The need for this Federal Reserve System became apparent after several failed attempts at establishing a uniform banking system in the United States. The first central bank was the First Bank that existed from 1791 to 1811. The Second Bank took over this role from 1816 to 1836. These two outfits proved to be the U.S. Treasury Department's only official representatives. This meant that they were the only organizations issuing and promoting the official U.S. currency.

Every other bank in the country ran under private auspices or as a state chartered organization. Each bank had its own bank notes which competed against the two U.S. banks as currency that could be redeemed for face value.

The first National Bank Act that Congress passed in 1863 allowed for a regimen of National Banks that would be supervised. Banks had to abide by certain operating practices, rules for making and issuing loans, and capital amount minimums kept in the banks. The Act effectively killed the non national individual bank currencies by creating a 10% tax on all state level banknotes.

Fiat Money

Fiat Money proves to be money that has no real intrinsic, or actual, value. It instead derives its worth from governments accepting it as legal tender. The concept of fiat money on a large scale is a relatively new one. Throughout practically all of history, the majority of currencies around the world derived their value from silver or gold. Fiat money is instead entirely based on trust and faith in the issuing monetary authority.

The problem with fiat money lies in the ability of the governments to inflate its value away. They can do this by over printing it. Since fiat currencies are not restricted by a requirement of hard reserve assets, they can be created in any quantity that the issuing government desires. As the supply continues to rise while the demand remains constant, its purchasing power will fall. When the supply is drastically increased, then hyperinflation will result. Fiat money that falls by hundreds of percent in value is deemed to be a victim of hyperinflation.

The other disadvantage is that only peoples' trust in it ultimately gives it practical value. It suffers from inflation and finally hyperinflation, then the confidence in it becomes shaken. Fiat money that lacks the confidence of its citizens will finally collapse in value and then no longer be of any trading use for daily transactions. When it fails, people either return to barter systems, or the government establishes a currency based on hard assets once again.

The history of money has proven on a number of occasions that governments debase currency to the point of fiat money when it suits them. They do this because it allows them to print as much as they need to pay for things. While this creates inflation for their citizens, it gives the money issuing government the ability to repay their debts with cheaper fiat money. Finally, as a society has had enough of the devalued money and currency instability, they force the government to return to asset backed money. This has happened before, and some monetary experts say that you are starting to see this happen again nowadays.

Financial Industry Regulatory Authority (FINRA)

The Financial Industry Regulatory Authority is a congressionally authorized independent and non profit outfit. Congress established them to safeguard the investors of America by ensuring that the stock market industry runs honestly and fairly for all participants.

FINRA is not an agency of the government, even though they have broad disciplinary and enforcement powers. The organization tirelessly works to ensure the integrity of the market and protection for investors by regulating the securities business.

FINRA carries out these duties in a variety of ways. They investigate brokerage firms to make sure they abide by the rules. The not for profit creates and then enforces these rules that govern the actions of more than 3,941 securities companies who have over 641,157 brokers on staff. FINRA also encourages transparency in markets and settles disputes. The group does all of this without taxpayers having to support them via taxes.

The authority works every day to make sure individuals selling securities are tested and licensed. They ensure all advertisements for securities utilized to sell the products are clear and truthful. FINRA holds companies to a high standard for only selling suitable investments to individuals that are appropriate to their needs. They ensure that every investor obtains full disclosure about their investment before they buy it.

The independent agency carried out 1,512 disciplinary actions on registered firms and brokers in 2015. This allowed them to collect fines of over $95 million. They mandated that $96.6 million be given back to investors who where harmed in these and other actions. The group handed over 800 different insider trading or fraud cases to other agencies like the SEC for settling or prosecuting the same year.

Ultimately FINRA's goals are to deter misconduct in the industry. They do this by enforcing rules for everyone. This is not only the rules that they create. The group also enforces the Municipal Securities Rulemaking Board's regulations and federal securities laws as well. They make the qualifying exams and require brokers to come to continuing education classes.

The organization puts hundreds of their own financial examiners in the field to check on the way these brokers carry out their business. Their main concern is for the investors and risks to the markets. They follow up on complaints filed by investors and other suspicious activities.

They also review all advertisements, brochures, websites, and communications to be certain brokers are fairly presenting their products. This amounts to approximately 100,000 different communications and advertisements they examine and approve between broker firms and their investors.

FINRA also disciplines rule breakers. They use their authority, technology, and professional experts to rapidly react to wrongs. The organization has the authority to fine brokers, suspend them, or expel them from the business.

The independent agency also possesses technology that is potent enough for them to be able to review various markets and pick up on possible fraud. They are able to gather data in such a way to keep tabs on insider trading or other practices that give broker firms advantages that are unfair. To this effect they process anywhere from 42 billion to 75 billion transactions daily to have a full picture of U.S. market trading.

The group is also involved in resolving disputes in the securities' business. This pertains to problems between investors and brokers. FINRA handles almost 100% of all mediations and arbitrations that are related to securities. They hear these disputes in 70 different locations. This includes one hearing center in every state, Puerto Rico, and London.

Financial Stability Oversight Council

The Financial Stability Oversight Council is an organization that was created by the Dodd-Frank Act following the financial crisis of 2008. It possesses a clear legal mandate that provides an accountability to look for risks and respond to perceived upcoming threats to the United States' financial stability.

This is the first time that a single organization has held such important responsibility. The group is actually headed by the Secretary of the Treasury. It combines the various experience and knowledge of state regulators, an insurance expert who is both independent and Presidentially appointed, and federal financial regulators.

The Financial Stability Oversight Council was granted first time powers by Congress to restrain and head off dangerous risks within the financial system. This Council can select a financial firm that is not a bank and mark it for intense supervision so that the firm can not threaten to blow up the financial system and its stability. As an aid in determining what qualifies potential risk to the country's financial stability, this FSOC is allowed to obtain information and analysis from and supply information to the recently established OFR Office of Financial Research that is headquartered in the Treasury building.

Before the financial crisis erupted, the financial regulation in the United States focused exclusively on specific markets and institutions. This permitted gaps in supervision to expand amidst inconsistencies in the regulation. Standards weakened as a result. There was no one regulator responsible for watching over and dealing with the various risks to American financial stability. The threats often revolved around various financial firms which functioned at once in numerous interrelated markets. Because of this, critical portions of the financial system remained unregulated. The Dodd-Frank Act dealt with these failures by creating the Financial Stability Oversight Council.

The Financial Stability Oversight Council has many roles. It facilitates and coordinates regulation. They are tasked with sharing information and coordinating action with the agencies involved to deal with examining, making rules, developing policy, reporting, and enforcing their actions.

They are also to encourage gathering and sharing information among their various member organizations. If they are unable to gather enough information, they are to turn to the OFR to obtain information from individual companies they need to evaluate. Gathering and evaluating such information is supposed to eliminate blind spots in the financial system. By doing this they are fostering a more stable and less dangerous overall financial system in the United States.

The Financial Stability Oversight Council is also to select nonbank financial entities that need to be consolidated. Dodd-Frank identified companies that did not receive appropriate supervision and then led to the outbreak of the financial crisis back in 2008. The act provides the Financial Stability Oversight Council the authority which it needs to force supervision on such companies at entirely its own discretion.

The council also has the power to make recommendations for harsher standards for those firms they deem to be the biggest and most interconnected operations which provide increased risks to the system. This includes both banks and non bank financial organizations. As the Council learns about activities and practices that are threatening financial stability in the country, they are able to recommend tougher standards to the appropriate financial regulators.

The extensive powers of this Financial Stability Oversight Council are most clearly shown in their ability to choose to break up companies at will which they perceive to represent a clear and present danger to the nation's financial stability. They can decide if action should be followed to break up these kinds of firms which they deem to be a grave threat to the United States and its financial stability.

Foreign Account Tax Compliance Act (FACTA)

Foreign Account Tax Compliance Act (FACTA) proves to be an American-issued and -rigorously enforced law. It requires all United States' citizens living either stateside or overseas to make annual report filings of any foreign bank account holdings they possess. This FACTA law came into effect back in 2010 along with the HIRE Act. The goal ostensibly was to encourage and foster greater transparency in the worldwide financial services universe. The ulterior motive lay in knowing any and all U.S. individuals' accounts which they might use to hide income or assets overseas. The ultimate goal is to maximize every last dollar in taxes form overseas-living Americans.

It was former U.S. President Barack Obama who signed the new HIRE Act into law in 2010. With this Hiring Incentives to Restore Employment Act, he was seeking to cut down the stubbornly high rate of unemployment that refused to disappear after the global financial crisis and meltdown of 2008-2009. Among the incentives they dangled in front of employers with the act was the ability to increase their business tax credits on every new staff member which a firm hired and retained for minimally a calendar year. There were still other incentive included in the bill. Companies benefited from a special payroll tax holiday advantage as well as a higher expense deduction limit on any new factory or production equipment which they purchased back in 2010.

Naturally the President and Congress required a revenue stream with which to pay for these business benefits and incentives. What they came up with was the requirement that all American tax payers report all of their assets maintained outside of the United States ever year. The idea was that in taxing such foreign-based accounts and assets, the country would boost its revenue sources enough to pay for the desperately needed corporate job stimulation programs. To provide a sufficient penalty incentive for American citizens to reveal these hidden assets, the IRS created a stiff regimen for any American resident or overseas-living U.S. citizen who chose not to report their international account assets and currency amounts which was greater than $50,000 value during the course of any tax year.

To grow the potential additional revenues by as much as possible, the government applied the new requirements not only to presumably wealthy and foreign-born individual Americans, but also to NFFE Non-Financial Foreign Entities and FFI Non-US Foreign Financial Institutions. These internationally based banks were then mandated to become compliant with the new revenue-catching law by revealing all American citizens' identities and the worth of any and all of their assets kept in their banks. Banks have to report this information to the IRS Internal Revenue Service or alternatively to the IGA FACTA Intergovernmental Agreement.

For those FFI's which elect to not comply with the Internal Revenue Service, they will summarily be banned from the United States' markets and banking system. They will also suffer a 30 percent deduction of any witholdable payments' amounts in the form of a tax penalty.

These payments relate to U.S. financial assets and income generated and kept in the banks. They include dividends, interest payments, remunerations, salaries and wages, profits, and compensations. Those NFFE's and FFI's which comply with the law have to report every year the identities of all their account holding U.S. citizens. This includes their names, addresses, and TIN tax identification numbers for every account. They also have to divulge the Americans' account numbers and balances, and all withdrawals and deposits made using the account during the calendar year.

The real goal behind FACTA is to eliminate tax evasion of American businesses and citizens who invest, earn, and operate in such a capacity as to gain taxable income overseas. It remains legal to own and operate an offshore account. It is in not properly disclosing it to the IRS that it becomes illegal. The reason is because the United States is the only major economy and jurisdiction to tax all of the assets and income from its citizens regardless of where they live, reside, and realize income in the world.

Fractional Banking System

The fractional banking system is also known as the fractional reserve banking system. This system is the way that virtually all modern day banks around the world operate. In a fractional reserve banking system, banks actually only maintain a small amount of their deposited funds in reserve forms of cash and other easily liquid assets.

The rest of the deposits they loan out, even though all of their deposits are allowed to be withdrawn at the customers' demand. Fractional banking happens any time that banks loan out money that they bring in from deposits.

Fractional banking systems are ones where banks constantly expand the money supply beyond the levels at which they exist. Because of this, total money supplies are commonly a multiple bigger than simply the currency created by the nation's central bank. The multiple is also known as the money multiplier. Its amount is determined by a reserve requirement that the financial overseers set.

This fractional reserve system is managed ultimately by central banks and these reserve requirements that they enforce. On the one hand, it sets a limit on the quantity of money that is created by the commercial banks. The other purpose of it is to make certain that banks keep enough readily available cash in order to keep up with typical withdrawal demands of customers. Even though this is the case, there can be problems. Should many depositors at once attempt to take out their money, then a run on the bank might occur. If this happens on a large national or regional scale, the possibility of a banking systemic crisis emerges.

Central banks attempt to reduce these problems. They keep a close eye on commercial banks through regulations and oversight. Besides that, they promise to help out banks that fall into difficulties by acting as their ultimate lender of last resort. Finally, central banks instill confidence in the fractional reserve banking system by guaranteeing the deposits of the customers of the commercial banks.

A significant amount of criticism has been leveled against this fractional reserve banking system. Mainstream critics have complained that because money is only created as individuals borrow from the banking system, the system itself forces people to take on debt in order for money to actually be created. They say that this debases the currency. The biggest problem that they have with the commercial banking system growing the money supply is that it is literally creating money from nothing.

Other critics associate fractional banking with fiat currencies, or money that is only valuable because the governments say that they are. They decry these as negative aspects of current money systems. They dislike that fractional banking systems and fiat money together do not place any limits on how much a money supply can ultimately grow. This can lead to bubbles in both capital markets and assets, such as real estate, stock markets, and commodities. All of these can be victims of speculation, which is made easier by the creation of money through debt in the fractional reserve system.

Freddie Mac

Freddie Mac is a semi-private company that Congress chartered in 1970. They created the entity to offer stability, liquidity, and affordable prices for the country and its housing markets. They have grown to be responsible for the home purchases of one out of four buyers.

Besides this the company is also among the biggest financing sources for multifamily housing in the nation. From 2009 to 2016, the company has dispersed mortgage market funding that amounts to over $2.5 trillion. This has enabled in excess of 13 million American families to refinance, purchase, or rent a home in that time frame.

In 1970 Congress was seeking to stabilize the mortgage markets of the country. They wanted to grow and improve opportunities for rental housing that was affordable and for home buying. Because of this, Freddie Mac's mission has always been to bring stability, liquidity, and affordability to the national housing market in the United States. They do this in a variety of ways. The company helps the secondary mortgage market. They buy both mortgage securities and mortgage loans outright as investments. They then package and sell these as guaranteed mortgage securities known as PCs. In this secondary market, there are entities which buy and sell mortgages as complete loans or as mortgage securities. Freddie Mac never makes loans to home owners directly themselves.

Because of the collapse of the mortgage backed securities markets in 2007 and 2008 and its impact on their finances, the company is now being run under conservatorship. The FHFA Federal Housing Finance Agency oversees their business to make sure loans are carefully scrutinized and securitized. They want to avoid the mistakes of the financial crisis becoming repeated here.

Freddie Mac operates in three main business areas to ensure that a continuous supply of mortgage funding goes through to the housing markets in the country. They make rental housing and home buying more affordable through their single family credit guarantee business, their multifamily business, and their investment business. They utilize all three of these to promote financing for affordable housing.

The single family line is essentially a recycling operation. They work with securitizing mortgages so that the entity is able to provide funding to millions of different home loans annually. This securitization proves to be the means where they buy up different loans lenders have made and then package these up into various mortgage securities. They then sell these on the worldwide capital markets. The money from the sale of these securities they next funnel back to the lenders. In this way home loan operations have sufficient mortgage money for lending.

The company is also interested in supporting renters as well. This is the role of their multifamily business. In this line, the outfit cooperates with a group of lenders to help finance the construction of various apartment buildings throughout the United States. The lenders make the loans and Freddie Mac buys them to package and resell. This way the lenders receive back the proceeds so they can issue more loans. This is a critical line as multifamily loans prove to be a few million dollars each and require unique underwriting from one property to the next.

Their investment business actually purchases some of their own mortgage backed securities which they and other financial entities like Fannie Mae guarantee. This portfolio further invests into individual loans which they guarantee but choose not to securitize. By bidding on some of their own securities, the investment business and portfolio serves the markets. It gives these mortgage backed securities greater liquidity and offers more funding for mortgages. They do this by issuing their own debt which creates net income for the company after they pay their interest to the bond holders.

Glass Steagall Act

Congress created and passed the Glass Steagall Act in 1933. This legislation arose because of the effects of the 1929 catastrophic stock market crash. Two congressmen came up with this solution in the Great Depression when many banks were failing. The law made separate all activities which involved commercial banking and investment banking.

Commercial banks had become heavily involved in the stock market. This activity received much of the blame for the stock market and financial crashes. Lawmakers felt that commercial banks had employed money from their depositors in speculation in the stock market.

The reasons this act came forcefully into law had to do with banks' activities. Commercial banks had bought new and unproven stocks to sell to individual customers. It was the greed of banks that led to the new legislation. The goals of banking were mired in conflict of interest. Banks would make loans to corporations in which they already had an investment. These loans were not issued based on good underwriting.

They would then push these investments to their clients. Their goal was to have their customers help support these companies. Such commercial speculation insured that when the companies failed, the banks and their customers all lost huge amounts of money. Finally banks began to collapse in the thousands as a result of this poor and unregulated activity.

The act actually came about because of Senator Carter Glass. Glass had served as Treasury secretary previously. He also founded the U.S. Federal Reserve System. The failing banks motivated him to act on a bill. He became the main driving force of this legislation. His partner on the project was Henry Bascom Stegall.

Stegall served as House Banking and Currency Committee chairman. At first he would not support the bill with Glass. They added an amendment to create insurance for bank deposits. This brought Congressman Stegall's critical support of the act.

The effects of this Glass Steagall Act erected a variety of barriers in the banking industry. A new firewall of regulation arose between investment bank and commercial bank businesses. The two types of banks experienced unprecedented oversight and control over their activities. All banks received one year to choose a specialty in either investment banking or commercial banking.

Those that chose commercial banking were heavily limited in their investment banking activities. Income from securities could not exceed 10% of the commercial bank earnings. Commercial banks were permitted to underwrite bonds the government issued. The ultimate goal was to stop banks from committing their depositors' funds to projects which were poorly underwritten and speculative.

Banks that were too big to fail at the time became significant targets for this act. JP Morgan and Company and rival financial empires were among these. Such outfits had to eliminate many services. This targeted a large and important part of their incomes.

Later on criticism of the Glass Steagall Act arose. This happened as different explanations became popular for the Great Depression. Many different individuals also saw that this act had created problems for financial services. They blamed the law for restricting financial firms to the point that they were not able to compete effectively.

Many opposed the act by the 1980s. Glass Steagall opposition grew into the 1990s. Congress finally repealed the act in 1999. The elimination of this act has been blamed for the Great Recession crisis that started in 2006.

Banks were again able to mix investment and lending activities. Close regulation of commercial banks had been largely eliminated. Because of this, banks again made many risky loans that were either liar loans or not properly documented for income.

Gold Standard

The gold standard represents a centuries' used system of money for backing up currencies with tangible, physical gold holdings in a central bank vault. Under the gold standard, the basic economic currency unit proved to be a pre set amount of gold by weight. Several different types of gold standards exist.

The Gold specie standard proves to be a system where the money unit itself is represented by gold coins that are in circulation. Alternatively, it could be represented by an exchange unit of value that is literally expressed in units against a specific gold coin that circulates, along with other coins that are minted from a metal with less value, such as silver or copper.

Conversely, the gold exchange standard usually has to do with silver and other valuable metal coins that are circulating. In this type of exchange system, the monetary authorities promise that a set exchange rate against the currency of another country practicing the gold standard will be maintained. This gives rise to a gold standard that is not literal but still de facto. The silver coins circulating then trade with a set external value in gold terms that stands independently of the actual silver value contained within the coins.

The most common gold standard that has been seen in the last few hundred years turns out to be the gold bullion standard. The gold bullion standard refers to a money system where no gold coins are actually circulating throughout the economy. Instead, the monetary authorities have consented to exchange a set amount of gold in exchange for their paper currency. This is done at a set price that is established for the paper currency that circulates.

The gold bullion standard existed in the world economy from the 1700's until 1971. During this span of almost three hundred years, the values of major world currencies proved to be exceptionally stable, as were the supplies of money in existence. This resulted from a restriction of the gold standard that only allowed such paper currency to be printed as greater amounts of gold existed in the respective nation's treasury and vaults. The positive of this proved to be that the world could count on currencies that did not fluctuate wildly in value or decline consistently over time. Governments disliked the gold standard as it kept them from increasing the money supply or spending more money than the country actually had. They found it too restrictive.

The gold standard in the world collapsed when President Nixon initiated what became known as the Nixon shock by unilaterally taking the country off of gold exchange and convertibility for dollars in 1971. The currency of both the U.S. and most countries of the world then became Fiat currencies, only backed up by the government decree. Since the gold standard was abandoned, the U.S. dollar has declined so severely that a single dollar in 1971 would today be worth $35 2010 dollars.

HM Treasury

HM Treasury stands for Her Majesty's Treasury. This is the United Kingdom's finance and economic ministry. It keeps control over the public spending and lays out the direction for the economic policy of Great Britain. Among its important mandates is to work towards a sustainable and strong level of economic growth.

The HM Treasury of today dates back to the time of the Norman Conquest in 1066. The kingdoms of the Anglo Saxons also had Treasuries which collected taxes and handled expenditures before this nation altering invasion occurred. The Danegeld was a tribute levied on Anglo Saxons to pay the Vikings to leave or not attack. Britain's first official Treasurer was likely one "Henry the Treasurer."

He held land from King William located near Winchester which proved to be the location for the royal treasuries of both late Anglo Saxon and Norman Britain. Henry is believed to have functioned as William the Conqueror's treasurer. He is mentioned in the Domesday Book, the very first systematic tax assessment of the entire nation which the Treasury carried out at the time.

Eleven Downing Street is the home of HM Treasury. In 1684, Mr. Downing obtained the permission from King Charles II to construct and name his new Downing Street development at St. James Park. These houses were finished in 1686. Even though Number 11 Downing Street did not become the official residence of the head of Treasury the British Chancellor of the Exchequer until 1828, a precedent had been set a generation earlier.

In 1806 and 1807, Lord Henry Petty dwelt there while he held the position as Chancellor of HM Treasury. Chancellors who have since elected to live over their office have experienced a house that is not only historic for Britain, but unique and quite comfortable as a home as well.

HM Treasury bears many important responsibilities today. They handle all aspects of public spending. This includes the pay for pensions and public sectors, spending of the various ministries, welfare policy, capital investment, and the AME annually managed expenditure. They carry out a number of functions in financial services. Among these responsibilities are to ensure the City of London remains competitive, to guarantee financial stability in the UK, and to regulate banking and other financial services throughout the nation.

Treasury also maintains responsibility for overseeing the various taxes in Britain. This includes indirect, direct, property, business, corporation, and personal taxes. The ministry handles encouraging private sector involvement and investment in national infrastructure and delivers infrastructure projects throughout the public sector. Finally, they must make certain that the growth of the British economy is ultimately both steady and sustainable.

In carrying out these critical responsibilities, HM Treasury has a range of priorities. They work towards strong growth which is sustainable. They attempt to utilize the tax money responsibly. Their goal is to rebalance the national economy while reducing the deficit. They strive to create a fairer and simpler tax system for all.

Treasury looks to develop safer and stronger British banks. They work towards levying the most competitive corporate taxes possible. They help to increase the ease and access to financial services for British consumers. Finally, they seek to better the financial sector's regulation so that it will safeguard both the national economy and members of the British public.

HM Treasury has its headquarters in London. They also maintain regional offices in Edinburgh, Scotland and Norwich, England.

HSBC

HSBC stands for Hong Kong Shanghai Banking Corporation. This largest international bank in the world by balance sheet has over $1.63 trillion in total assets. The British London based banking giant counts more than 47 million customers as part of its international network spanning 71 countries and territories and 6,000 offices around the globe.

HSBC was founded by a British businessman in 1865 to finance the growing trade between the West and Asia, and especially China. Today HSBC remains among the largest and most impressive banking and financial services conglomerate groups in the world by any relevant measure. Their stated goal is to be recognized as the globe's foremost and best respected international bank.

HSBC is operated globally through four major divisions. These include its Commercial Banking, Global Banking and Markets, Private Banking, and Retail Banking and Wealth Management divisions. Among the banking group's many achievements over the centuries, the group was responsible for setting up the modern day Chinese currency and banking system back during the reign of the last Chinese imperial dynasty. This financial and currency system which HSBC established for China is still used today.

HSBC Commercial Banking operates throughout 55 different nations and territories. Their operation covers both developing and developed world markets that are most important to their many customers. The division serves a great variety of customer types, ranging from major multinational corporations to small outfits to medium sized companies. It offers them the financial tools they need to run their operations effectively.

One of the bank's most appealing features is that it can call upon its vast and multinational financial strength to support clients with term loans, project and acquisition finance, and daily working capital. The bank also offers its customers the financial and legal know how to assist them in engaging in effective stock and bond issues and offerings.

The commercial banking group supports specialist staff in four primary fields. Global Liquidity and Cash Management provides businesses with tools to effectively manage their liquidity. The online platform helps the customers to transact payments seamlessly between currencies and countries. Global Trade and Receivable Finance offers financing to suppliers and buyers in the trade cycle so that they can cover their supply chains.

Global Banking offers its commercial customers a variety of services such as capital financing via equity, debt, and advisory services. Insurance and Investments provides protection in the form of financial, business, and trade insurance. It also offers wealth management for corporations, employee benefits, and other commercial insurance products to protect against risk.

The Global Banking and Markets division works with customers to help them access commercial opportunities for developed and developing markets. This division operates in three groups including the corporate sector group, the resources and energy group, and the financial institutions group. Services and products are comprised of financing, advisory, research and analysis, prime services, trading and sales, securities services, and transaction banking.

HSBC Private Bank delivers global private banking services that include wealth management, investment, and private banking services to its individual, business, and executive clients. The division's goal is to become the world's foremost private bank for business owners who are high net worth individuals leveraging the group's longstanding globally leading commercial services and heritage.

Retail Banking and Wealth Management provides its tens of millions of customers with a broad range of products and services. These include personal banking, internet banking, loans, mortgages, savings, insurance, investments, and credit cards. They offer a variety of proprietary services and accounts that include HSBC Premier, HSBC Advance, personal online banking, financial planning, and wealth solutions.

ING Group

The ING Group is the largest Dutch and Benelux based bank in the world. The acronym ING translates into International Netherlands Group in English. This global bank and financial institution draws on its important European base to provide services on a global scale. Their customers include governments, institutions, major corporations, smaller businesses, families, and individuals. ING is famous for its world class service and well known brand that put their customers at the center of all their endeavors.

Over 52,000 staff work for the ING Group to deliver wholesale and retail banking and financial services and products to their customers located in more than 40 countries. The group calls its advantages the important financial positions it enjoys, its international network, and its all channel distribution strategy. They claim their greatest asset is their brand that is both well recognized and well liked by customers in a number of different countries. They are honored as one of the leading institutions found in the Banks industry sector of the Dow Jones Sustainability Index.

The ING Group acts as a European network bank that extends its range around the globe for its many customers. They boast a range of global franchises as well. ING concentrates on growing into the main bank for new customers. This strategy is to increase the number of customers with recurring income payment accounts that have another product minimally included. ING starts customers with retail banking and offers other anchor products such as lending, wholesale banking transactions, and investments.

The bank's business transformation program is working to help the bank grow into an optimal operating model of Wholesale Banking. To do this, they are increasing their customer base in industry transaction and lending financial services. To better focus on this goal, they divide their principal and target markets into market leaders, challengers, and growth markets.

The market leaders group are those countries of Benelux - the Netherlands, Belgium, and Luxembourg. These are the nations where the ING Group is market leading in wholesale banking and retail banking services. The strategy here is to expand in certain segments and to continue developing into their direct first bank model. They are investing in digital capabilities and providing excellence in their operational programs to this effect.

Challenger markets are those where they are working consistently to increase their current market share. These markets include the important countries of Germany, France, Italy, Spain, Austria, and Australia. The businesses in these nations provide wholesale and retail banking. The focus with retail here is to offer online direct banking services. This gives them a price advantage versus other traditional banks.

In the challenger markets, ING is working to use their already recognized savings vehicles to grow into payment accounts and to create primary banking relationships. They are striving to launch from their expertise in direct banking to build up the consumer lending and small to medium sized business lending. They are also working on diligently increasing their corporate customer base in these countries through new abilities in industry lending and transaction services here.

ING Group's growth markets include their businesses in Turkey, Poland, Romania, and Asia. Here they provide a comprehensive line of wholesale and retail banking. These rapidly expanding economies provide them with solid opportunities for growth. This is why they are investing heavily to build a sustainable market share here. To do this, they are concentrating their efforts on digital technology leadership and also are pushing their direct first bank model.

Interim Financing

Interim financing is a way of obtaining funding on a short term basis for a project. It can also be called gap financing or bridge financing. People or companies elects for this kind of financing for a specific purpose.

They may be seeking to get funding so that a project can be finished and start creating revenues. This would keep them from having to take resources away from other projects. This concept generally refers to loans. There are also cases of interim financing where companies utilize grants or other types of financial assistance.

A short term loan proves to be among the most frequently employed types of interim financing. These kinds of loans can be crafted so that the borrower will pay back the entire principle of the loan along with all of its interest in twelve months or less from the loan issue date.

This is the opposite of long term financing. In the longer term variety, the borrower receives several years to repay the loan. Loan deals on gap financing often come with interest rates that are a little higher than with longer term loans. For individuals or companies with excellent credit, financing companies can often offer extremely competitive interest rates on these short term loans.

A common use of interim financing is with construction projects that need to be finished. On an individual level, a consumer may wish to renovate either a room in the house or the entire home. The borrower may decide to obtain a short term loan at a better interest rate to cover the costs of labor and materials at the beginning of the project. This can save the borrower on the more substantial interest rates and fees for using credit cards or store credit with the various vendors. The end result is that the consumer spends significantly less money on the improvement project than he or she would by not utilizing the interim financing.

Real estate deals are another common use for this interim financing. A home owner may wish to move forward and buy a new house. The owner may need their present house to sell first. Short term loans like these can prove to be an optimal answer to the problem. Using the bridge loan the owner buys the house. The borrower can then repay the loan once their original house sells. This kind of strategy will help to push through the sale of the original house as well. The previous owners have already moved, which means the new owners can occupy the property without delay.

The goal of interim financing is to offer a short term bridge loan for the individual or business concerned. Despite this, sometimes a situation develops where the borrower will not be able to repay the loan as quickly as hoped. In this case, longer term or additional financing becomes necessary. Many lenders will work with the borrower in such a case to come up with a longer term financing program.

This will completely pay off the short term original loan. Additional money will usually be provided so that the borrower has the funds necessary to complete the project. This is especially the case with construction companies. It works out better for the borrower to engage in a rollover longer term loan than to take out another short term loan. The reason for this is that the longer term loans' finance rates are nearly always lower than the most competitive rates lenders will offer borrowers for short term bridge loans.

International Bank Account Number (IBAN)

IBAN is an acronym which stands for the International Bank Account Number. This standardized numbering system for identifying bank accounts around the world with precision was first conceived of and implemented by the banks of Europe. They wanted to make simpler the means of transacting between bank accounts of financial institutions based in different countries.

This internationally agreed to system for identifying the world's banks and bank accounts was critically needed for banking across international borders. European banks found it necessary to come up with a way to effectively process the cross border transactions. They wanted to dramatically lower the dangers of errors in transcription and subsequent transmission problems which sometimes resulted.

It was the ECBS European Committee for Banking Standards that first adopted the IBAN concept. It later evolved into a global standard under the auspices of ISO 13616:1997. This standard became updated with ISO directive 13616:2007 that now utilizes SWIFT as the official registrar. The system originally arose as a means of facilitating payments made throughout the European Union. It has now been put into place by the majority of European nations along with many countries throughout the globe, especially in the states of the Caribbean and Middle East. Sixty-nine different nations utilized the IBAN account numbering system as of February 2016. More sign up all the time.

The IBAN account number is made up of several components. The two letter national code comes first. This is followed up by the two check digits which enable an integrity check of the IBAN number to be sure it is correct. Finally come as many as thirty alphanumeric characters which are also called the BBAN, or Basic Bank Account Number. Each national banking association decides which BBAN will become the standard for their own national bank accounts. In general, the remaining thirty characters include such information as the domestic bank account number, branch location identifier, and additional routing information.

While the IBAN concept has taken hold effectively throughout the continent of Europe, it is not a universal global standard yet, though it is the closest thing to one. The practice of working with such standardized account numbers as these is growing and gaining in popularity in other countries of the world. This is proven by the fact that nearly forty non- European countries now employ the International Bank Account Number system for themselves on only the twentieth anniversary of the concept being introduced originally.

Before the rise of the IBAN, every country utilized its own national standard to identify bank accounts within their own borders. This proved to be confusing in Europe, particularly as the borders between the 27 different EU countries began to blur thanks to the EU. Free movement of people, capital, and goods meant that money was being drawn from and transferred back and forth between the banks and bank accounts of different European states on an increasingly common basis. Sometimes important and even critical routing information was simply missing from transfers and payments.

SWIFT's routing information does not require transaction specific formats which identify both account numbers and transaction types specifically. This is because they leave the transaction partners to agree on these. SWIFT codes also lack check digits, meaning transcription errors can not be detected nor can banks validate the routing data before they submit the payments without these two digits. Continuous costly routing errors were creating delays on payments and transfers as the receiving and sending banks were also working with intermediary banks for routing.

The ISO International Organization for Standardization overcame these problems in 1997 by creating the IBAN in association with the European Committee for Banking Standards. Because the ECBS simplified and better standardized the original format proposed by the ISO, an update was issued with ISO 13616:2003 and then again in ISO 13616-1:2007.

As of 2017, the United States' banks do not employ IBANs themselves. Instead, they utilize either Fedwire identifiers for the banks or the ABA Routing Number.

International Bank for Reconstruction and Development (IBRD)

The International Bank for Reconstruction and Development proves to be a principal and original organization within the World Bank. It loans money to help out middle income nations as well as poorer countries that are creditworthy. It derives the majority of its funds from selling bonds on the global capital markets.

Over 180 countries participate as members of the IBRD. Every member has a certain amount of voting power. This is based on its subscription of capital. The United States possesses a full sixth of all the IBRD's shares. Besides an enormous amount of voting clout, the U.S. also owns the exclusive rights to veto any changes which are proposed for the bank itself.

The origins of the International Bank for Reconstruction and Development hail back to the end of the Second World War. The United States founded it in 1944. The initial purpose of this organization lay in assisting Europe to rebuild itself from the devastation brought on by World War II. The role of the bank has since shifted to offering loans along with technical assistance, knowledge, and advice to mostly middle income nations.

As the first institution within the World Bank, the IBRD cooperates closely alongside the other institutions within the World Bank Group. Together they serve to encourage economic growth, to assist developing nations in reducing the poverty of their citizens, and to help spread prosperity.

The bank itself is owned by the 189 member nations' governments. A board and directors represent these countries for routine decision making and administration. This board is comprised of 25 members who are Executive Directors. Five of these are appointed and 20 of them are elected by the owning members.

Developing nations are able to benefit greatly from the technical services, knowledge, and strategic advice that the bank provides. This is beyond its financial resources which it distributes as guarantees, loans, and risk management products. The World Bank serves in this capacity its beneficiaries who are also shareholders and global actors as well as being clients of the bank.

Not only national but sub national levels of governments can participate and benefit. The International Bank for Reconstruction and Development finances a wide variety of projects spanning every sector. It simultaneously offers its expert knowledge and technical support for varying phases in an ongoing project.

Some of the financial services and products which the IBRD delivers assist countries with developing resilience to external shocks. They help with product access for alleviating negative affects of interest rates, currency exchange rates, destructive weather and natural disasters, and volatility in commodity prices. The bank is different from a traditional commercial lender in that it does more than serve as a financier. It also has an important role in the international transfer of knowledge and technical assistance.

In times of crisis, the International Bank for Reconstruction and Development serves to help preserve the financial strength of its borrowers to limit the negative effects on the poor. It also works to provide financial market access to these nations at better terms than they would be able to attain by themselves. This helps with attracting private capital as well by encouraging a positive investment environment.

Many of the longer term social and personal development projects that the bank supports, private creditors would not consider. The bank also helps with promoting institutional reforms in areas like anti-corruption and public safety.

International Financial Institutions (IFI)

International financial institutions (IFIs) are international financial organizations which multiple nations founded. They are subject to international law instead of the laws of any one single country. The IFIs are usually owned by national governments of the founding members.

Sometimes other international institutions or organizations are stakeholders as well. Even though there are IFIs that two or three nations created, the best known ones were developed by numerous national participants. The most famous international financial institutions arose following the Second World War in order to help rebuild Europe, as well as to offer the means of multinational cooperation in overseeing the world's financial system.

The largest international financial institution in the world today proves to be the European Investment Bank. In 2013, this organization possessed a balance sheet that amounted to 512 billion euros. This compares to the main component parts of the World Bank, the IBRD with $358 billion in assets as of 2014 and the IDA with its $183 billion in assets as of 2014. By means of comparison, the world's biggest international commercial banks boast assets each totaling between $2 - $3 billion, as with Britain's HSBC and the United States' JP Morgan Chase Bank.

Arguably the most important international financial institutions in the world today remain the ones which the Bretton Woods agreement founded in 1944. These are the World Bank and the International Monetary Fund. Both are participating members of the United Nations system. Their goals are to improve the standards of living in their respective member nations.

Each of these two organizations has its own approach to achieving this mandate, yet they complement each other. The IMF concentrates its efforts on larger macroeconomic issues. The World Bank instead focuses on developing the economies and reducing the poverty of member states over the longer term.

The World Bank and IMF came into being in July of 1944 at the internationally attended Bretton Woods Conference held in New Hampshire. The conference had a goal to build up a new framework of development and economic cooperation which would help to establish a more prosperous and stable global economy. Over 70 years later, this goal is still critical to the operations of both international financial institutions. Only the means they use to reach the goals has changed as different economic challenges and developments arise.

The World Bank mandate is to encourage poverty reduction and economic improvement longer term. They do this by offering financial and technical assistance to aid countries which are trying to reform sections of their economies or to develop particular projects. These projects could be delivering electricity and water, constructing health centers and schools, safeguarding the environment, or fighting disease. Such help as the World Bank provides is typically longer term in nature and funded by contributions from member nations as well as by issuing bonds. The staff of the World Bank is typically specialized in certain sectors, issues, or methods.

The IMF on the other hand operates under a mandate to foster monetary cooperation on an international level while it offers technical assistance and policy advice to help countries to develop and keep more prosperous and stronger economies. As part of this, the IMF offers loans. They also help nations to create policies and programs that will address their imbalance of payments if they are unable to obtain affordable term financing to meet their international financial obligations. These loans are either medium or short term. The funds come from the quota contributions' pool provided by member states. The staff of the IMF is mainly economists who possess vast experience with financial and macroeconomic issues.

Investment Banking

Investment Banking refers to a particular subdivision of banking. This investment type of banking pertains to developing capital for governments, organizations, and corporations. Investment banks will come up with new equity and debt securities to float and sell them on behalf of any corporation. They also facilitate mergers and acquisitions and company reorganizations. They help to sell the securities and broker major trades for private investors and institutions. Besides this, they give guidance to those issuing stocks on the placement and floating of stock issues.

A great many of the bigger investment banks prove to be associated with (or wholly or partially owned by) bigger financial and banking institutions. A number of them have evolved into house hold known names. The biggest of these famous investment banks are Goldman Sachs, JPMorgan Chase, Morgan Stanley, Bank of America Merrill Lynch, HSBC, and Deutsche Bank.

In general, such investment banking fosters huge, complex, often international in nature financial transactions. This might come with advisory services on the best ways to structure deals when the customer is interested in engaging in a sale, merger, or acquisition. Other firms may want to know how much a certain company is worth. The investment banks may need to float and sell securities in order to raise money for the groups of clients. Someone will have to develop the documents which the SEC Securities and Exchange Commission requires in order for companies to be taken public.

The investment banking groups hire investment bankers who assist their clients (the governments, organizations, and corporations) in planning for, setting up, and managing enormous projects. This saves a great deal of money and time for the clients through identifying any risks common to the project before the project starts. The idea is that investment bankers are highly trained experts in the financial services fields. They are supposed to have a wealth of knowledge, background, and advice to offer their clients for the best way to plan developments so the company can pursue the best recommendations for the current state of economics pertaining to the company's particular project.

One can also think of the investment banks as not only an advisor but a middle man. They offer the useful go-between for companies and the investing public who want to purchase such new bond and stock issues. Investment banks package together financial securities and instruments so that the companies can optimize their revenues and safely come through the often complex regulatory environments.

For example, in many cases where companies launch their first IPO initial public offering, the underwriting investment banks will purchase most or all of the new shares straight off of their client the company. They then re-sell these IPO shares on the stock markets. The company gets a big single payday upfront this way and the investment bank acts as a contractor for the actual IPO underwriting. The investment banks typically profit well, as they usually re-price the shares with a nice markup on their original purchase price. This also entails a serious amount of risk though. If they overprice the stock shares, then they may not be able to sell all the shares and instead could end up selling them at a loss to the price they initially paid for them in the first place.

It is not at all uncommon for various investment banks to compete with each other for the best new IPO underwriting opportunities, and sometimes they end up working together on enormous ones. It could lead to a higher per share price being realized for the company which is going public. When the competition for the project becomes particularly intense, it can hit the investment bank's profit margins. In these cases what often happens is that several of the major investment banks will underwrite a portion of the securities, often in different jurisdictions such as EuroNext, NYSE, and London Stock Exchange. The advantages to the investment banks are that the risk becomes spread around and reduced this way.

Japanese Bankers Association (JBA)

The Japanese Bankers Association is also known by its internationally recognized acronym the JBA. This is the elite financial institutions' umbrella organization. Its membership is comprised of bank holding companies, banks, and banker associations throughout Japan. Their purpose is to promote planning for the best operating of payment systems, to reinforce compliance and promote CSR, to encourage appropriate transactions for consumers, and to support the individual banking endeavors and operations of its member banks.

Every year the Japanese Bankers Association elects both a chairman and a number of vice chairmen to oversee the organization. It is the JBA's Board of Directors which confers each March to hold this election. The various board members actually vote to decide who will become the two heads of the umbrella banking organization. President and Chief Executive Officer Takeshi Kunibe of Sumitomo Mitsui Banking Corporation is the current chairman of the JBA, as of February 2017.

In Japan, the various financial institutions are actually broken down into a few important categories. These groupings come from characteristics which include either the historical backgrounds or the primary business functions of the institutions in question. Such categories include city banks, regional banks, and member banks from the Second Association of Regional Banks (or regional banks level II). These are not legally binding definitions. Instead they are classifications used to help with publishing statistics and administration efforts.

City banks prove to be extremely large in their geographical representation and size. Their headquarters lie in the major cities of the Japanese islands. They also boast branches in the important and large population centers of Tokyo, Osaka, and other important cities and surrounding suburbs. Today there are only five of the large and impressive city banks remaining in Japan. These are as follows: Bank of Tokyo-Mitsubishi UFJ, Resona Bank, Mizuho Bank, Sumitomo Mitsui Banking Corporation, and Saitama Resona Bank. Mergers and acquisitions in the field have helped to narrow this important category down from the original 13 city banks to the present five.

By contrast, regional banks are typically found and headquartered within the primary city of a given prefecture in Japan. They naturally conduct the overwhelming majority of their business endeavors in their home regional prefecture. It follows that they would have important local ties with area governments and locally based businesses. Today's Japan boasts 64 regional banks such as Hiroshima Bank, Shikoku Bank, and Bank of Okinawa.

The final category of the Japanese based banks is the regional banks level II. Such financial institutions tend to provide services to individuals and smaller companies in their principal geographical regions. The vast majority of the Regional Banks II was once mutual savings banks at some point. There are 41 Regional Banks II in Japan today. Among them are banks including Towa Bank, Aichi Bank, and Ehime Bank.

The banking classification picture has become more clouded in 1999 with the rise of certain specialty financial institutions which were not traditional banks at all. These entered into the banking universe in Japan through founding different kinds of banks like those which are internet based or specialize in settlements. They do not fall under a traditional category of the three mentioned above and so are referred to by the Japanese Bankers Association as "other banks." There are five banks in this non-traditional banking category. These are as follows: Citibank Japan, Aozora Bank, Norinchukin Bank, Shinsei Bank, and Seven Bank.

There is only one single foreign based banking member of the Japanese Bankers Association today. This is the United States' headquartered JP Morgan Chase Bank, National Association. Citibank Japan is of course classified as one of the "other banks" so does not fall under this category as determined by the JBA.

One of the primary ancillary functions of the Japanese Bankers Association is to calculate up and publish the JBA TIBOR. Since 1995, they have released this Japanese Yen TIBOR rate as well as the Euroyen TIBOR rate from 1998. Such rates reveal the unsecured call markets' prevailing rates as well as the interest rates on the offshore market.

JP Morgan Chase

JP Morgan Chase turns out to be among the oldest financial institutions or banks that are based in the United States. The firm's history hails back more than 200 years. Today, the company boasts assets that exceed $2.4 trillion, and it is a leading global banking and financial services outfit. JP Morgan Chase has a presence in over 100 countries and maintains more than 235,000 employees around the globe in over 450 corporate offices.

JP Morgan Chase counts millions of individuals and small businesses as customers of the banking group. They serve some of the most important governments, institutions, and corporations in the world. JP Morgan proves to be one of the global leaders in financial services for individuals and small businesses, investment banking, commercial banking, asset management, and financial transactions and processing. One of their proudest achievements as a testament to their importance in the United States is the fact that their company stock is one of the only 30 company components of the famed Dow Jones Industrial Average.

JP Morgan Chase & Company proves to be not only one of the oldest and biggest financial institutions in the world, but also among the best known such organizations on earth. The earliest predecessor of the banking group received its charter in New York City in 1799. The company has an aggressive history of mergers and acquisitions that have seen over 1,200 predecessor banking and financial institutions merged into the present day form of the banking behemoth.

Among its most important legacy firms are J.P. Morgan, Chase Manhattan Bank, Chemical Bank, and Manufacturers Hanover of New York City as well as Bank One, National Bank of Detroit, and First Chicago in the Midwest. These institutions each held important ties for their day and age to progress in finance and the expansion of both the American and world economies.

The mega mergers of the banking group began in 2000 when J.P. Morgan & Co. Inc. merged together with the Chase Manhattan Corporation. In this merger, J.P. Morgan, Chase, Manufacturers Hanover, and Chemical became one enormous financial conglomerate. This at last combined four of the biggest, most important, and oldest banking center groups of New York City together under the single entity name and ownership of J.P. Morgan Chase & Co.

The activity continued in 2004. J.P. Morgan Chase & Company merged with Chicago's Bank One Corporation. At the time, the New York Times newspaper claimed that the combination would remake the competitive landscape of banking as it tied together the commercial and investment banking prowess of J.P. Morgan Chase with the significant consumer banking abilities of the Midwestern-based Bank One.

In 2008, JP Morgan Chase acquired the world's largest savings and loan Washington Mutual Bank as a result of the biggest bank failure in history. Gaining control of Washington Mutual's substantial banking operations meant that the banking group expanded its consumer branches into Florida, California, and Washington State for the first time. This formed the second biggest network of bank locations in the United States whose branches reached an astonishing 42% of all people living in the U.S.

That same year in the depths of the financial crisis, JP Morgan Chase took over the collapsing Wall Street firm The Bear Stearns Companies. This improved the group's swelling abilities in a wide variety of businesses such as global energy trading, cash clearing, and prime brokerage. The group rounded out its presence in the United Kingdom in 2010 by gaining full ownership of its original British joint venture J.P. Morgan Cazenove. This joint venture was among the most premier investment banks in Britain.

Lloyds Banking Group

Lloyds Banking Group represents the biggest financial services consortium in the United Kingdom. As a financial services provider that concentrates on business and retail clients, they count millions of customers throughout the country. They have a presence in practically every community of the U.K.

Part of the impressive size and strength of Lloyds Banking Group centers on its major household name brands. Among the most important of these are Lloyds Bank, Bank of Scotland, Halifax, and Scottish Widows.

The main businesses of the Lloyds Banking Group help it to touch so many customers in their daily lives. They provide retail, business, and corporate banking. The group also delivers general and life insurance. They provide investment opportunities and pension plans as well.

The shares of the Lloyds Banking Group trade on the London Stock Exchange as well as the New York Stock Exchange. The company is one of the biggest in the main British stock market benchmark index the FTSE 100. It also ranks among the largest banks in the world.

Lloyds Banking Group also runs the biggest retail bank in the United Kingdom. This was formerly known as Lloyds TSB but is now simply called Lloyds Bank. It claims the highest number of bank branches in the country. This gives them access to a diversified and massive base of customers. It helps them to cross sell products and services so that they are able to offer a total package of financial services and products for their clients. Their mobile, telephone, and digital services are comprehensive.

The history of this leading member in the Lloyds Banking Group, Lloyds Bank, goes back three centuries. Founded in 1765, the bank celebrated its 250 year anniversary back in 2015. This also makes it among the oldest of the largest banks in the world.

Lloyds Bank started its first branch in Birmingham where it operated as a single branch for a hundred years. In the twentieth century, it pursued decades of mergers to grow into first a national and then an international bank. The 1995 merger with TSB changed its name to Lloyds TSB Bank for a time. In the process of its expansion, the bank gained control of the company which invented Travelers Checks, opened the first British ATM machine, and had a foremost part in launching among the first credit cards in the United Kingdom.

Bank of Scotland is headquartered in Edinburgh. It turns out to be the oldest bank in Scotland. The Scottish Parliament founded it in 1695. It has remained a cornerstone of Scottish business since the act created it. The Parliament originally established the bank to increase the trade of Scotland with nearby trading partners. These included neighboring England and the Low Countries (now Belgium, the Netherlands, and Luxembourg).

The Bank of Scotland also claims a number of pioneering firsts in the industry. It became the very first European commercial bank to issue banknotes with success. It continues to do this today. The bank became the first in the U.K. to put in a computer for processing accounts in 1959. In 2009 the bank joined the Lloyds Group.

The banking group also owns the Halifax brand. This is a building society that arose in 1852. A little group set it up in meetings at the Halifax based Old Cock Inn. They created this investment and loan society to benefit the area working people. Individuals with extra money were able to invest it while others could borrow these funds to build or buy their own house. Eventually Halifax grew into the largest building society around the globe. It counts over 18 million customers today.

London Interbank Offered Rate (LIBOR)

LIBOR is a main global benchmark interest rate. It stands for London InterBank Offered Rate. This rate represents how much banks actually charge each other for loans based on one year, six months, three months, one month, and overnight timeframes. Banks all over the world use this benchmark rate. Reuters news service publishes this critical rate every day at 11 am. They do this in five different currencies of the U.S. dollar, the Euro, British Pound, Swiss franc, and Japanese yen.

Historically the BBA British Bankers Association oversaw and compiled this rate. The IBA ICE Benchmark Administration assumed this responsibility on August 1st of 2014. They figure up this rate using contributor bank submissions. In every currency for which they calculate it there are between 11 and 18 contributing banks who act as an oversight board.

LIBOR does more than provide a rate for the interbank loans. It is utilized as a bank guide for their setting of credit card rates, interest only mortgages, and adjustable rate loans. Bank lenders add in between one and two points to make money. An incredible $10 trillion in loans are determined at least in part by this interbank rate.

Besides these uses, this rate also serves as a base price for credit default swaps and interest rate swaps. These contracts are a type of insurance in case loans default. The swaps also created the 2008 financial crisis. Hedge funds and banks believed that risk did not exist in the mortgage backed securities because they were protected by this insurance.

The problem arose as the subprime mortgages that underlay the mortgage backed securities started defaulting. AIG and other insurance companies discovered they did not have enough cash available to pay off the swaps. In order to save all swap holders from bankruptcy, the Federal Reserve was forced to rescue AIG with a bailout. Despite the fact that these swaps were supposed to be dispersed after the financial crisis, the LIBOR rate remains the basis on over $350 trillion of such credit default swaps.

Banks created LIBOR in the 1980s in response to a demand for a standard interest rate to establish derivatives. The original rate came out in 1986 in the three currencies the U.S. dollar, British pound, and Japanese yen. The BBA later expanded it to include the additional currencies of Swiss franc and Euro.

A scandal plagued the LIBOR rate starting in 2012. The British Bankers' Association figured out the rate using its panel of banks that acted as representatives from every one of the currencies involved. BBA queried the banks about the rate they would charge in the set currencies for different amounts of time. The BBA's downfall was that they believed the rates the banks provided them with were true.

This unraveled in 2012 as British bank Barclays became charged with deliberately providing lower rates to the BBA then the ones they actually received from 2005 to 2009. They suffered a $450 million fine and the CEO Bob Diamond had to resign. When Diamond went down he told authorities the majority of other banks engaged in the same practice and that the Bank of England was aware.

The reasons that Barclays and others were lying about their rate was for better profits. Lower rates made the banks look stronger and more attractive to borrowers than banks with higher rates. The end result had three bankers found guilty of manipulating rates in 2015 while six others were acquitted of their charges in 2016. The guilty bankers all worked for Rabobank. The rate was taken away from the British Bankers Association and given over to the care of the ICE Benchmark Administration because of the scandal.

Money Market Account (MMA)

Money Market Account refers to a type of savings account which commonly includes advantages such as a debit card and check writing privileges. Besides this, it usually has interest rates which are higher than those which normal savings accounts provide. Such money markets generally have a higher minimum account balance than the average savings accounts do. These accounts are sometimes referred to by their acronym of MMA.

For those individuals who are contemplating a safe depository vehicle for bigger sums of cash and who wish to earn some interest while keeping the funds entirely liquid, these money market accounts can be an optimal solution. Among their pros are that the balance funds are available without advance notice, that they earn a relatively higher interest rate, that they provide the capability of writing as many as six checks each month, and that the debit card attached to them can be utilized as many as six times every month.

For any person who is going to place at least a few thousand dollars into a bank account and desires the clear cut safety provided by the FDIC Federal Deposit Insurance Corporation guarantee of funds, these can be a solid choice. Both credit unions and banks offer them as a reliable place to keep customers' emergency day purpose funds. The money is kept segregated from an account holder's daily utilization checking account funds this way. It can grow quicker than money kept in a comparable savings account thanks to the higher interest rate commonly attached to these MMAs. They provide the added convenience of check writing, which allows for easily covering any unexpected or emergency expenses.

Yet these accounts should not be confused with either checking or savings accounts. In fact they have stark differences from either of the two competing types. For starters, MMAs are not at all checking accounts. They may include the debit card maximum use feature or limited check writing privileges. Yet as with a savings account, they are Federal Reserve-regulation limited to maximum of six monthly withdrawals or transfers in a given month. This includes transactions made by check, debit card, or online/in person transfer. For those individuals who will need more than these half a dozen uses, interest bearing checking accounts make more practical sense than do money market accounts.

Besides this MMAs are similarly not strictly savings accounts either because of their debit cards and check writing capabilities. For those people who do not feel the need of having checks or even the debit card convenience with the account, there are sometimes better interest rates on balances available through what are known as high yield online savings accounts.

One of these types is the CD or certificate of deposit. Cd's may require that the owners agree to tie up their funds for as little as from months to as long as for years. MMAs will certainly permit more convenient and immediate time framed withdrawals than this. Yet CDs will pay better rates for those who can afford to lock it down for some time.

Finally, such money market accounts should not be confused with money market funds. The latter are instead investments whose principal value will decline if the market plunges. All MMAs carry the full FDIC backing when they are operated by banks, and by the NCUA National Credit Union Administration when they are held at credit unions. This amount of protection is equal to $250,000 per depositor or account.

For those individuals who decide that money market accounts are well suited for them, the best policy is to pursue those that come without any associated monthly fees and that pay the highest possible interest rates. It is also critical to ensure that they do not require too high a minimum account balance. This is critical to pay attention to since some financial institutions mandate that depositors open the account with and maintain a $10,000 account balance for these MMAs.

Money of Zero Maturity (MZM)

Money of zero maturity represents a way of measuring the money supply. This measurement for money which is circulating in an economy only covers money that is available to be spent and utilized. As such, this MZM is really a counting of all of the money supply that is liquid in a given economy.

Individuals can figure up the money of zero maturity with some basic math. This starts with obtaining the M2 measure of the money supply. From this M2 figure, all time deposits must be subtracted, such as with certificates of deposit. Next this result must be taken and added to the amount of money market funds which are available. This sum finally provides the MZM.

In practical terms, this measure of money includes several different components. All physical currency, including bank notes and coins, are a part of it. Checking account balances are also included. Savings account totals similarly comprise the MZM. Finally, money market accounts round out the figure. These are all configurations of money which are immediately available for par value to both companies and individuals.

Other forms of money are not included in the measure. Money of zero maturity never considers money held in accounts such as certificates of deposit or any other types of time deposits. This is because these funds contained in such financial instruments can not be instantly accessed for full par value. Similarly investments held in stocks and bonds must be first sold and settled before they can be obtained.

A number of analysts like to utilize the money of zero maturity because it proves to be an extremely liquid measurement. In fact this has grown to become among the most preferred means of measuring the country's money supply exactly because it does more completely depict the readily available money in the economy that can be employed for consumption and other spending. The name for this money measure comes from its combination of all available liquid and money with zero maturity that the three M's contain in M1, M2, and M3.

There are practical applications for the money of zero maturity measurement. The figure presents a reliable indicator of a nation's actual money base for the entire economy. As such it depicts the quantity of money which is literally moving throughout the economy as a whole. Since the Federal Reserve quit tracking and following the M3 number for money supply back in 2006 on March 23rd, this has become a preferred measurement of money supply, if not the most popular one.

When economists and analysts are aware of the amount of money which is moving throughout the economy, they can develop a feeling for two important trends. They are able to learn at a fairly quick glance whether or not the economy is growing or is instead contracting. By studying this figure, they can also determine how high the danger for inflation is over the near term.

When economists look at a chart of the MZM, they are interested in the rate of growth on a year to year, quarter to quarter, or month to month basis. As this growth rate improves, the economy is likely to expand along with it, and the threat of inflation increases apace. If instead the growth rate in the MZM decreases, the economy stands a solid chance of shrinking. This would mean inflationary threats are lower.

Money Supply

Where business and economics are concerned, the money supply proves to be the complete quantity of money that is available throughout the economy at any given moment in time. Money can be defined in a few different ways. The commonly accepted definitions are comprised of both circulating currency and demand deposits. Demand deposits are the assets of depositors in banks that are easy for them to access, such as checking accounts.

The statistical data on money supply is recorded and made available to the public by the government. In some countries, the central bank publishes such information. Analysts are always interested in any changes to the money supply total, since it has great impacts on inflation levels, prices, and the business cycle.

There are now several different measurements of money supply published within the U.S. These range from narrow to broad money supply totals. While narrower calculations only measure the most liquid of assets that are easy to spend, such as currency itself and checking account deposits, other broader measures include assets that are not so liquid, such as certificates of deposit.

The MB is the complete monetary base as it pertains to all currency. It proves to be the money supply figure that is the most liquid. M1 is the measure that leaves out bank reserves. M2 is the measurement that is given as the main economic indicator in figuring how high inflation will become. Both money and its near substitutes are included in this category. M3 used to be the main figure for money supply in the Untied States, until the Fed elected not to release it any longer after 2006. It included the M2 measure plus longer term deposits.

Inflation commonly results from changes to the money supply. The evidence demonstrates the direct correlation between the growth of the money supply and longer term rising prices. This is particularly the case when the money supply increase is rapid within an economy.

The latest example of how the growth of the money supply can ruin a currency and destroy an economy is demonstrated by Zimbabwe. This African country witnessed dramatic increases in the national money supply and then became a victim of hyperinflation, or a dramatic gain in prices. Because of this, the money supply has to be responsibly controlled and overseen.

The money supply is actually controlled through monetary policy. Central banks such as the Fed determine the money supply in part through their reserve ratios that they make banks observe with percent of deposits kept on hand. They can also adjust it with the interest rates that they set for the country.

Many critics have pointed to the rapid growth in the money supply of U.S. dollars in the years of the financial crisis and the Great Recession as dangerous. From the years of 2007-2010, the dollar money supply has been grown by in excess of three hundred percent. At the same time, the economy has a whole has barely grown. This is the consummate recipe for inflation, and many economists have suggested that you will see high inflation, and potentially even hyperinflation, within the United States in the next several years as a direct result.

Monte dei Paschi di Sienna Bank

Monte dei Paschi di Sienna Bank is the oldest bank in Italy, Europe, and the world. It is also among the most important financial institutions in Italy as the third largest Italian bank. As the flagship brand of the MPS Group (Monte Paschi Sienna), it leads the domestic market and lending market in market share percentages. It trades on the country's most impressive and respected index, the FTSE MIB in Milan, the nation's financial center.

The bank is affectionately known as "il Monte" by millions of Italians who are customers, investors, or creditors to it around the country. Founded in 1472 by merchants in the then Republic of Sienna, the bank has evolved into the ideal reminder of the once-glorious medieval banking and mercantile traditions of both Sienna and the formerly independent Italian city states.

Unfortunately for Monte dei Paschi di Sienna Bank, the world's oldest lending institution has lost its luster and is no longer solvent. Il Monte's financial woes began back in the wake of the American-bank caused financial crisis of 2007. Since then, the Monte dei Paschi di Sienna Bank has announced bad loans to the tune of an eye-watering 28 billion Euros (almost $30 billion US). It has been recapitalized three previous times and yet still desperately trying to secure 5 billion Euros in new capital in order to fund continuing operations. As of end of December 2016, the bank had failed to successfully come up with more than half that amount. Its shares ceased trading on the Italian stock market on the news on December 22nd, as Italian lawmakers urgently approved a 20 billion Euros rescue package fund for the listing bank.

Despite the fact that European Union regulations frown on public bank bailouts since the banking law reforms enacted following the financial and European Sovereign Debt crises, Italy is doggedly pursuing such a rescue. The reason is because of contagion fears to the rest of the Italian banking system, which may easily also spread beyond the national boundaries into the continental European bank powerhouses of embattled German largest financial institution Deutsche Bank, French titans BNP Paribas and Societe Generale, and Swiss behemoths UBS and Credit Suisse.

The Italian banking system is critically important because it is the life blood of the third largest economy in the Euro Zone. Italy is at the same time the second biggest debt to GDP ratio holder in Europe. This is also a scary concern for investors, who know all too well that Italy is the world's third largest sovereign bond market after the United States and Japan. Millions of investors and financial institutions in Italy, the EU, the U.S., and the rest of the world even have exposure to the Italian government bond markets. Besides this, Italy is a member of the G7 great nation economies of the world, with a trillion dollar plus economy whose health and financial future has a very material impact on both the EU and the world economy as a whole.

The global economy can not survive an Italian banking crisis. Italy has become too big to fail as a nation. Italy's largest bank Unicredito remains one of the world's systemically critical global banks. Yet the country is fully in a banking crisis anyway you look at the situation. If Monte dei Paschi di Sienna Bank can not be saved, the resulting Italian banking system crash could cause the entire Euro zone to unwind and the world economy to enter yet another Great Recession as in 2007-2009.

Despite feeble attempts to curb their government debt, the Italian government has only watched it grow to 133 percent of their entire GDP. The most current Bank of Italy provided data proved that the nation's total public debt increased to an astonishing €2.22 trillion through October 2016. With this enormous public debt burden saddling down Italy, the nation faces a literal ticking time bomb thanks to the boiling bank crisis.

This is why the fate of Monte dei Paschi di Sienna may rule the futures of not only its countless Italian pensioner investors and creditors, but also citizens of the whole world. Two decades before Christopher Columbus found the Americas, the bank that holds the key to the stability of the world banking system today first arose. Now the venerable Tuscan-based lender is threatening to overturn the very Western world economies it helped to usher into the modern era of banking and finance as people know it today.

National Bank Act

The National Bank Act refers to three different congressionally passed acts which set up a regime of national banks for the disparate state banks across the United States. These three Federal Banking Acts enabled the U.S. National Banking System to arise. The idea was to foster the creation of a nationwide currency which would be backed up by U.S. Treasury securities held by banks.

The Office of the Comptroller of the Currency under the umbrella of the U.S. Department of the Treasury wanted to be the sole issuer of American currency. To this effect, Treasury authorized the Comptroller of the Currency to start examining and regulating the nationally chartered U.S. banks. These series of acts were responsible for determining the system of national banks in place today and supporting a cohesive banking policy for the United States as a whole.

The first such effort to create a central bank since the First and Second Banks of the United States had failed began with the National Bank Act of 1863. This became the model which was used in the Federal Reserve Act of 1913 eventually. This first act permitted national banks to be created, gave the Federal government permission to sell securities and war bands, and established a plan for creating a unified national currency backed up by government securities.

The Federal government itself directly chartered these subsequent national banks which became subjected to tighter regulation than other banks were at the time. The national banks had to maintain larger capital requirements and could not loan out in excess of 10 percent of their total deposits. The government discovered they could discourage the competition by levying a burdensome tax on the state banks. It only took until 1865 for the majority of the state banks to apply for national charters or to fail altogether.

In 1864, the Federal government waded into the realm of active supervision of all commercial banks. They did this using the National Bank Act of 1864, which was itself based on a law from New York State. This important act created the Office of the Comptroller of the Currency. This office carried the responsibility for chartering, supervising, and examining every national bank.

A year later Congress added still more to this new legislation in the form of the Banking Act of 1865. This July 13, 1866 passed legislation expanded the law to more than simply mandating a 10 percent tax on all of their own state bank proprietary notes. It extended the tax from state banks, national banking associations, and state banking associations so that individuals who utilized such proprietary state bank notes would also be subjected to an additional 10 percent tax.

The act became challenged and subsequently strengthened as a result of the court case known as *Veazie* Bank versus *Fenno*, supra. Thanks to the Chief Justices of the Supreme Court electing to rule with Congress on the matter, all final resistance offered by the state banks to the National Bank Acts of 1865-1866 collapsed.

The 10 percent taxed proved to be so onerous that the majority of state banks chose to change their charters for national ones in order to sidestep the heavy handed tax. This led to the decline for a few years of state banks. In the 1870's and 1880's, state banks saw a resurgence once again as state bank created checks allowed them to get around the failing profitability and importance of their own proprietary bank notes.

OCC

The OCC is the acronym for Office of the Comptroller of the Currency. This independent bureau falls under the United States Department of the Treasury. The U.S. President appoints an individual to serve as Comptroller of the agency for a term of five years. The American Senate must approve this appointment. The Comptroller serves as one of the directors of the Neighbor Works and the FDIC Federal Deposit Insurance Corporation.

The OCC has its headquarters in Washington, D.C. They also maintain four district offices throughout the U.S. as well as London office to monitor the national banks' international activities. The United States Congress created the agency with its 1863 National Currency Act. The group celebrated its 150 year anniversary back in 2013.

There are important responsibilities that the OCC has regarding banks. It charters, supervises, and regulates every national bank and federal savings association. Besides this, it also manages the foreign banks' federal agencies and branches. It has a mission to make certain that all of these financial institutions run according to sound, safe practices and abide by all relevant regulations and laws. It also ensures that there is sufficient access to financial products and services and that customers are treated fairly.

This government agency operates as a foremost financial supervisor. Its vision is to improve the value of financial institutions by offering supervision that is both proactive and detects risks. It works to ensure a healthy and well rounded banking system that helps the economy as a whole and businesses, consumers, and communities. The group is frequently sought out for its expertise and knowledge.

One of the main functions of the bank examiners who work for the OCC is to go on site to national financial institutions and hold on location reviews. They continue their supervision after this as well. The examiners study the funds management, investment and loan portfolios, earnings, capital, liquidity, and market risk for all of these organizations. Any national financial institution that has under $10 billion of assets falls under their enforcement of consumer banking laws. In pursuit of this, they examine external and internal audits and internal controls along with compliance to the laws. The examiners also check on the ability of the bank managements to identify and manage their own risk.

Where these federal thrifts and national banks are concerned, the OCC has substantial powers. This starts with examining the institutions. They can then deny or approve applications the banks put in for new charters, capital, branches, and other forms of change to their banking or company structure.

There are a number of actions this supervisor can take regarding national financial institutions. They can remove offending directors and officers at these banks. They may also deliver financial penalties and cease and desist orders when banks will not change their unsound or illegal practices. The agency prefers to negotiate changes to such practices first.

The bureau has tremendous powers in implementing the banking laws. They may create regulations and rules. They also provide legal interpretations of them. Finally they issue binding decisions that govern bank lending, investments, and other activities.

Congress does not provide the OCC with a budget. The agency derives all of its revenues from several activities. They receive assessments from the national financial institutions. Banks must pay the agency to conduct examinations that they undergo. Financial institutions also pay fees for having their applications processed. Finally the bureau has revenues that come in from their investments which are mostly U.S. Treasuries.

Offshore Account

Offshore accounts are accounts that you have in a bank that is located in another country. The term originally came from banks and accounts that were found in the Channel Islands, which were literally off shore from Great Britain. Interestingly enough, the majority of offshore banks and offshore accounts are still found on islands to this day.

Individuals and businesses might use offshore accounts for a variety of purposes. The popular conception of offshore accounts is that spies and criminals utilize them as places to store their cash. In fact, most offshore accounts are completely legitimate. People and even businesses have them as places to deposit their money, make investments, or use as trading accounts. When they are used as trading accounts, the person utilizes them to place online trades in stock markets.

Offshore accounts can also be employed to hide assets from governments and taxes, even though this is not the case for most such offshore accounts. A number of offshore banking accounts exist, such as HSBC Offshore Banking in Gibralter, Barclays Offshore Banking in the island of Jersey, and Griffon Bank in the island of Dominica in the Caribbean. These accounts provide all types of services for the banking needs of people and businesses, one of which is Internet banking.

Among the advantages of offshore accounts is privacy. Offshore banking institutions keep offshore account information secret. Such banks are forbidden to declare this information concerning the status of the account or any of its particulars to any individual or entity who is not the account holder. The only exception to this is when offshore banks believe the holder of an offshore account may be using the account for illegal purposes like drug trafficking, support of terrorism, or criminal money laundering.

Another good reason for putting your money into an offshore bank account is because they typically offer better interest on money. It is a well known fact that offshore banks provide better interest rates for their customers. Such rates depend on the location and the offshore bank in question. Reasons for higher interest rates have to do with the lower operating costs in these islands or other locations, as well as the higher interest rates in the prosperous countries where they are based.

Tax advantages prove to be another motivating factor for offshore banking and having offshore accounts. A number of countries will provide tax benefits to investors who are foreigners in order to attract their money. While this is different for every location too, many offshore banks and their hosting countries will not levy taxes on investment returns and interest earned in such offshore accounts.

Offshore Banking

Offshore Banking is a means of banking by keeping your funds in a bank that is outside of the country in which you primarily reside, or literally "offshore." These days it has acquired a negative connotation consistent with money laundering, criminal activities, or tax evasion. Yet none of these mental pictures are accurate any longer. All an offshore bank account truly means is that it is overseas or international. When individuals choose to keep part of their bank deposits internationally, this is a sensible, legitimate, and legal practice.

The old model of the Swiss Offshore Banking account has expanded to numerous other countries. Today places as far flung as Singapore, Hong Kong, Panama, Malta, Liechtenstein, Bermuda, Jersey, the Isle of Man, Gibraltar, and the Cayman Islands all participate in the concept. Some of the highest-rated and most financially stable Offshore Banking centers are Singapore, Hong Kong, and Liechtenstein.

There are a number of good reasons why ordinary people (as well as wealthy clients) opt to move their checking and savings accounts overseas to an Offshore Banking center. For starters, this protects assets from legal or government malfeasance. It is not an exaggeration to claim that any individuals who choose to maintain all of their assets and funds within the exact same country in which they work and live are taking on substantial legal (and hence financial) risk. The United States proves to be by far the most litigious society and nation which has ever arisen in all of world history. It is the shocking truth that any government agency or court can freeze any individual's private bank accounts with only one phone call and with no due process.

A second good reason for using Offshore Banking concerns the fact that the banks in other countries outside of most Western nations are far safer and sounder financially. Many banks in the so-called first world or developed world are in perilous financial condition. This became painfully obvious back in 2008 during the Western-based Financial Crisis and Great Recession. Some of the largest American, British, and European banks failed or went to the brink of bankruptcy. Examples of this are Wachovia Bank, Washington Mutual Bank, Bear Stearns, Lehman Brothers, and

Merrill Lynch.

Many others would have gone under but for desperate and generous government support of the likes of Citibank, Royal Bank of Scotland, and Lloyds TSB. While many of them have recovered somewhat, others like Credit Suisse, UniCredito, and Deutsche Bank remain in dangerous financial condition. In fact in Europe there are even entire banking systems as in Italy, Greece, Spain, Ireland, and Cyprus that had to receive sometimes multiple bailouts in order to survive at all. The jury is still out on the large and too big to fail Italian banking system.

American banks also keep dangerously low levels in their liquidity. This means that they do not have nearly enough cash and cash equivalent assets to pay their depositors back in the event of a customer "run on the bank." Yet in Offshore Banking centers like Malta, Singapore, Hong Kong, and Liechtenstein, the banks are conservative to a fault. They practice extreme caution with their depositing customers' money and keep huge and conservative liquidity and capital ratios. Many of these same jurisdictions are governments with little to no debt and highly solvent and very well-capitalized banking insurance funds.

Finally, Offshore Banking centers often pay significantly higher interest rates for U.S. dollar deposits. While major Western central banks in the United States, Great Britain, Europe, and Japan have absolutely slashed their interest rates to historic low rates or even negative interest rates, others are still paying decent returns overseas. In some of these, investors can receive even in excess of four percent on U.S. dollar-denominated deposits in low to no risk banks and regulatory regimes and jurisdictions.

Open Market Operations (OMO)

Open Market Operations are also called by their acronym OMO. These describe both the purchasing and selling of open market-based government securities. The Federal Reserve central bank of the United States has a committee which engages in these transactions with the goal of expanding or contracting the total quantity of money flowing through the banking system.

When the Fed buys up instruments, it forces money into the banking system to stimulate growth. When it sells its various securities, this has the opposite effect and contracts the economy. The idea behind the Federal Reserve's thinking with this technique is to tweak through manipulating the federal funds rate. This rate represents the price for which the banks will loan money to each other.

This Open Market Operation proves to be the most frequently deployed and highly flexible tool from the toolkit of the Federal Reserve. It permits them to both control and implement their monetary policy for America. They also work with the reserve requirements for the banks and the discount rate. While they have all three tools at their disposal, the buying and selling of government securities proves to be their favorite and also most often deployed tool. This permits them to precisely control the amount of bank reserve balances. It assists the Federal Reserve in decreasing or increasing the short-term interest rates as they deem to be appropriate for any given time.

The Federal Reserve committee which determines the monetary policy is called the FOMC Federal Open Market Committee. They carry out this monetary policy through actually setting the target for the federal funds interest rate and also by implementing their Open Market Operations, along with manipulating the reserve requirement and discount rate strategies to get the federal funds rate to their desired levels. This fed funds rate turns out to be incredibly important for them to finely control since it impacts practically every other interest rate found in the United States today. Among these are the prime rate, car loan rates, and home loan mortgage rates. Only the London-based LIBOR is more important today.

When the FOMC is attempting to attain a desired federal funds rate, they first fall back on the Open Market Operations. They carry out either the contractionary or expansionary monetary policy to achieve their desired movement and ultimate ends.

When the Fed sets its sites on expanding the economy this way, they want an expansionary policy. They need to reduce the fed funds rate in order to facilitate this goal. They will buy government securities off of private bond dealers to deposit funds into the accounts for the financial institutions, entities, and investors who sold them the government bonds. These deposits then became a component of the commercial bank held-cash on account with the Federal Reserve. It grows the money supply available to commercial banks for their various lending operations. It is these commercial banks which seek to loan out their cash reserves. To do this, they will lower their interest rates to bring in more customers.

The Fed also occasionally has moments when it seeks to cool off an overheating economy in the U.S.A. To do this they will begin their contractionary monetary policy and seek to boost the federal funds rate. In practice, this involves them selling off their seemingly limitless supply of government securities to the financial institutions and banks. It reduces the amount of money the commercial banks have left to loan out. This makes the cost of money more expensive and so boosts the associated interest rates, including the federal funds rate too.

Origination Fees

Origination fees are also known as activation fees. These are the costs pertaining to setting up an account with a mortgage broker, bank, or other firm that will go through the tasks of collecting and processing all documents and requirements for getting a loan, in particular a mortgage on a house.

These origination fees are generally amounts that are pre determined for any new account. Origination fees can range from half a percentage point to two percentage points of the entire loan total. This variance has to do with where the loans come from, off of either the prime or the subprime loan market. On a subprime mortgage for $200,000, the origination fee would likely amount to two percent, equaling four thousand dollars in this particular case.

The average origination fee comes in at approximately one percent of the total mortgage loan dollar amount. This fee goes to the firm that originates and processes your loan. It defrays their expenses that arise from developing, putting together, and finally closing on your mortgage.

The rise of the Internet has allowed for an alternative compensation scheme for companies that put together and originate mortgages. While the vast majority of mortgage brokers and banks still charge these loan origination fees, there are some Internet based brokers who use a different model. These entities do no charge origination fees at all; instead they pass the savings directly on to you the customer. The way that they get paid is by selling your loan to an investor once it is closed. The investor pays them a premium for the packaged loan, which covers the origination fees, and the online mortgage broker is compensated for his or her work and time.

The origination fees can be deducted from taxes. The year that the transaction closed and the origination fees were charged, they can be used to reduce actual income on income tax forms. The Internal Revenue Service permits this reduction to income no matter who pays the origination fees, meaning that a person who employs a broker that does not charge them origination fees will still be able to deduct the fees that the investors who later buy the loan are subsequently paying to the mortgage broker.

This means that if you take out a $200,000 mortgage, then you are able to deduct the $2,000 in loan origination fees, even if you did not have to pay them, but an investor in the loan did instead.

Origination fees are listed on the HUD-1 Settlement form. They are tallied beneath the sub-heading of lender charges. Discount points that are used to bring down interest rates either permanently or temporarily are also listed on this form under the category.

Overdraft

An Overdraft refers to the extension of credit where a bank or other lending institution allows for debits to be paid after an account has hit zero dollars. Thanks to these overdrafts, individuals are able to keep drawing down the account value below zero, although there is no money left in it or an insufficient amount to resolve the withdrawal. Another layman's definition of this term is when the bank permits its clients to borrow a given sum of money.

When individuals possess an account with overdraft facilities, the bank will courtesy cover any checks that will put it into overdraft instead of returning them unpaid (bouncing them back to the check depositor). Naturally the outstanding overdrawn balance will have interest charged on it, as with any loan. Typically such interest rates prove to be far lower than those offered by credit cards though. Sometimes there may be other fees for utilizing the overdraft protection. This would decrease the overdraft protection amount available. Some of these could be per withdrawal or per check insufficient funds assessed fees.

Such overdrafts on money market savings accounts, regular savings accounts, and checking accounts happen when the customers do not keep sufficient funds within this account to cover the incidents such as check and ATM withdrawal transactions. In order for it to equal an overdraft, the bank will have to be willing to process and cover the transaction regardless of the shortfall of funds.

Many banks will pay overdrafts on four kinds of banking transactions. These include recurring transactions of debt cards, checks and related transactions that rely on the account number, online banking transfers and payments, and auto bill payments.

Banks might decide to utilize their own corporate funds in order to pay a client overdraft. They might also have customers link the overdraft on to one of their credit cards. When banks deploy their own money in order to pay an overdraft, then this does not usually impact a client's credit score. As credit cards are utilized to cover overdrafts, this could increase the client debt to the amount where the credit score became negatively impacted.

This does not directly result from checking account overdrafts however.

The problem comes when the overdrafts do not become repaid in a prearranged time frame. The bank might opt to hand over the account into the hands of a collection agency. Such a collection activity might negatively impact the credit score if it becomes reportable to any or all of the three primary credit agency bureaus of TransUnion, Experian, or Equifax. This comes down to how the collection agency reports its accounts to the agencies. It will determine whether the overdraft protection on a checking account shows up as a problem or not.

Such Overdraft protection will deliver a useful tool to help manage the checking account on a day to day basis. For example, a person might easily forget that they drew out money for a Starbucks or Costa Coffee run. The overdraft protection will make sure that the ATM is not turned down or that the ATM Debit card purchase does not get rejected at the merchant point of sale. Banks will commonly assess an overdraft fee and use this to make money from the convenience they are delivering. This is why such protection should not be too commonly used and over-utilized. Instead it is to be reserved for emergency needs and situations.

Every overdraft protection dollar amount is not equal. Each bank and type of bank account will vary the level of protection they deliver. This could also vary on a case by case basis. When such protection is overused, the bank or other financial institution may simply elect to remove the courtesy off of the bank account. Getting it reactivated after such a penalizing move is never easy.

Peer to Peer Lending (P2P)

Peer to Peer Lending helps consumers who have some extra money to invest to help out those who need to borrow it. It is often abbreviated as P2P Lending. The idea behind peer to peer lending is not a new one. It has grown exponentially online in the past ten years thanks to the Internet. The benefits of this form of lending are that it reduces usurious interest rates dramatically. This means that both consumers and the overall economy benefit as it decreases the amounts of payday loans.

Prosper is one of the largest P2P lending companies in America. It loans out amounts as high as $35,000. For this they charge a closing fee of 5%. Their interest rates range from 5.9% for extremely good credit to 30% for credit that is only fair. These rates are often lower than what credit card companies charge and substantially lower than payday loan companies which can command over 600% in a single year.

Loans with Peer to Peer Lending companies like Prosper are unsecured. The applicants' credit history earns the approval, though it does not require perfect credit to obtain them. The money itself comes from surplus money which normal people across America wish to invest.

These Peer to Peer Lending companies generally allow their loans to be utilized for most any type of need. They encourage ones that are financially responsible. Debt consolidation is one of the big reasons why individuals take out these loans. The interest rate is often more affordable than the ones the credit card companies charge. Such a loan helps individuals to pay off loans quicker and with a larger amount of the money attacking the principal rather than interest.

Home improvement is another commonplace reason that consumers employ these peer to peer loans. The traditional means of financing such loans comes from bank issued home equity loans or lines of credit as well as from credit cards. The home equity loans often require a great amount of time for approval and commonly include expensive fees. This has encouraged smart home renovators to seek out Peer to Peer Lending companies.

Small businesses like these loans which help them to increase their capital for expansion. Traditional banks will often require a lot of paper work and documentation in order to issue an approval. P2P lending operations such as Prosper only need credit scores that are decent.

Many consumers have turned to these companies for financing for car loans as well. Having this money pre-approved and in hand can save more than just dealer approved financing costs. It can strengthen the buyer's hand in negotiating the final price on the vehicle as the money for the purchase is effectively offered to the dealer in cash instead of financing.

One of the many advantages to these Peer to Peer Lending companies is that they do not charge early repayment penalties. This makes them effective financing vehicles for many different types of needs. Individuals have employed them in place of short term loans and to pay for surgeries not covered by insurance, among other uses.

Besides this, P2P lenders do not require the prime credit scores that most banks do. Consumers can access substantial loans of as much as $35,000 with credit scores that start at a fair 640.

Plunge Protection Team (PPT)

The Plunge Protection Team is a nickname given to the President's Working Group on Financial Markets. It came into existence to make economic and financial recommendations on the economy when there are periods of economic chaos. On the team are the heads of the most critical U.S. financial regulatory organizations. This includes the Secretary of the U.S. Treasury, the SEC Securities Exchange Commission Chairman, the Chairman of the Federal Reserve, and the Chairman of the CFTC Commodity Futures Trading Commission.

The Washington Post newspaper created the nick name Plunge Protection Team only a decade later in 1997. President Ronald Reagan originally convened the team as a response to the terrible Black Monday stock market crash. The government was desperate to restore investor confidence in U.S. financial markets. President Reagan called together the group to improve on the efficiency, integrity, and order of them.

The Working Group on Financial Markets was instructed to find out what happened with the financial markets in the U.S. on and around trading day October 19, 1987. They were told to come up with government actions for coordinating efforts and making contingencies to prevent them from happening again when possible.

To carry this out they were told to talk with various representatives from the business world. This included individuals from clearing houses, exchanges, significant market players, and regulating bodies to learn what the market might suggest for non-government solutions.

Finger pointing at first characterized the investigation. The NYSE held the various futures exchanges responsible for the crash. The CME group engaged in a number of studies to refute this by having market experts rationally analyze the events. They refuted the accusations for the problems with these studies.

One positive mechanism came from these initial meetings with the Plunge Protection Team. NYSE and CME group worked to establish circuit breakers between the securities and futures markets. This slowed down or stopped wildly erratic moves in the market. These circuit breakers remain in effect to this day.

The PPT had 60 days from the Executive Order to give this initial report to the President. They were to report from time to time after this as they reached more findings and solutions for recommended changes to the legislation. When the report and finished recommendations were completed, the President did not disband the group as many had expected.

Instead it stayed together to be reconvened on any subsequent crisis and threat to the financial system. This caused some observers to believe that the group had a secret purpose to manipulate markets and ensure they stayed higher. The group covered such issues as the almost collapse of Long Term Capital Management, Terrorism Risk Insurance from September of 2006 and Over the Counter Derivatives Markets and the Commodity Exchange Act in November of 1999.

Most famously the group reconvened during the financial crash of the Great Recession in 2008. In March, 2008 they issued their Policy Statement on Financial Market Developments. It had the PPTs analysis and report on what continued to plague the markets and cause the ongoing market turmoil.

Their final conclusions had to do with the subprime market mortgages. The determined that the main cause of the destructive chain of events started with the rise in delinquencies of these mortgages. They issued another statement on the continuing crisis on October 6 of 2008. In this they announced that the situation in worldwide financial markets continued to be very strained. They assured investors that they were working with global regulators and market participants to take on the problems and restore stability and confidence to markets.

Prime Brokerage

A prime brokerage refers to a particular category of different financial services which a number of brokerages provide to their important clients. Services they deliver under this umbrella cover a number of different types. Among these are leveraged trade orders, loaning of securities, and cash management assistance. The majority of the bigger brokerages offer such prime broker services. This includes Goldman Sachs, Morgan Stanley, and Paine Webber.

The demand for such prime brokerage services originally came from the hedge funds. These special investment pools often place enormous trades. Because of this fact, they require particular attention from the major brokerages. These prime brokerages are also called prime brokers sometimes. They are usually comprised of enormous financial institutions. They tend to have business transactions with similarly large financial institutions as well as the hedge funds.

Prime brokers and their services are not mutually exclusive. While these financial services broker companies provide a wide range of such services, the clients do not have to participate in all or even most of them. The large clients have the choice to receive some of their financial services at other institutions that best suite their needs.

There are many such prime brokerage services the broker dealer may deliver to its best clientele. Whichever brokers are assigned to these important accounts will be expected to offer services as settling agent and gratuitous financing for leveraged trades. They could provide assets custody and even everyday account statement preparation. These prime brokers have the advantage of enjoying substantial and varied resources that smaller to medium-sized financial and brokerage institutions simply can not match within their own operations. This means that the prime brokers deliver a means for many of the bigger and more important financial institutions to "outsource" a range and host of their administrative investment activities so that they can instead concentrate their best efforts on strategy and on their investment goals and returns.

As an example, there may even be concierge types of services offered by the prime broker. There are a wide range of such highly specialized offerings the broker might include in an effort to keep their largest, most important clients satisfied. Among these are cash financing, securities financing, capital introduction, and even risk management services. There are also services that go above and beyond what would be expected of a typical broker. These could include the ability to sublease space within their offices and to obtain free access to other benefits based within their facilities. These are non- traditional services, and participation in them is completely voluntary for any client.

Some of these services require the hedge fund or other important client to post collateral. This is especially the case where brokerage securities are lent out to the customer. In this way, the prime brokerage is able to reduce its risk it takes on and also to obtain faster recourse to funds should they be required.

The truth is that the overwhelming majority of such clients of the prime brokerage will be comprised of bigger financial institutions, funds like hedge funds, and bigger private investors. It is true that hedge funds and money managers are some of the most important clients which attain the minimum qualifications to participate. Others who might meet the threshold for participation in the program include a range of professional investors and those who engage in arbitrage. Hedge funds know all too well that the level of these prime broker services will often play a substantial part in the success or failure of their fund.

Among the more common kinds of clientele that participate in and attain the standards for prime broker services are commercial banks and pension funds. Both of these groups will typically handle enormous quantities of money which they must invest. They also have in common that they lack the in-house resources to adequately invest and maintain such large dollar investments by themselves.

Prime Rate

The Prime Rate is the most typically utilized shorter term interest rate for the United State banking system. All kinds of lending institutions in the United States employ this U.S. benchmark interest rate as a basis or index rate to price their medium term to short term loans and products. This includes credit unions, thrifts, savings and loans, and commercial banks.

This makes the Prime Rate consistent around the country as banks strive to be competitive and profitable in their lending rates which they provide to both consumers and businesses. A universal rate like this simplifies the task for businesses and consumers as they shop around comparable loan products that competing banks offer. Every state in the country does not maintain its own benchmark rate. This makes a California Prime or New York Prime identical to the U.S. Prime.

Commercial and other banks charge this benchmark rate to their best customers. These are those clients who have the best credit ratings and loan history with the bank. Most of the time banks' best clients are made up of large companies.

The prime interest rate is also known as the prime lending rate. Banks typically base it on the Federal Reserve's federal funds rate. This is actually the rate that banks loan money to each other for overnight purposes. Retail customers also need to be aware of the prime lending rate. It directly impacts the lending rates that they can access for personal and small business loans as well as for home mortgages.

The federal government and Federal Reserve Bank do not set the prime lending rates. The individual banks set it. They then utilize this base rate or reference rate to set the prices for a great number of loans such as credit card loans and small business loans.

The Federal Reserve Board releases a statistics called "Selected Interest Rates." This is their survey of the prime interest rate as the majority of the twenty-five biggest banks set it. It is this publication which reveals the Prime Rate periodically. This is why the Federal Reserve does not directly set this important benchmark rate. The banks more or less base it on the target level of the federal funds rate that the Federal Open Market Committee sets and changes at their monthly meetings.

Different banks adjust their prime lending rate at the same time. The point where they change it is generally when the Federal Open Market Committee adjusts their own important Fed Funds Rate. Many publications refer to this periodically changing reference rate as the Wall Street Prime Rate.

A great number of consumer loans as well as commercial loans and credit card rates find their basis in the prime lending rate. Among these are car loans, home equity loans, personal and home lines of credit, and various kinds of personal loans.

The rates above the prime lending rate that banks charge their less then prime (or subprime) customers depend on the credit worthiness of the borrower in question. The banks attempt to correctly ascertain the risk of default for the borrower. For the best credit customers who have lower chances of defaulting, banks can afford to assess them a lower interest rate than others. Customers with higher chances of defaulting on their loans pay larger interest rates because of the risk associated with their loans not being repaid.

As of June 15, 2016, the Federal Open Market Committee voted to maintain its target fed funds rate in a range of from .25% to .5%. As a result of this, the U.S. prime lending rate stayed at 3.5%. Once per month the Federal Reserve committee meets to determine if they will change the fed funds rate.

Principal

Principal has several different meanings. It most commonly pertains to the initial amount of money that a person either invests or borrows with a loan. A secondary meaning has to do with a bond and its face value. Sometimes the word pertains to the owners of a company or the main participants in any type of transaction.

Where borrowing is concerned, this term relates to the upfront amount of any loan. It also is utilized to describe original amounts which the individuals still owe on the loan in question. Looking at a clear example always helps to clarify the concept. When people obtain a $100,000 mortgage, this Principal is the same $100,000. As the individuals pay down $60,000 of this amount, the remainder of $40,000 that is left to pay off is similarly referred to as Principal.

It is the original Principal that decides how much interest borrowers will pay. If borrowers take out a loan with an initial amount equaling $20,000 that comes with a yearly interest rate at seven percent, then they would be required to pay $1,400 in annual interest for each year that the loan remains open. As borrowers pay the monthly payments to the loan servicer, the interest charges for the month will first be paid off. What remains goes toward the initial amount which the individuals borrowed. Paying down this original amount borrowed remains the only means of lowering the interest amount that accrues on a monthly basis.

Another form of mortgage that operates differently has the name of zero principal mortgages. Bankers think of these as interest-only loans. They represent a unique form of financing where the routine monthly payments of the borrower only apply to the loan's interest. This means that the initial loan amount never gets paid down unless the borrower makes extra payments. It also translates to no equity building up in the property which backs the mortgage loan.

Because of this, financial advisors will typically not recommend these types of mortgages to home buyers as they are rarely in the true interest of the purchaser. Despite this fairly obvious assessment, there are a few unusual cases when they could work out for certain people. When a home buyer is starting out on a career path that pays very little initially but will later on earn substantially more in the not too distant future, it could be worthwhile to lock in the home price now while it is lower. Once the income increases apace, the borrowers always have the ability to refinance into a more traditional mortgage which would cover payments on the initial amounts borrowed as well.

Another scenario where these loans make sense relates to unusual and fantastic opportunities for a particular real estate investment deal. When huge returns on investment dollars can be anticipated, it is practical to go with these mortgage's far lower payments that are interest-only. Meanwhile the borrower can plow the additional monthly payment money savings into the exceptional investment opportunity.

Principal also finds use describing the first initial outlay on an investment. This does not take into consideration any interest that builds up or earnings on the investment. Savers might deposit $20,000 at a bank in a savings account with interest. After a number of years, the balance will grow to $21,500. The principal remains the original $20,000 the savers gave the bank. The additional $1,500 will be called interest or earnings on top of this initial outlay.

It is interesting to note that inflation will not change the nominal value of a loan or financial instrument's principal. Yet the effects of inflation do very much reduce the real value of the initial amount.

Private Banking

Private Banking refers to an intensely personal form of banking and related financial services which a bank traditionally delivers to its HNWI high net worth individual and UHNW ultra high net worth individual clients. In terms of wealth management, it is these two principal types of banking customers who have amassed significantly greater wealth than the common man or woman. This means that they can gain easy access to a greater range of traditional and alternative banking solutions and creative high-yielding investments than the typical banking customer can. Such private banks make huge efforts to effectively match up these types of high value customers with the best possible investment options and banking solutions.

Private banking goes far beyond managing investments anymore. In fact, these financial institutions provide a veritable wealth of investment-related advice and consulting as well. The goal is to offer comprehensive solutions for the clients' whole financial picture. This means that besides growing and protecting the assets in the present, they are similarly interested in offering creative and legal strategies for future financing needs, offering retirement strategies, and bequeathing wealth which is not tax-encumbered to the next generations of the family.

It is possible for more ordinary individuals who possess $50,000 in liquid net worth to engage in a form of private banking. Yet there are many more exclusive (mostly Swiss) private banks that only take clients who boast a minimum $500,000 in investable assets. This represents a large sum of wealth that permits such families and private parties to become involved in lucrative alternative investments like speculative real estate and hedge funds. This amount of wealth is considered to be essential for avoiding liquidity issues with investments. In today's banking world, Credit Suisse, UBS, HSBC, Morgan Stanley, and Bank of America Merrill Lunch are all well-known and -regarded examples of such private banking institutions.

Among the most notorious and important advantages to private banking are its legendary standards of anonymity and privacy. These institutions go way above and beyond the call of duty to maintain anonymous transactions for their clients. In fact, these types of elite banks usually deliver HNWIs and

UHNWs with specially designed solutions about which they keep quiet in order to stop an important customer from going over to a major competing institution. This long-standing tradition and culture of privacy delivers the additional advantage of bringing in newer customers who value the exclusive treatment.

It is this legendary standard of banking and financial management services that appeal to HNWI's and UHNW's. They will all receive their own special and specific relationship or account manager. He or she will then strive to create a specifically crafted personalized approach to managing their particularly unique assets. It permits the clients to interface personally with the bank's management if they need to urgently.

In fact the HNWIs and UHNWs often obtain discounted pricing at the major private banks because their considerable assets are a prize to be competed for and gained. As an example, clients who run exporting and importing companies could obtain an advantageous rate of foreign exchange from their private banking institution. The banks will similarly endeavor to deliver superior outperforming returns on investments as well. This is in their own best interest since such clients can easily leverage down on their vast resources in response to great private banking returns. A UHNW individual might receive limited access to a best in class hedge fund because of their connection to a certain private bank which has a relationship with the hedge fund directly and personally.

Thanks to the big picture-altering Global Financial Crisis of 2008, private banks have suffered the wrath of the financial regulators around the developed banking world. A new highly restrictive regulatory regime has arisen to deliver a punishing level of accountability and higher than anticipated transparency requirements. As an example, the licensing requirements nowadays are far stricter for the professionals working at the private banks than they used to be. This ensures that the clients receive appropriate types of advice for managing their vast financial resources and empires.

Private Equity

Private Equity refers to an investment capital source that comes from those institutional investors and accredited individual investors who boast high net worth. The goals of these investors are to gain a significant equity ownership in corporations. The partners at these firms raise funds and then manage them to gain higher than average returns for their client shareholders. They commonly pursue this goal via an investment time frame of from four to seven years. Private equity is therefore not for those who require that their investment positions be readily liquid.

Such mega funds are often utilized to buy private companies or to privatize publically listed corporations in order to de-list them from the stock market exchanges in a go private arrangement. Each firm sets its own minimum investment threshold for the fund investors. This ranges depending on the needs of the funds being raised. There are many funds with a minimum $250,000 in smallest investment permitted, while still others look for at least millions of dollars per contributing investor.

The private equity industry has a long and storied history of gaining the best possible talent from the corporate world throughout America. This includes top-delivering CEOs and directors even from Fortune 500 firms as well as the best management consulting and top strategy firms. This is why private equity hiring managers often scout out major corporations, law firms, and accounting companies when they go recruiting for new talent. They require legal experience and accounting skills to provide the many support services that such large enterprises require in order to put together major corporate mergers and acquisitions and to properly advise the management companies on the effective management of their newly acquired portfolios holdings.

There are quite high fees involved with such firms. Typically they receive first a management fee and then a performance fee. This generally amounts to annual management fees at around two percent of all assets under management. The performance fees add up to 20 percent of all gross profits when they sell a company. There can be a great deal of variety in the ways that such firms receive their compensation and incentives to outperform.

It is not hard to understand why private equity has been so successful at recruiting and keeping the very best talent based upon the money they have to offer by way of compensation for performance. Consider that these firms which have a billion dollars' assets under management would likely have around only two dozen professional investment personnel. They receive $20 million in annual fees just for the assets under management. Add on to this the 20 percent performance fees based on all gross profits, and it is not hard to understand how they generate additional tens of millions of dollars in performance fees for the company.

Middle market level managers and associates generally expect to earn six-figure salaries and bonuses. The vice presidents pull down half a million dollars easily. Principals rake in a cool over million dollars per year in both realized and unrealized compensation.

Given the incredible rewards at stake, it should not come as any surprise that there are a range of types of private equity firms operating today. Many choose the route of passive investing to be strictly financiers. They depend on their appointed management to increase the size and profitability of the firm in which they invest so that the owners will realize generous, outsized returns. Other kinds of these firms choose to be more active investors. They deliver operational support to the management to ensure that they can build up a stronger and more profitable firm which they can then resell or spin off.

These private equity firms pride themselves on their expansive list of contacts and relationships with corporate boards. They leverage these CFO and CEO relationships to help them grow the company revenue as well as to recognize synergies and operational combination opportunities. One of the kingpins of private equity remains Goldman Sachs, the legendary investment bank. They facilitate the biggest deals and concentrate their time on forging acquisitions and mergers that have billions of dollars in notional values. For other smaller investment banking companies, the majority of deals run in the range of from $50 million to $500 million, while lower middle-market transactions vary from $10 million to $50 million in total.

Quantitative Easing

Quantitative easing is the policy where the government purchases bonds and financial instruments by printing money in order to stimulate the economy. Quantitative easing proves to be a monetary policy that the Federal Reserve and other central banks around the world utilize in order to grow the money supply. They do this by boosting the cash reserves in the banking system. This is accomplished via purchasing the government's issued bonds in order to raise their prices.

Since prices and interest rates of bonds move inversely, higher bond prices lead directly to lower long term interest rates. Quantitative easing is commonly employed only after other more traditional means of dominating the supply of money have not worked. These other methods involve lowering discount rates, bank interest rates, and even interbank interest rates to around zero.

Once these traditional means have failed to stimulate the economy, the Fed then steps into the market and directly buys financial instruments. The assets that they purchase include agency debt, government bonds, corporate bonds, and mortgage backed securities, which they purchase from banks and institutions. This entire process is called open market operations. By depositing electronically created money into the banks' accounts, the banks gain additional reserves that permit them to create still additional money from thin air. The Fed hopes that this multiplication of deposits accomplished through the fractional reserve banking system will allow greater amounts of loans to be made to businesses and individuals in order to stimulate the economy.

This quantitative easing policy is not without its risks. It could be too effective or not sufficiently effective, should banks decide to hoard their extra money to boost their capital reserves. This is particularly the case in an environment of rising defaults in the banks' mortgage and other types of loans' holdings.

Recent examples of quantitative easing abound. This subtle form of printing money became more and more common as the financial crisis of 2007 to 2010 grew worse. In these years, the United States engaged heavily in it, tripling the world wide dollar reserves by creating money both at home and abroad. Other Central Banks, such as those of Great Britain and the European Union, similarly engaged in the practice to help mitigate the effects of the crisis and resulting Great Recession. These countries and economic blocks had all already lowered their interest rates to zero or near zero amounts, and they found quantitative easing to be their best remaining option for restarting economic growth.

Quantitative Risk Management (QRM)

Quantitative Risk Management represents the discipline which deals with the ability of an organization to quantify and manage its risk. This scientific approach to business is becoming increasingly critical in today's world as organizations need to satisfy stakeholders who demand it.

Government regulators similarly insist on clarity within organizations now, especially regarding the amount of capital financial institutions are holding. The firm executives are hunting for the best allocation of capital. Corporations and their boards are seeking justification to control expenditures. Project managers need to be assured they will make their timelines and meet budgets. All of these individuals and entities are looking for effective QRM nowadays.

These QRM capabilities give decision makers the facilities to both analyze their applicable risk data as well as to forecast the likely positive and negative effects in the future. It provides the organization with enormous advantages. Analyses that are more dependable and finely detailed will deliver information which management requires to make superior decisions that are ultimately better informed. As the Quantitative Risk Management process yields higher quality information and becomes more easily accessible to the relevant organizational members, the decision makers are able to more effectively utilize the techniques of QRM to decrease the amount of guesswork involved in the daily decisions of their business operations.

This allows them to obtain valuable insights into possible risks, so they can estimate their overall exposure to them and discern any weaknesses in their oversight controls. It also permits them to determine how practical new services and products will be and to consider the opportunities for up selling and also cross selling of company goods, information, and services. Finally, organization leaders will be able to evaluate any degrees of variance in their company cash flow so that they can streamline and better their ultimate operations.

Quantitative Risk Management is important as every one of those activities just mentioned contains at least some degree of risk. By quantifying and considering them all using a combination of techniques such as trending, modeling, stress tests, and metric evaluations, company decision makers can create faster and more effective responses. This allows them to benefit from any uncovered opportunities and simultaneously to deal with any possible negative effects before they actually materialize and cause significant damage.

There are numerous examples of the uses of and needs for Quantitative Risk Management in business organizations. Cash flow at risk, or CFaR, represents one of the most significant drivers of business. Company leaders require effective prognoses of their future cash flow in order to firm up important decisions for the business. These include confirming or pushing off investments, reducing expenses, reinvesting capital in the business model, or choosing to reengineer their critical operations. Correctly extrapolating cash flow involves proper understanding of such underlying factors as currency changes, sales, pricing of products and services, vendor viability, and operational costs.

Value at Risk, or VaR, is another critical measurement in an organization that benefits from Quantitative Risk Management. Bigger, international, and more complicated financial institutions such as JP Morgan Chase, Citigroup, HSBC, Standard Chartered Bank, BNP Paribas, and Banco Santander have to constantly evaluate where their risk exposures are in order to appropriately allocate the correct capital amounts to be capable of absorbing losses which they do not anticipate.

Project risk management is another area where this Quantitative Risk Management can save the day. So many projects exceed their allocated budgets, deadlines, and milestone markers simply because there is not a sufficient evaluation of the variables, uncertainty, and risk involved with the project itself. This is where the process of QRM can save enormous amounts of time, frustration, and ultimately resources by delivering on deadlines and budgets.

Rabobank

Rabobank refers to the Dutch banking giant whose full name is the Coöperatieve Rabobank. This Dutch international banking giant is a full-scale financial services organization whose headquarters today lies in the city of Utrecht in the Netherlands. The banking group is a world leader for agriculture and food production financing as well as in banking based on sustainability. Their motto is "as large as necessary, as small as possible."

The group Rabobank is a unique form of banking organization and structure in many ways. It is made up of 120 fully independent local Rabobanks in the Netherlands as of 2013. These banks actually own the parent central organization called Rabobank Nederland. They also operate a significant number of subsidiaries and specialized international operations and offices. The main international concentration of the Rabobank Group proves to be agribusiness and food-related.

By their assets, this bank remains the second biggest Dutch bank. When measured by their Tier 1 Capital, the bank proves to be in the top 30 biggest financial institutions on earth. Current as of December 2014, their aggregate assets equaled €681 billion (Euros) while they claimed a net profit amount of €1.8 billion. The banking and finance industry publication Global Finance ranks Rabobank at an impressive number 25 for "world's safest banks."

The bank's historical and current day roots remain in agriculture. As a confederation of local credit union banks which deliver banking and financial services to their local markets, the company operates on a bottom up model which is most unusual in banking. This means that the central organization and all of its countless subsidiaries and international offices throughout the world are a huge subsidiary of the local Dutch branches. With the overwhelming majority of commercial banks in the world today, the central organization proves to be the owning parent entity.

The roots of the bank came from the founder of the credit union cooperative movement Friedrich Wilhelm Raiffeisen, whose name is today immortalized in the enormous central and Eastern European, Austrian-based Raiffeisen Bank. He was the one who started the original farmers' bank within

Germany. The local countryside town mayor was aghast at the dire poverty he saw in the local farmers, their families, and communities. Though he attempted to deliver charity to alleviate their suffering, he soon discovered that helping them to be more self-reliant would yield better results over the long term. He did this by establishing his farmers' banks which gathered up the countryside residents' savings in order to offer them out as loans to enterprising farmers who needed capital to expand. Among his early followers was Father Gerlacus van den Elsen. He founded and inspired many of the local farmers' banks throughout the south of the Netherlands.

The bank had traditional dual headquarters in both Utrecht and Eindhoven. It was in the year 1898 that two different cooperative banking conglomerates formed as the Utrecht- based Coöperatieve Centrale Raiffeisen-Bank and the Eindhoven-based Coöperatieve Centrale Boerenleenbank. The former proved to be a co-op of six different area banks, while the latter existed when 22 local banks formed their co-op. Even though the two banks were largely the same, they still operated as separate competitors alongside one another for around 75 years. It was ironically the differing Christian religious bents of the two banks that kept them apart for so long. While the Eindhoven co-op was strongly Catholic, the Utrecht based Raiffeisen-Bank had Protestant roots. It explained why the Catholic based-bank was heavily centralized while the Protestant-based bank encouraged local autonomy of its branches.

The two were cooperating by 1940 and merged together in 1972 as Rabobank. The name changed to Rabobank Nederland in 1980. Overseas expansion came through many acquisitions in farming-oriented countries. They bought Primary Industry Bank of Australia in 1994 and reformed this as Rabobank Australia Limited by 2003. In 1997 they acquired Wrightson Farmers Finance Limited of New Zealand and converted this in 1999 to Rabobank New Zealand. They entered Indonesia decisively with the buyout of Bank Haga and Bank Hagakita. In 2011 and 2012, they opened online banks in Poland and then Germany. A savings business in Ireland followed. They also expanded into the Western U.S. with the purchase of Mid-State Bank & Trust in 2007 and Pacific State Bank in 2010.

Repayment Penalty

A repayment penalty is commonly associated with paying back a loan before the end of its term. If you are contemplating paying off your loan balance in advance of its due date, then you should be aware that a number of loans come with these repayment penalties for liquidating the balance early. Different types of loans utilize different names for these same fees. Repayment penalties can also be called redemption charges, early redemption fees, prepayment penalties, or financial penalties.

The fees associated with repayment penalties vary depending on the loan in question. These repayment penalties are commonly stated as a percentage of the balance that is outstanding when prepayment is offered. Alternatively, they might be figured up as a certain number of months of interest charges. In general, when they are figured up using months of interest, they are comprised of one to two months' interest in fees. The sooner in the loan's life that you choose to repay the loan, the greater amount of charge you can expect to pay. This is because the anticipated interest portion of the loan comprises a great part of the repayment earlier in the loan's time frame. Early repayment penalties might increase the total cost of your loan significantly.

If you wish to avoid a repayment penalty in paying off your loan in advance of the term's end, then you will have to be aware of the loans that come with these fees and the ones that do not. Even if you change a currently existing loan into a loan for debt consolidation, you will have to cover the early repayment penalty if one is in the terms. The only way to avoid early repayment penalties is by selecting loans that specifically do not have ones attached to them. It is ironic that some of the least expensive loans out there do not include repayment penalties for early pay off actions.

Another factor of repayment penalties involves a gradual disappearance of the provision over time. With many mortgages, these repayment penalties gradually go down over the years of the mortgage. After the fifth year, the majority of repayment penalties no longer even apply. In many cases, repayments of as much as twenty percent of the original balance are permitted in a given year without you having to be penalized.

Besides this, there are different kinds of penalties for repayments. Penalties that only apply to your refinancing of the mortgage are called soft penalties. Penalties that include the sale of the house and a refinancing are known as hard penalties.

Reserve Requirement

The reserve requirement proves to be the quantity of funds which banks are required to hold on hand each and every night. This is expressed as a percentage of the bank's total demand deposits. A country's central bank is responsible for setting out the effective percentage rate.

Within the United States, it is up to the Federal Reserve's Board of Governors to determine the member banks' reserve requirements. Such a requirement is applicable for commercial banks, savings and loan associations, savings banks, credit unions, Edge corporations, U.S. based branches or agencies of foreign banks, and agreement corporations.

The banks are allowed to keep their cash physically within their proprietary on-site vaults or keep them deposited with their area Federal Reserve Bank. When banks lack sufficient cash to fulfill their reserve requirements, they are able to borrow cash from other banks with extra to spare. They could also obtain a loan from the discount window of the Federal Reserve alternatively. Money which banks lend or borrow from one another in order to meet their own requirements is called the Federal funds.

Among the many tools which the Fed counts at its disposal, the reserve requirement is the underlying basis for all of them. They are able to employ this to precisely control cash liquidity within the economy. Smaller reserve requirements prove to be expansionary types of monetary policy. This is because they permit a greater amount of money to flow through the banking system into the real economy. Higher reserve requirements conversely are contractionary. They soak up money from the pool of available liquidity and tamp down on economic activities.

It is also true that the greater a reserve requirement is, the smaller the profits will be for a bank deploying its customers' money. Higher requirements are particularly challenging for smaller banks. This is because they begin with a smaller pool from which to lend out money. Because of this reality on the ground, small banks are usually exempted from such onerous requirements. Smaller banks are those which have fewer deposits than $12.4 million.

The Fed does not often actually change the reserve requirement. This is because it is expensive to do so. Banks are forced to rectify their policies to compensate when this is done. Because of this, the board avoids changing the requirements on its member banks. It is far easier for them to tweak the amounts of deposits which are subjected to the various reserve requirements every year.

For example, since October 12, 2012, the Federal Reserve has mandated that every bank possessing greater than $79.5 million in deposits must keep a minimum reserve amount of 10 percent of total deposits. Those banks which count under $79.5 million but still greater than $12.4 million only have to keep three percent of deposits on hand. Again those banks with fewer than $12.4 million in deposits fall under the pre-determined exemption amount. They enjoy a zero percent reserve requirement.

The Federal Reserve does raise the levels of deposits which are subject to its various ratios each year. This provides the banks with an incentive to become larger. From June 30 to June 30, the Fed is able to raise its low reserve tranche and accompanying exemption amount by 80 percent of the amount that deposits increase in the previous year.

Deposits which are considered for these reserve requirements include a number of different types. These are automatic transfer service accounts, demand deposits, NOW accounts, telephone or authorized transfer accounts, share draft accounts, ineligible bankers' acceptance, and affiliate-issued obligations which mature in seven or fewer days. Banks are only required to accept the net amount. They are not expected to cover any amounts owed to them by other banks or any cash that remains outstanding. As of December 27, 1990, deposits do not comprise Euro-currency liabilities or non personal time deposits.

Retail Banking

Retail banking is also called consumer banking. This form of banking is most easily described as the common everyday activities of financial service firms. In this definition their individual clientele utilize the local area branches of the more significant and bigger commercial banks. They provide a wide range of services to their customers through this division of financial services. These include checking and savings accounts, personal loans, mortgages for homes, lines of credit, credit cards and debit cards, and CDs certificates of deposits investment opportunities for customers. The main concentration is on the one on one consumer relationship.

Within the United States, the phrase commercial bank refers to a traditional bank. This term distinguishes it from the competing concept of investment bank. Following the Great Depression of the 1930s, the American Congress mandated that banks were only allowed to participate in traditional deposit and lending banking activities as opposed to investment activities. This Glass Steagall Act similarly required that investment banks could only participate in activities pertaining to the capital markets.

This important separation prevented another severe financial crisis like the Great Depression from erupting. Unfortunately for Americans everywhere, the Congress chose to repeal these protections afforded to markets and individuals by Glass Steagall when they canceled out the act in the 1990s. This allowed commercial banks to once again dabble in investment bank activities with depositors' money. It was considered to be a main factor which led to the financial collapse of the Great Recession in the years 2007-2009.

Commercial banking also relates to a division of a bank, or even an entire bank, that focuses on larger businesses and corporations. They handle these huge entities' loans and deposits. This would separate the concept from retail banking which only addresses the ordinary individuals along with their banking needs and accounts.

The idea behind retail banking is to be a one size fits all, single stop shop which provides all the financial services which they possibly can to their retail customers. Bank clients demand a full lineup of essential banking services from these retail operations. Included in this are such expected products as savings and checking accounts, lines of credit, personal loans, home loans, credit cards, debit cards, and CDs. The majority of retail banking customers visits their local bank branch in order to receive these services. Such centers deliver the consumer demanded onsite client service to provide for each of these retail customer requirements.

Financial representatives also work in these local area branches. They offer their clients of the bank both financial advice and customer service. Such financial reps prove to be the primary contact for garnering credit related applications for these products which help the banks to generate their revenues and profits.

These types of banks have begun to offer expanded retail services so that they can capture more business from their retail customers. Besides the typical bank accounts and accompanying customer service that the in branch financial reps deliver, banking centers have added various combinations of financial advisors. They provide a wide array of product offerings. Some of these are investment services like stock brokerage accounts, wealth management services, retirement planning, and even private banking for High Net Worth Individual clients and families.

There are occasionally insurance products and services offered through the in-branch retail banking network as well. Sometimes, such ancillary products and services will be provided out of third party affiliated institutions like insurance companies and investment firms. The idea behind such broadened offerings is to both provide customers greater convenience and to develop more points of financial interaction between them and the bank. This allows for clients of the bank to have greater and more convenient access to their funds and to engage in personal banking transactions both faster and easier.

The Internet has also made possible online retail banking. Many banks now offer partial banking services online. A few are actually banks which are entirely structured to provide banking services over the Internet alone. Among these are GoBank, Moven, and Simple. They offer lower fees as they have significantly smaller overheads with no in-branch personnel, buildings, and networks to support.

The top five biggest American commercial banks possessed more than half of the retail bank customer deposits for the entire country in the year 2015. These five largest institutions were JPMorgan, Bank of America/Merrill Lynch, Wells Fargo, Citibank, and U.S. Bank.

Revolving Credit

Revolving Credit refers to lines of credit that customers draw on and then make payments on to their creditors. In order to have such a facility, the debtor must pay a commitment fee. This enables them to utilize the funds on an as-needed basis. Such a facility is typically deployed for operating expenses. It would therefore vary every month according to the present day cash flow requirements of the customer. Both individuals and corporations alike are able to take out these revolving lines of credit.

An agreement would be established upfront between the bank and the customer. Such a contract would guarantee the maximum potential amount that the bank will loan out to the client. Besides the initial commitment fee, there will naturally be interest costs for the corporate borrowers. These are called carry forward charges when the accounts are set up for consumers.

Banks and other financial institutions will contemplate a number of factors concerning the borrower and its ability to repay such a line before these revolving credit lines become issued. Where individuals are concerned, this means that his or her current income, credit score, and stability of employment will all be evaluated. Where organizations and corporations are concerned, the bank will typically review the income statement, balance sheet, and cash flow statement before making its final decision on approval and maximum line amount.

For those business entities and individuals who suffer from commonplace fluctuations in non-anticipated expenses and cash balance fluctuations, this revolving credit can be crucial and even lifesaving. They provide flexibility, versatility, and convenience, though this comes at a cost. The price for this is a more expensive interest rate which banks and lending institutions levy for revolving credit than they do on more traditional installment types of loans. Many times, this revolving credit facility will come alongside interest rates which are variable and can be quickly adjusted as appropriate.

The credit limit proves to be the highest dollar amount which the financial institutions will allow the borrower to draw. While there are many different examples of revolving credit facilities in the market place today, the most frequently cited ones are the personal lines of credit and the home equity lines of credit. These are also called HELOCs.

It is important to understand the differences between revolving credit and installment loans. Installment loans typically involve a pre-determined and –set number of payments which will be made on a monthly or quarterly basis over a fixed amount of time. By contrast, revolving funds only involve interest payments along with fees which are applicable per the contract established between the actual bank and the client.

When an individual or corporation receives this revolving credit line, it means that a customer has been pre-approved for receiving a loan. It is more convenient to use than taking out loans again and again, as one does not need to have his credit reevaluated or a new loan application taken every time they draw upon the revolving facility funds. This is why revolving facilities were created for smaller loans that are shorter term in nature. With more massive sized loans, the banks will want a better laid out structure that comes complete with installment payments.

There are differences between business credit cards and revolving lines of credit. No physical credit card is necessary with revolving credit lines. Also revolving lines do not require a preset purchase or amount. This credit can be transferred into the company or personal account for whatever reason they wish. This makes the revolving facilities more like cash advances with funds immediately available upfront and without questions asked regarding the purchase. The interest rates on revolving facilities are also commonly substantially less than are those associated with even business forms of credit cards.

Run on the Bank

A run on the bank is the vernacular expression for a bank run. Runs on the banks actually happen as a result of many bank customers deciding to take out their deposits at one time. They do this out of fear that the bank is either broke or on its way to becoming insolvent. When runs on the banks get started, they have a tendency to create their own terrible momentum that leads to a self fulfilling prophecy. The more customers who take out their money, the greater the odds of bank default become, which leads to still more customer deposit withdrawals. If this happens long enough, it will likely upset a bank's finances to the point that the bank encounters bankruptcy as a result.

Runs on the bank can often lead to bank panics. These financial crises result from a large number of banks experiencing bank runs all at once. If the bank panics are not dealt with swiftly and convincingly, then a systemic banking crisis can develop. In such a banking crisis that is system wide, it is not uncommon to witness practically all, or even all, of a country's banking capital disappear.

Once this occurs, numerous bankruptcies follow, many times ending up in a deep and painful economic recession or even depression. Bank runs created a great amount of the economic damage that you saw done in the Great Depression. Associated costs of fixing the mess related to a systemic banking crisis are enormous. Over the last forty years, these expenses around the world have averaged fully thirteen percent of the respective countries' Gross Domestic Products in fiscal costs, leading to losses of economic output that averaged twenty percent of Gross Domestic Product.

Runs on the bank are able to be prevented with a few different strategies. Withdrawals can be suspended. More effectively, deposit insurance systems can be put in place, like the one that the Federal Deposit Insurance Corporation operates in the United States. The Central Bank may also help out banks by performing the function of the lender of last resort in times of banking crises. Such strategies are commonly effective, but not always. Even when countries possess deposit insurance, the bank depositors could still be fearful that they will not have instant access to their bank held deposits while the bank is reorganized by the FDIC.

The reason that runs on the bank are able to happen in the first place is because of the fractional reserve banking system. Modern day banks only keep a small percentage of their demand deposits in cash on hand, typically ten percent in developed nations. The rest of these deposits are tied up in loans that have longer terms than demand deposits. This leads to a mismatch of assets and liabilities. Though some banks keep better reserves than others do, no modern bank keeps sufficient reserves in its vaults to handle the majority of their deposits being withdrawn at a single time.

Savings and Loan Crisis

The most significant collapse of banks since the Great Depression in 1929 became the Savings and Loan Crisis of 1989. In 1989, over a thousand of the Savings and Loans in the country had collapsed. This brought to a close a route that had long been a secure means for obtaining home mortgages. It turned out that half of the failed S&Ls in the country came from Texas.

This pushed the Lone Star state into a recession. Poor investments in land and housing were auctioned off and crashed prices. The vacancy rate for offices increased to 30%. Crude oil prices plunged by 50%. Cases emerged of illegal practices. Empire Savings and Loan and other Texas banks were charged with criminal activities such as flipping land illegally.

The government had established the FSLIC Federal Savings and Loan Insurance Corporation to insure the S&L deposits as the FDIC does with regular banks. The problem arose as the S&L failures cost $20 billion from the FSLIC. They could not cover all of the costs which bankrupted them. Over 500 of the bank failures had been insured by other insurance run by state funds. Their collapse created costs of more than $185 million. This ruined the ability of state run insurance funds to protect bank depositors.

The crisis also took down five American senators called the Keating Five. They had taken campaign contributions of $1.5 million from the president of the Lincoln Savings and Loan Association Charles Keating. These senators pressured the government regulator Federal Home Loan Banking Board to not look into suspicious and potentially criminal involvement by Lincoln S&L.

The S&L crisis erupted because of a relaxing of standards that governed them. S&Ls had been unique banks which were allowed to receive funds from low interest deposits from savings accounts to make mortgages. In the 1980s a challenger to these savings accounts became popular in the form of money market accounts. They offered higher interest rates to savers. The S&Ls could not compete and were losing their funding source. They went to Congress to request a lifting of restrictions on their low interest rates they paid.

The Garn-St. Germain Depository Institutions Act resulted in 1982. S&Ls could then offer higher interest rates and were not limited to mortgage loans any longer. Now they could make consumer loans and commercial loans as well. Bigger problems came from the lifting of loan to value ratio restrictions. Also the Reagan Administration cut back on budget for the Federal Home Loan Bank Board which caused them to cut their regulatory staff. They no longer had the man power to look into potentially risky loans.

The S&L banks engaged in risky activities to try to raise capital for lending. They became involved with speculative commercial and real estate loans. In only a few years to 1985 they built up their assets of these types of speculation by 56%. Forty different S&Ls in Texas tripled their size by expanding as much as 100% annually.

In 1983 as many as 35% of the S&Ls in the nation were not making money and 9% had been bankrupted technically. Federal and state insurance money proved to be insufficient as the banks continued to fail. A number of unprofitable S&Ls kept operating and making poor loans as losses mounted.

President George H.W. Bush and Congress bailed out the S&L industry with the FIRREA Financial Institutions Reform, Recovery, and Enforcement Act in 1989. This gave $50 billion of tax paper money to shut down the failed S&Ls. It also created an agency called the RTC Resolution Trust Corporation to sell off these bad assets. Proceeds went to pay off depositors who had lost money. In the end the crisis cost $160 billion, of which $132 billion came from tax paper money.

SDR Denominated Bonds

SDR denominated bonds are a fairly recent phenomenon. These are bonds issued in special drawing rights currency units. SDR units are a basket of the world's most important currencies including the U.S. dollar, Euro zone euro, Japanese Yen, British pound sterling, and the Chinese Yuan. The International Monetary Fund's executive board approved a framework to issue such bonds to member nations and central banks back on July 1, 2009.

The principle of these SDR denominated bonds was intended to be allocated in SDRs. The market for such bonds was established initially as the official sector of IMF members. This meant it was to include primarily the member nations, relevant central banks, and another 15 holders of SDRs.

Included in these 15 prescribed holders are four central banks which were regional, eight developmental organizations, and three monetary agencies which were intergovernmental. Others allowed to trade in them were the fiscal agencies of the members. This means that a number of sovereign wealth funds were allowed to participate as there are not always distinguishing lines between national monetary authorities and their sovereign wealth funds. This is the case with Hong Kong and Saudi Arabia.

The IMF issued SDR denominated bonds were to start with three month maturities that could be extended to as long as five years. Interest payments on these instruments were quarterly. China signed an agreement to buy upwards of $50 billion of them, while Russia, India, and Brazil intended to buy as much as $10 billion each.

SDR denominated bonds again gained the international spotlight in August of 2016 when the World Bank's IBRD International Bank for Reconstruction and Development priced the first such bond in the Interbank Bond Market of China. This bond raised 500 million SDR units, which were equal to about $700 million US dollars. These bonds came with a three year maturity date. Their coupon interest payment rate was .49% per year. What made them most notable was that the payments are issued in Chinese Yuan.

This group of bonds is only the first batch. The full size of the issue approved by the World Bank SDR Denominated Issuance Program in August 12, 2016 is for 2 billion SDR's, making them equal to roughly $2.8 billion US dollars.

Even in China, placing so many SDR denominated bonds is a challenge. This is why the joint lead managers for the Interbank Market were several important banks with great depth in China. These included HSBC Bank of China Company Limited, the Commercial Bank of China Limited, China Development Bank Corporation, and China Construction Bank Corporation.

The issue was a great success. The significant interest in them led to a 2.5 times oversubscribing. Orders amounted to roughly 50. Fifty-three percent of them came from bank treasuries, 29 percent from central banks and official institutions, 12 percent from asset managers and securities firms, and six percent from insurance companies. These bonds will mature on September 2, 2019 with all payments coming from the World Bank's IBDR to be made to bond holders in Chinese Yuan.

Securitization

Securitization is a financial engineering procedure. In this process, sponsors take an asset or group of assets that is illiquid and turn them into a saleable security. Mortgage backed securities are common instruments that result from securitization. These MBS products are backed by assets. The security that underlies them are a group of mortgages.

The securitization process works in a series of steps. It begins with a bank or other financial institution originating a number of mortgages. The mortgages themselves are backed up by the specific properties the home buyers purchase. Next, these single mortgages become combined together into what is known as a mortgage pool. The pool of mortgages remains in trust for the MBS collateral.

MBS are sometimes put together in the securitization process by an investment bank or other third party independent financial firm. They could also be issued by the original bank that underwrote the mortgages in the beginning. Large aggregators like the government sponsored entities Freddie Mac, Fannie Mae, and Ginnie Mae put together many of these mortgage backed securities themselves.

Whichever group undertakes the effort, the end result is identical. Securitization creates a new financial security that is underpinned by the legal and financial claims on the assets of the mortgagors. Sponsors then take the new security and sell it investors or other interested parties in the secondary mortgage market. This proves to be a very large and liquid market. It offers substantial tradability to the securitized mortgages that would have little to no liquidity as stand alone investments.

When these mortgage backed securities are being created through the securitization procedure, issuers have options. Many times they decide to break up their pool of mortgages into a group of different components. They call these tranches. With tranches the issuers are able to put together the security however they would like.

This means they can craft one MBS into a range of tolerance for risk. Some buyers like pension funds are only interested in investing in mortgage backed securities with high credit ratings. Other investors like hedge funds have a higher tolerance for risk. They will be willing to take on tranches with lower credit ratings in exchange for higher returns.

Individual investors who want to participate in these mortgages have several choices. They can take a participation certificate share in a pool of mortgages. This pass through participation provides a pro rated share of interest and principal payments that come back into the pool when the issuers obtain the borrowers' monthly payments. There are also pools of such pass through mortgages called CMOs collateralized mortgage obligations.

Many individuals would like to become involved in mortgage investing but are unsure of all the research involved with the various kinds of MBS. An ideal way to participate without having to understand the detailed mechanics is through mortgage mutual funds. These funds could invest in a single kind of MBS like a Ginnie Mae issued one.

Still other funds are comprised of a range of mortgage backed securities as part of a group of holdings in government bonds. Mutual funds provide a better diversification in loan holdings than individuals might afford on their own. They also offer the ability to reinvest all payments of principal and interest into other MBS. This helps to reduce the risks of changing interest rates and prepayments. It also permits investors to receive yields that vary with current interest rates.

Sovereign Debt

Sovereign Debt refers to the amount of money which the government of a given nation owes its various domestic and foreign creditors. It is a synonym to country debt, national debt, or government debt since the word sovereign simply equates to an independent national government. Another way of thinking of this term is that it is the amount of money which the nation owes its outside creditors. This is a good reason why it is commonly interchanged freely with the phrase public debt. Sovereign debt is similarly the total accumulation of the yearly deficits run by a government. For this reason, it reveals the additional amount of money which governments spend over what they realize in revenues cumulatively.

It is mostly through issuing bonds that governments are able to finance their deficit spending. A good example of this is the United States' Treasury notes and bills. These instruments come with terms ranging from as little as three months to as far out as 30 years. Governments will pay the holders of the notes interest in order to give them a return for loaning the government the money.

As the likelihood of the bond being paid back increases, the interest rate which accompanies it decreases. This leads to a lower cost for carrying sovereign debt for nations which are perceived as trustworthy and financially viable longer term. Besides this financing avenue, governments are able to take out loans from private businesses, commercial banks, and other nations as well as from international individual financiers.

It is not so simple to compare the various sovereign debts of differing nations. Each debt ratings agency has its own emphasis in figuring up debts for sovereigns. As an example, Standard & Poor's' as an investors and business measuring debt ratings agency only considers those debts which the country owes its commercial lenders. It will not consider the money the country owes other countries, the World Bank, or the International Monetary Fund. It also will only include the national debt, and not the amount that provinces, states, cities, and counties in the nation owe.

With the European Union, it measures debt more broadly. It restricts the total amount of debt that its member states are allowed to maintain while being members of the EU. This would include local and provincial governments' debts and any amounts of future social security types of obligations that have been promised to citizens.

The United States itself considers debt still differently. Money which it owes other departments of its own government, called intra-governmental debt, it does not count. It also never includes any debts that the states, counties, and cities have incurred. As the overwhelming amounts of city and state governments are not permitted to run up deficits, it is generally a non-issue.

It is true that expanding the national debt increases growth. The simple explanation is that when governments increase their spending on health care, social security, or for new warships, they are rapidly flushing money through the economy as a whole. This increases economic growth (even if only temporarily) since businesses will then expand in order to keep up with the government spending-driven, rising demand.

This generally leads to new jobs. A multiplier effect becomes created as this increases growth and demand still more, leading to a virtuous cycle. This is why deficit spending is always considered to be a potent stimulant economically since the demand appears instantly while the cost for the debt is delayed into the future.

So long as the amount of sovereign debt is at a reasonable level the lenders to the nation are not worried. The higher growth means that they can be more easily paid back with their owed interest. The leaders in government want to spend constantly for the very simple reason that expanding economies equate to happy voters who will vote them back into office next election. Motivations for cutting spending simply do not exist in democracies.

Structured Finance

Structured Finance refers to the possibility of and procedures for issuing loans because of a reliable history of strong corporate cash flow. Instead of using assets for a loan's collateral, the funds are given out based upon the past history that shows a consistent cash flow in the business of the borrower. This cash flow will provide for the orderly and on- time pay back of the loan principle and interest. This type of financing is usually opted for when the more traditional methods either fail or are simply not practically available to a business.

It is also fair to say that structured finance proves to be an intricately involved and even complex financial instrument. This vehicle permits big companies and financial institutions such as banks to access complicated means for financing their needs. Such needs often will not be good matches for traditional financial products.

This structured finance has grown dramatically from the middle of the 1980s decade. It has evolved and expanded since then to be a significant player in the financial universe. Classic examples of such finance are CDOs collateralized debt obligations, CBOs collateralized bond obligations, synthetic financial instruments, and syndicated loans. Alongside CBOs and CDOs, there are also fairly new instruments like CMOs collateralized mortgage obligations, CDSs credit default swaps, and even hybrid forms of securities which may involve elements of both equity and debt instruments.

In fact it is most often corporations which find themselves in need of this structured finance funding. Many times they discover that a typical loan or even conventional instrument of finance (like corporate bonds) simply will not adequately meet their needs. Sometimes this is because the transaction needs to be discretionary and discreet. In order to accomplish this, creative solutions utilizing riskier instruments are employed.

The reality is that traditional types of lenders do not commonly offer such structured finance solutions and products. It is often up to investors to come up with the major cash infusions for organizations or businesses when such financing is required. Another interesting feature of these products is that they usually can not be transferred. This simply means that they can not be altered from one form of debt to another as with a standard loan.

On an increasing basis and frequency, governments, corporations, and financial intermediary organizations utilize such structured finance securitization programs. They are often deploying these to help manage risk, expand their reach of the business, develop one or more financial markets, or create new means of funding projects. In such scenarios, employing structured finance turns cash flows into lump sum payments. It also has the side effect and consequence of changing the liquidity of financial books and portfolios.

It is the process of securitization that actually creates these complex financial instruments. The magic of this process is that it creatively combines various financial instruments and assets into a single package. These repackaged instruments are rated according to a few tiers. The tiers then get sold on to investors. The advantage to this is that it encourages and fosters liquidity in markets and for businesses.

A typical example of the process of securitization is the MBS Mortgage backed security. When individual mortgages are grouped into a single pool, the issuer gains the ability to break up the large pool into various component pieces. They do this according to their risk of default. Smaller pieces can be sold off to investors, often for a better and more advantageous price by parts than the whole pool would fetch alone.

Utilizing structured finance is often appealing to a company that may lack significant physical assets which they can pledge as collateral. Yet they may possess a substantial base of clients as well as a documented, consistent history of both billing to and payments from their customers. Many times investors will loan money to these kinds of corporations. This is often true even if the companies are small. Investors will generally loan the company money on this basis for a better interest rate than a traditional bank loan would cost the firm to obtain. It also is a faster process with less administrative paper work than a typical business loan from a bank.

Subordinate Financing

Subordinate financing refers to that type of debt finance which ranks behind the primary finance. It is second in importance and position to debt that senior or secured lenders hold. This is important when a default occurs, as it determines who gets repaid first from any bankruptcy proceedings or foreclosure. The term signifies that senior lenders who are secured will be repaid before the debt holders that are subordinate.

Lenders who participate in this subordinate financing take on greater risk than the lenders considered to be senior. This is because they have a lower claim on the business or property assets. Sometimes this type of corporate finance is comprised of both equity and debt financing. A lender would be interested in this because it would offer them potential stock options or warrants that would reward them with extra yield as a means of compensating for the greater risk they take.

Where consumer borrowers and loans are concerned, subordinate financing would be a second mortgage. It takes second priority below the original first mortgage. First mortgages have the property to secure their loan and the debt. While nearly every mortgage is backed by the underlying property, first mortgages receive special seniority ahead of subordinated mortgages. This means the senior mortgage lender is repaid first in a foreclosure. With mortgages, subordinate financing could be a mortgage that is 80/20. In this case, the first mortgage would be 80 percent while the second mortgage that was subordinated represents 20 percent.

This means that only the lenders which are first mortgage holders are likely to get at least a portion of their money back if a borrower defaults in general. Should a borrower only default on the subordinate mortgage, this lender is able to foreclose on the property to regain its principal. Subordinated lenders could work to make their mortgage the senior one and then foreclose. They could do this by buying out their borrower's first mortgage. Afterwards, they could choose to subordinate the original first mortgage so that their once second mortgage became senior in the foreclosure.

Consumers should think carefully before participating in subordinate financing to obtain their houses. There are several disadvantages involved. Home owners will usually have to write two different mortgage payments each month if they do. They will also typically pay a higher interest rate on the second mortgage since these rates are usually greater than the first mortgage rates. There are also often two different loan fees, costs, and even discount points when first and second mortgages are used. Finally, this type of finance will often lead to a greater monthly payment when the two are combined than only one mortgage payment would.

The main reason that a home buyer would be interested in employing subordinated financing to purchase a home is because an 80/20 mortgage would not require them to come up with any down payment. It might also eliminate the need to pay for PMI private mortgage insurance which can be a substantial component of the monthly mortgage payment. This would depend on how the mortgage financing was originally structured.

Consumers will generally require a high credit score of minimally 700 in order to qualify for this subordinated financing. When borrowers have two mortgages, it will likely be impossible to obtain a home equity loan or line of credit at a later time.

SWIFT

SWIFT Network is the internationally relied upon system for transferring money. It underlies the overwhelming majority of security and international money transfers. This vast network for financial messaging is employed by financial institutions such as banks to rapidly, securely, and accurately receive and send information that includes instructions for money transfers. In any given day, almost 10,000 different member institutions of the SWIFT system deploy around 24 million unique financial messages throughout this truly impressive worldwide network.

SWIFT is an acronym that actually means the Society for Worldwide Interbank Financial Telecommunications. This messaging network securely transmits both instructions and sensitive information for financial institutions using a standardized operating system of codes. In order for this amazing system to work, SWIFT itself gives a one of a kind identification code to every financial institution in the world which participates. These codes are comprised of either 11 or eight characters. Names for this code range from SWIFT Code and SWIFT ID to BIC bank identifier code and ISO 9362 code. It should not be confused with the similar yet still different IBAN International Bank Account Number.

An example of one such SWIFT code for a member institution is helpful to look at in order to better understand how SWIFT puts these identifiers together. Consider UniCredit Banca based in Milan, Italy. The eight character SWFT code for UniCredit Banca proves to be UNCRITMM, which stands for UNI CREDIT ITALY Milan (Milan is identified with two Ms). SWIFT always takes the first four letters from the institution's name, making up the institute code. The second two letters are the national code. The next two characters represent the city location code. Another optional three characters stand for the individual branch within a large bank, as in using ZZZ to represent a particular branch location.

Thought SWIFT is undoubtedly a powerful institution and system in the world today, it does not ever hold or touch any securities or cash. It also never manages accounts for clients. Instead it is simply a financial transaction messaging system. Yet this service is critical in today's fast moving world of finance, business, and banking.

This is because the world before SWIFT was a ponderous place in which to do international wire and bank transfers. Before the advent of SWIFT, there was only the Telex system to send the international wire transfer message confirmations. Telex was fraught with problems. Among these were it had security issues, was terribly slow, and lacked a unifying system of standardized codes as SWIFT possesses for naming both the banks and the types of financial transactions being conducted.

A sender with Telex was forced to detail out each and every transaction utilizing sentences that had to be first interpreted then executed by the receivers on the other end. As these people often spoke other languages besides the lingua franca English, it led to countless human errors and mistakes in ultimate transmission.

In order to get around these many problems, seven of the biggest international financial institutions came together to create a cooperative society and system whose entire reason of being was to run a global financial network with would relay such critical financial messages utilizing both speedy and secure means. It only took SWIFT three years to grow rapidly from the original seven founding banks to 230 banks in five nations.

Despite the fact that competing financial messaging services such as FedWire, CHIPS, and Ripple exist, SWIFT has continued to enjoy its now-dominant market share and position. Many observers have noted that this stems in large part from the way it constantly comes up with newer message codes for various financial transactions.

Besides the simplified payment instructions SWIFT arose to deliver, the network additionally delivers messages for a significant and broad-based number of treasury and security transactions throughout the globe. Almost half of the SWIFT worldwide traffic still stems from the traditional heart of the network, the payment messages. An impressive 43 percent today pertain to security transactions. The other under ten percent deals with treasury transactions.

SWIFT has continued to evolve and grow into other related businesses. Today it also deploys its lengthy data maintenance history to deliver reference data, business intelligence, and compliance information services. An area it is addressing now is the delivery and implementation of software automation for its financial transaction messaging system. The company has successfully created and tested such software, but its use and deployment will come at a higher cost to participating banks.

Swiss Banking

Swiss Banking is unusually concentrated into two main banks. These are UBS and Credit Suisse. Together they control an enormous amount of the accounts and assets in all of Switzerland.

The Swiss Banking tradition used to be shrouded in secrecy. Under the administration of American President Obama, many Swiss banks were investigated and charged with helping Americans to illegally evade taxes. This is not a crime in Switzerland, and the country's laws had long protected their banks for engaging in the activity.

Starting with justice probes that investigated around a dozen of these Swiss banking outfits, the U.S. began handing out sentences and fines in 2013. Two banks at least were destroyed by the legal wrangling with the United States' justice department. These included Wegelin & Company and Bank Frey.

Wegelin & Company proved to be the oldest existing Swiss bank when the fines came out. It was the first foreign or Swiss bank to receive a criminal sentence and penalty for helping Americans to avoid taxes. The U.S. Justice Department levied $74 million in fines and forfeitures against the bank. The bank was already being wound down by the Swiss authorities because it had suffered so much financially from the struggle with the American government.

Bank Frey & Co was a boutique lender in the Swiss banking tradition. Its principal office was on the most important banking street in Zurich. In October of 2013 it had to close its doors as well in large part because of the lengthy and costly tax dispute with the U.S.

The main players in Swiss banking today UBS and Credit Suisse operate under similar models as universal Swiss banks with important overseas operations. UBS as the larger of the two has a greater number of banking assets. It is headquartered in Zurich and Basel and boasts operations in over fifty countries. It maintains more than 60,000 employees around the globe. It has offices in every major financial center of the world. About a third of the bank employees work in the Americas division. Slightly more than another third call Switzerland their base of operations.

In just over 150 years of history, UBS has managed to expand and acquire more than 300 different banks. They have over 300 branches and more than 4,500 employees in Switzerland alone. Over a third of all Swiss homes and 120,000 Swiss companies call UBS their bank. Their reach extends to 80% of all the wealth of the Swiss.

Credit Suisse is the second largest Swiss bank in the world after UBS. The bank dates back to 1856. Since then it has grown immensely to achieve a global presence. The bank counts operations in more than 50 different nations. It employs over 48,000 staff who hail from in excess of 150 different countries. In 2006, it started operating as a globally integrated universal bank.

This broad footprint has enabled both banks to create a well balanced revenue stream and to capture many new assets geographically. It provides them with significant opportunities to grow throughout the globe today.

The Credit Suisse and UBS strategies work off the banks' three critical strong positions. They are both leaders in worldwide wealth management. The banks are also standouts for specific investment banking abilities and skills. Finally they have a powerful regional footprint in the home nation of Switzerland.

The banks employ a well balanced strategy of gaining opportunities for wealth management in key emerging markets. This largest focus for them centers on the most important growth area of Asia Pacific. They also strive to serve critical already developed markets while focusing on the original country Switzerland.

Swiss Interbank Clearing (SIC)

Swiss Interbank Clearing is the interbank clearing system that Switzerland uses for payments within the country and between its banks. SIX Interbank Clearing Limited launched the system on June 10, 1987. They have been operating it since then for the Swiss National Bank.

The primary eligible users of the SIC are all of the Swiss banks along with German Post Finance. Cash handling companies, insurance companies, and securities dealers which are based in either Switzerland or Liechtenstein are also able to participate. The system allows for foreign based banks to utilize it once they fulfill the added requirements and conditions which the Swiss National Bank sets.

Swiss Interbank Clearing handles large transactions as well as retail transfers that connect service providers to the banks. This includes automatic debits, card payments, and bank transfers. The system has grown continuously in the amount volume it settles and quantities of transactions it processes since SIX first launched it.

Ten years after SIX created and launched the Swiss Interbank Clearing, they developed a similar system to enable the Swiss financial center and Liechtenstein to have access to the European Union's TARGET2 clearing system. This is called the euro Swiss Interbank Clearing, or simply euroSIC. It permits Swiss banks settle any payments in Euros between themselves quickly, simply, and cheaply. Thanks to this expansion of the system, they do not have to keep mutual euro accounts. It saves them the additional trouble, paperwork, and expense.

EuroSIC also makes it possible for Swiss and Liechtenstein banks to send payments in real time to other Euro zone banks. The participating members can process Euro payments across borders with almost any Euro zone institution. The system works effectively both ways. Euro zone banks and institutions gain convenient access to more than 3,200 banks and branches throughout both Switzerland and Liechtenstein.

Banks and financial institutions which the Swiss National Bank supervises may participate in euroSIC. This also applies to any of their branches, joint institutions, or clearing organizations that are located outside the country of Switzerland. These groups must be able to demonstrate that they have a comparable amount of operational and legal standards in the countries where they are based as do their partners or parent organizations in Switzerland.

The Swiss Euro Clearing Bank manages the system. This joint venture between SIX, UBS, Credit Suisse, and Post Finance bears the responsibility for both monitoring and supervising the euroSIC system. SECB has the advantage of being a German licensed bank as well. This means it provides a link to the real time clearing system of the Deutsche Bundesbank.

The system manager the SECB Swiss Euro Clearing Bank provides access to make rapid payments to Germany. The payments which euroSIC processes must be non urgent payments. Banks can send as much as much as 50,000 euros on behalf of their clients with reasonable transaction costs thanks to the system that the Deutsche Bundesbank provides. This is handled through the German EMZ bulk payment system. The SECB also provides its euroSIC members with a means for making inexpensive transfers and payments using the STEP2 system. This is the European Union wide bulk payments system.

Euro Swiss Interbank Clearing operates using the settlement accounts of the member institutions. SIX actually runs the system in Zurich, the Swiss financial center. Every transaction processes through the settlement accounts. There must be enough funds in the bank's account in the system at the Swiss Euro Clearing Bank for the transaction to go through in real time. Otherwise, the transaction is put aside until enough funds are present to cover the transaction.

Swiss National Bank (SNB)

The Swiss National Bank is one of the important central banks of the world. It carries out its monetary policies and other roles independently of the government of Switzerland. In 2007, the SNB celebrated its one hundred year anniversary from its founding in 1907.

Switzerland's central bank has a wider mandate than some other national central banks do. The mandate of the Swiss National Bank is to conduct itself per the best interests for the whole country. It does have a main goal to guarantee price stability for Switzerland by considering the impacts of economic developments. Beyond this it also performs numerous other functions.

Switzerland has adopted a goal of price stability that is comparable with other internationally important central banks. The goal of the SNB is to see under 2% per year increases in the cost of consumer prices. They are concerned with inflation not getting out of hand as it misallocates capital and labor and also unfairly distributes wealth and income. The bank also has a special concern to avoid deflation, the continuous decline in the levels of prices. It is the middle ground of just below two percent which they work towards with their monetary policy decisions.

The SNB actually implements monetary policy to control inflation by guiding the interest rates for on sight deposits and by directing the money market liquidity. This influences the country's overall interest rate. The bank uses the three month Libor measured in Swiss francs for the interest rate it references. One thing the SNB is not shy about is participating in the foreign exchange markets. They do this whenever necessary to impact monetary levels as they deem appropriate.

The Swiss National Bank also issues the Swiss franc notes and coins. The banknotes are created according to high standards for security as well as quality. They determine how many banknotes to issue based on payment purpose demands. As far as cashless payments go in Switzerland, the bank participates in the SIC Swiss Interbank Clearing System. They hold the accounts for the various institutions to clear the checks and other cashless payments.

Asset management is an area in which the Swiss National Bank is proactive. They manage both the country's currency reserves and their gold reserves. Switzerland is unusual in keeping a 25% gold to franc note gold reserve and standard. They keep enough of currencies on hand to have ample room to adjust their monetary policy.

For several years, the bank instituted a 1.20 floor on Euro to Swiss franc exchange rates. Defending this level required massive purchases of Euros and sales of Swiss francs as conditions in the Euro zone deteriorated. Finally, Switzerland abandoned this three year old policy without warning in 2015. This caused massive chaos in world foreign exchange markets as speculators had built up enormous positions in Forex based on the SNB's policy.

Like many central banks, the SNB is tasked with maintaining stability for the national financial system. They analyze risks to the system and find areas where they need to respond. They are also responsible for assisting with both designing and implementing the regulatory framework that governs the financial sector. The bank regulates financial market institutions that are considered to be systemically important.

Another interesting role that the Swiss National Bank carries out is as the banker to the Swiss Confederation. This means that it handles payments for the Confederation. The bank also issues any bonds and money market debt and is custodian for their securities. They carry out all transactions in foreign exchange on behalf of the Confederation as well.

The SNB is renowned for cooperating on the international monetary stage. They offer technical assistance and advice as needed, participate actively in the IMF, and coordinate international monetary actions in crises.

Finally, the Swiss National Bank compiles and releases statistics. These cover financial markets and banks in the country, direct investment, Swiss financial accounts, the balance of payments, and the country's international investment position.

Systemic Risk

Systemic Risk refers to those dangers that threaten the entire financial sector, another segment of the market, or the entire market. Analysts and economists also call this volatility, "undiversifiable" risk, and market risk. Such risk is especially dangerous because it can not be entirely avoided nor accurately predicted or forecast. There is no practical way to mitigate such risks to the entire system by diversifying assets. Instead, it can only be managed (though never perfectly) via effective hedging strategies or through the optimal allocation of assets.

Another way of considering such Systemic Risk is that it entails the very real possibility that a company-level or bank-level failure could set off serious volatility and instability. It might begin a chain reaction that leads to collapse in a whole industry, market segment, or even entire national or multinational economy. This risk to the system caused much of the Global Financial Crisis of 2008. At this tumultuous time in American and Western economic and geopolitical history, there were a number of financial companies in particular that were labeled too big to fail simply because they posed a real risk to the entire system.

This is the case because institutions like these are extremely large and systemically important in their own market industries. In extreme cases they might represent a dangerously large portion of the entire economy of a nation. Firms that are highly entangled with a number of other ones also prove to be systemically risky.

The federal government of the United States engages in the study of systemic risk so that it can justify becoming involved in the national economy from time to time. They do this with the idealism that they can lessen the impacts of company-centered events that cause sometimes severe ripples. The Feds feel with surgically- and precisely-targeted actions or regulations that they can reduce the severity of the consequences of these failures on a macroeconomic level. One example of this was the Dodd-Frank Act of 2010. This massive package of additional rules, regulations, and laws was intended to stop another Global Financial Crisis and Great Recession from happening. The heavy-handed regulation of important banks and other financial companies is supposed to reduce risk to the system.

It is instructive to look at the historical real-world examples of which companies posed such Systemic Risk in the middle of this greatest financial crisis since the Great Depression of the 1930s. It was the so-called "Lehman Brothers moment" that nearly brought down the entire Western-based financial and banking system in 2009. The size and scope of Lehman Brothers and its connectedness to the entire American economy caused it to be a massive source of risk to the system.

As the company collapsed the effect of this spread far and wide through the entire national and even international financial system. In the United States first, the capital markets froze. This meant that companies and individuals were no longer able to access loans. In some cases, they still could obtain them, but only if they had the highest standard of creditworthiness so they would not entail any risk of default for the embattled banks and other lenders.

At the same time, AIG the American International Group insurance company experienced intense and insurmountable financial problems. As the world's largest insurance company, they were overly connected to the other banks and financial companies of the globe. This made them a serious Systemic Risk not only to the American financial system, but also to the British, European, and Asian financial systems.

Their own portfolio of highly toxic assets connected with subprime mortgages and residential MBS mortgage backed securities meant it suffered from repeated calls for collateral, a downgrade of its credit rating, and an evaporation of liquidity. This only worsened and became a vicious downward spiral as the values of these poisonous assets declined further every month.

For some unknown reason, the same U.S. government that would not prop up Lehman Brothers intervened dramatically to save the AIG by loaning them over $180 billion. It may have been because various regulators, analysts, and economists, were convinced that the failure of AIG would have led to many additional banks, insurance companies, and financial firms collapsing.

Term Auction Facility (TAF)

In response to the bank lending freeze that followed the outbreak of the banking and financial crisis in 2007, Ben Bernanke created and launched his Term Auction Facility TAF in December of 2007. The Fed was able to utilize its long mostly dormant discount window from December 2007 through to March 2010 as a creative new means of helping out struggling banks to access extra funds. They were then able to loan out these additional funds to consumers and businesses at their discretion. A primary new way of lending out such money to the banks lay in this Term Auction Facility.

Using the Term Auction Facility TAF, the Fed set up a system to auction out term funds to interested banking institutions. Any bank or credit union that already was able to borrow money via the primary credit program had eligibility to be a participant in these TAF Fed auctions.

The Fed was willing to accept bad loans as collateral for these funds. At every TAF auction, the Fed loaned out a set amount of money. They utilized the auction process starting with minimum bid rates in order to set the interest rates on these loan facilities. Banks could participate in the bidding process via phone through their local area Reserve Banks. The last of these TAF auctions occurred back on March 8 of 2010.

For the nearly three years that it ran, the Term Auction Facility worked according to a set out regular process. On a two weekly basis, the Federal Reserve would decide on the amount of money which it would then loan out on any given day. They would determine the minimum interest rate at which they would consent to loan out the funds. Banks which were interested in extra funds could then make bids for the dollar amount of money they wished to obtain at the interest rate they would agree to pay. Next the Federal Reserve sorted out the various competing bids by the level of interest rate that each participating bank offered them.

The Fed started with the greatest interest rate and then went on down from there, adding up the totals of money requested until they reached the maximum dollar amount which they were willing to lend out. Interest rates on each loan equaled the lowest interest rate which had been offered by the banks that had bids accepted.

The Fed was willing to do this so that there would not be funding shortfalls at a single institution which might cause the circular flow of credit and money in the whole American banking system to seize up and stop. In reality, most of the banks who borrowed from the Fed through the Term Auction Facility ended up leaving this money in their accounts with the Federal Reserve.

The Term Auction Facility served a useful purpose as the Federal Reserve Bank was willing to offer loans to member banks at rates that were lower than the associated market rates in exchange for putting up collateral in the form of bad loans that no one else would accept. On March 11, 2009, the banks had drawn total credit in the amount of $493.145 billion. The balance sheet of the Fed swelled to nearly a trillion dollars worth of collateral at its maximum extent.

In the end, the program proved to be successful for increasing confidence the banks had in each other, even though they did not loan out these borrowed funds generally. The TAF was originally intended to be more temporary than it turned out to be. Bernanke never envisioned it reaching the trillion dollar mark by June of 2008. All TAF funds have been repaid without taxpayers having to subsidize any of these loans which the Fed issued to the various banks.

Term Loans

Term loans refer to those loans a bank makes to a business or corporation for a set amount of time. These loans come with either a floating or a fixed interest rate and a pre-arranged schedule for repayment. There are numerous banks that offer such term loan programs to businesses so that they can access the funds they need for monthly operating expenses. Many times such a small business will utilize the cash they receive from this kind of a loan in order to buy equipment or other forms of fixed assets that they need for their production or manufacturing process.

Term loans are utilized for either working capital, purchases of real estate, or equipment purchases. These must be paid back in a time frame ranging from a single year on up to 25 years from issue. Payment schedules will either be quarterly or monthly. The maturity date will also be fixed on the loan. Actual interest rates could be pre-set or could vary with the floating interest rate benchmarks. Obtaining this kind of a loan will need appropriate collateral to be posted.

The approval process is exacting and extensive in order to lower the chances of default on such a loan. Small businesses which are established and that possess solid financial statements will find such loans to be appropriate for their situation. Banks will be more likely to approve them if the business is able to make a good faith down payment on the loan. This helps to lower the aggregate loan cost by reducing interest amounts and to decrease the minimum quarterly or monthly payment dollar amounts.

Funding amounts for these common commercial loans can range from $25,000 and higher. Bank loan officers usually subdivide such term loans according to one of two different categories. These are intermediate and long term loans. With intermediate loans, the loan maturity date is typically under three years. Such loans will commonly be paid back in monthly time-frame installments. There can be balloon payments due as well. Businesses expect to pay them out of their cash flow. The American Bankers Association states that repayment will typically be tied to the asset which is being financed and its useful life.

Conversely, longer term loans will last for more than three years and extend on up to ten or even 25 years long. The assets of a business will often serve as collateral for these bigger commitment loans. Usually either quarterly or monthly payments will come due. Businesses repay these installments utilizing either their cash flow or company profits.

Such longer-term commitment loans will generally come with clauses that restrict the number of other financial commitments the firm may assume in the form of debts, officers' salaries, and dividend payouts. Sometimes they will mandate that a given percentage of company profits must be put off to the side in order to pay back the loan.

While there are countless ways a business could deploy the resources from a term loan, some are more appropriate. The smartest ways to use them are through important capital improvements to the business, construction projects, large investment in capital, or buying other businesses. Working capital is another sensible use for such a loan.

The rates for these types of loans are typically competitive and not expensive relative to other forms of borrowing. They commonly cost approximately 2.5 percentage points over the prime lending rate for those loans which will be shorter than seven years. For the ones that are longer-term than this, around 3 percentage points greater than prime rates is normal. There will also be fees for such loans that usually amount to around one percent. Construction loan fees are often higher.

Too Big To Fail

Too Big To Fail refers to the disturbing but proven concept that some businesses have become so enormous and systemically important that the jurisdictional government has no choice but to save them from failing with whatever means necessary. The governments feel they must deliver material assistance to the firms in order to prevent a catastrophic rogue wave effect from reverberating across the entire economy.

The simple explanation for how a company can be so important to an entire economy is this. When such an enormous firm fails, all of the companies that count on it for parts of their revenue can also be compromised and fail, as well as its debt holders and ancillary services providing companies that work with the failing massive firm. Jobs then become eliminated en masse. For this reason, the expenses involved with a simple bailout or government backed guarantees of the mega corporation are significantly less than the cost of overall widespread economic failures. It explains why governments will often opt for the bailout as the less expensive answer to the moral problem.

Too Big To Fail especially pertains to commercial banks and financial services firms. These financial companies are so critical for the United States' and other Western economies that it would create havoc and spread financial ruin if they declared bankruptcy. Because of this, the American and British governments especially opted in the Global Financial Crisis of 2008-2009 to spare the banks and other financial service firms.

They saved the bank creditors and holders of counter party risk. As an unwished for side effect, they allowed the managers and company board members to keep their enormous salaries and incredible bonuses. Throughout the last years of the 2000's, the United States' Federal Government doled out approximately $700 billion in order to shore up such critical failing corporations as Bear Stearns, AIG, and the major banks which stood on the edge of financial ruin.

It was investors' total evaporation in confidence of the major financial institutions that led to their near-downfall back in the years 2008 and 2009. Especially the investment banks ran into trouble as they had become unbelievably leveraged (to the tune of from forty to one and eighty to one) when suddenly their mortgage loan-based assets and derivatives plunged in value as the subprime mortgage crisis spiraled out of control. Both stake holders and creditors quickly began to have doubts in their financial solvency as their balance sheets crumbled.

The defining moment in the Too Big To Fail crisis erupted when the government did not step in to prevent Lehman Brothers investment bank from failing. This has become widely known as the "Lehman moment." As widespread chaos erupted in the financial markets, regulators suddenly became painfully aware that these largest companies were so intricately connected that it would take enormous financial bailouts in order to stop literally half of the U.S. financial sector from collapsing.

Once the bailouts had intervened to save the major Too Big To Fail investment banks, only two remained standing. Even the survivors Morgan Stanley and Goldman Sachs were both forced to convert to traditional commercial banks so that they could be backstopped by the FDIC. Bear Stearns was effectively wound down, Lehman's skeleton was bought out by Barclays of Great Britain, and once-mighty Merrill Lynch became a subsidiary of Bank of America. The shadow banking industry had all but disappeared overnight.

The government then attempted to address the issues of Too Big To Fail financial firms. The U.S. Congress passed the Dodd-Frank Wall Street Reform and Consumer Protection Act of 2010. The idea was to create restrictions which would make it far more difficult for such conditions to flourish again. They hoped to sidestep having to extend other bailouts in the future.

The Act made the financial institutions create forms of "living wills" so that their plans are in place in order to rapidly liquidate assets if they have to file for bankruptcy. An internationally based consortium of financial regulators came up with a new set of rules in November of 2015 to force the major global banks to raise their capital by $1.2 trillion more in additional debt funding which they are able to convert into equity or write off if they suffer catastrophic losses again.

Transaction Fee

Transaction Fee describes a cost that companies have to pay every time they process a debit card or credit card transaction. These can also be called per transaction fees. Such fees range typically from .5 percent to five percent of the full transaction amount plus another .20 to .30 handling fee per transaction. Every merchant service provider assesses its own specific fees. As an example, when customers charge a $100 amount, the fee for the merchant to process this transaction could vary from a low of .70 to a high of $5.30. This is why those merchants which encounter many debit and credit card payments from their customers are best advised to shop the most advantageous deals and lowest fees from the various service providers.

Such transaction fees are set by two different participants. The first is the actual card payment firm, such as Visa, MasterCard, American Express, or Discover. The other fee setter comes from the provider of the merchant services. These wholesale or payment card transaction fees cannot be negotiated and do not vary from one merchant to the next. Yet the fees of the service providers do range. Service providers group them according to one of three main categories. These are interchange plus, tiered, or subscription.

With interchange plus, the structure of fees breaks out according to the service provider and payment card company fees individually on the monthly statement of the merchant. Tiered structures levy their fees on the type of transactions in question. This might be online or in person based transactions. With subscription fees, these are either annually or monthly assessed. Such per transaction fees reimburse the financial service firms for processing the payment card transactions.

There are more than just transactions fees that merchants have to pay in order to accept credit and debit card payments from their customers. The merchants also have to cover terminal fees, annual fees, and network fees. The contract dictates the terms of the payment processor and what the merchants might be capable of negotiating with the processors. These per transaction fees prove to be the main reason why some companies require consumers to spend a minimal amount in order to charge a purchase on their debit or credit cards.

As an obvious example, there is simply no justification for allowing a .50 charge on a credit card if the per transaction fee will amount to .30 of this. This is why many merchants elect to establish a between $5 and $10 minimum for payments by either debit or credit cards. The fact is that those smaller companies which simply cannot self-absorb the high credit card fees will be the ones who most frequent enforce such minimum transaction amounts for credit or even debit card payments in their stores. They simply lack the high volumes of credit card processing transactions necessary to obtain the rebates and other discounts which the mega payment processors give out to their larger and higher volume payment processing merchants as an incentive to keep them charging away.

Transaction fees could also apply to purchasing or selling stocks, bonds, mutual funds, ETFs, and other financial securities. These are sometimes known as simply commissions when investors encounter them. Both the buying and selling sides of trades will encounter such fees whatever the underlying instrument they are purchasing proves to be. The relatively high cost of commissions on trades (as a percentage of the total trade dollar amount) has created the rise of a whole class of discount brokers in both the stock markets and Forex markets. Charles Schwab was the first and best known national discount broker which arose in the world of stocks and mutual fund trading for individual investors back in the late 1970s.

Troubled Asset Relief Program (TARP)

The Troubled Asset Relief Program is also known by its clever acronym the TARP. This represented a series of national relief programs which the United States Treasury Department developed and administered. They did this to attempt to restore stability to the American financial system, to rebuild economic stability and growth, and to forestall housing foreclosures after the 2008 Global Financial Crisis and Great Recession wrecked the national and Western portion of the global economy. The idea was to buy up threatened firms' equity and toxic assets so that they could continue to operate and make loans.

In the first round, the Troubled Asset Relief Program provided Treasury with an mind boggling $700 billion of purchasing ability with which to purchase the dubious and at that point entirely illiquid MBS mortgage-backed securities as well as additional assets. They were to buy these from systemically important banks and financial institutions with an eye on rebuilding the shattered liquidity of the stricken money markets. It was the congressionally approved Emergency Economic Stabilization Act they passed on October 3rd in 2008 which allowed them to develop the program. With the Dodd-Frank Act for banking reforms, the Congress reduced their $700 billion amount of authorization down to a still-impressive $475 billion.

The series of events that led to this de facto bank bailout originated from the freeze up of the worldwide credit markets that ground to a screeching halt in September of 2008. This became worse as a few of the systemically important financial institutions like American International Group, and the GSE government sponsored enterprises Freddie Mac and Fannie Mae became victims of intense financial trouble. Lehman Brothers' went bankrupt which nearly overthrew the global financial system. At the same time Goldman Sachs and Morgan Stanley altered their charters to evolve into commercial banks which provided them with the backing of the FDIC Federal Deposit Insurance Corporation. This did stabilize the attacks on their two market capitalizations and shore up their capital positions, though it required some time to have effect.

It was with the Troubled Asset Relief Program that the government through the U.S. Treasury was finally able to buy up the root of the crisis, the Mortgage-backed securities. In decreasing the possible unknown toxic asset losses from the financial institutions which held them, they saved the banking system in not only the United States but likely the entire Western world.

Critics of the Troubled Asset Relief Program called it the largest bank bailout scheme in the history of the world. Without these cash infusions into the important national banks throughout the U.S. though, they would have been unable to continue operating at all. When the program had successfully stabilized the banking system and the too big too fail, systemically all-important banks, and the market had sufficiently calmed down, TARP was allowed to expire on October 3rd of 2010.

Treasury utilized the TARP funds wisely and well. They deployed some of them to make loans, others to invest in companies in need of cash infusions, and still more to guarantee toxic assets like the MBS. They received bonds or shares off of the collapsing financial companies and banks in consideration for this accommodation. The first program was known as the Capital Repurchase Program. In this initiative, Treasury purchased preferred shares of stock in eight major banks. These included Citigroup, Bank of America/Merrill Lynch, Goldman Sachs, Morgan Stanley, Bank of New York Mellon, Wells Fargo, J.P. Morgan Chase, and State Street Bank.

The banks had to provide the government with a full five percent dividend return which had to increase to nine percent in 2013. This gave the banks huge incentive to purchase back their own stock from Treasury before the conclusion of the five year windows. Then-Treasury Secretary Hank Paulson understood the government would make money off of the program in the end as he believed the stock prices of the banks would rebound at least somewhat by or before 2013.

Four other groups and entities would have collapsed without additional help from the Troubled Asset Relief Program and Treasury. Each of these received either direct cash infusions via preferred stock purchases or loans. AIG (the largest insurance company in the world) received $40 billion. Various community banks obtained a collective $92 billion. A number of these did fail in spite of this help. The American Big Three car makers got

$80.7 billion collectively. Bank of America and Citigroup also received an additional $45 billion between them. TARP also loaned out $20 billion to the sister TALF program which the Federal Reserve managed.

Though critics heavily maligned the government for saving the banking system and national banks, the bailout did not cost the government anything by the time it had been concluded. In fact, by May of 2016, the banks had paid the government back all of their principal (collectively, despite some failing anyway) plus $25 billion in profits for a total repayment of $275.04 billion.

Trust Account

A trust account refers to a type of account which a trustee holds on the behalf of the beneficiary. The trustee does not have the ability to utilize the funds in any personal capacity, but merely to safe keep, disburse, and invest them for the advantage of the beneficiary.

An example of this type of arrangement is when an attorney holds funds for the benefit of the client. The attorney will not be able to draw upon the funds until after a certain protocol takes place. As the attorney earns the lawyer fees, the client will have to first review and then actually approve the bill from the attorney before he or she can transfer the client funds from this trust account over to the general account of the attorney for settlement of bills.

There are a number of reasons and situations in which individuals may opt to establish a trust account. In some scenarios, people wish to disperse a pre-determined sum of money to their family or other loved ones over a number of years or throughout the remainder of their natural lives.

As a real world example, consider the following. Parents may wish to establish some trust accounts which will provide money to their dependents and/or children every month if and when they die. In such a scenario, it would normally be banking brokers who would manage such accounts. In fact these broker trustees would draw down the account values by the appropriate amount every month or year as they disbursed the either monthly or yearly funds to the beneficiaries for the individuals who originally formed the trust.

There are other common kinds of trusts as well. One of these is a property tax trust account. Such accounts will be established by entrepreneurs of real estate who own a variety of properties. Rather than have to be concerned about the property tax funds and disbursements to the appropriate taxing authorities themselves, they elect to form a trust account which will pay the taxes. This prevents the entrepreneurs from forfeiting their valuable properties because they forgot to pay the property taxes. There are a number of monetary benefits to having such an account. One of these is that estate taxes will not apply to properties contained in such a trust when the owner dies.

There are two different main types of trust accounts. These are revocable and irrevocable trusts. With revocable trusts, these represent deposit accounts whose owners chose to name one or several beneficiaries. These beneficiaries would then obtain the deposits in the account once the holder of the account died. As the name implies, such revocable trusts may be terminated, revoked, or altered on demand whenever the holder of said account wishes. In this particular case, the owner is the trustor, settlor, or grantor of the revocable trust in question. These types of trusts will be established as either informal or formal. While trustees are powerful and have a broad scope of authority over the assets of the beneficiary, they are not omnipotent, but must be bound by the laws and regulations of the jurisdiction which pertain to trust accounts.

Irrevocable trusts on the other hand are similarly deposit accounts but they are not titled in the name of the owner. Instead these become titled as an irrevocable trust for the name. The owner, trustor, settlor, or grantor also makes deposits of money or other valuable assets to the trust account. The principal difference is that the owners forfeit all ability to alter or cancel the trust once they have established it. These types of trusts also become created once an owner of a revocable type of trust dies. They can be set up through a judicial order as well, or even by a statute as appropriate.

Trust Fund

A trust fund proves to be a specific kind of legal entity. It contains property or cash which it holds to benefit another group, individual, or organization. Numerous different kinds of trusts exist. They are governed by almost as many provisions that determine how they work. Every trust fund involves three critical parties. These are the grantor, the beneficiary, and the trustee.

A grantor is the individual responsible for creating the trust fund. Grantors can do this with a variety of assets. They might give stocks, bonds, cash, mutual funds, real estate, private businesses, art, or other items of value to the fund. They also determine the terms by which the trustee will manage the fund.

Beneficiaries are the individuals who receive the benefit of the fund. The grantor sets it up on their behalf. The assets the grantor places inside of the trust fund are not the property of the beneficiary. The trustee oversees them so that the financial gain benefits this individual according to the rules laid out by the grantor at the time he or she establishes it.

Trustees are the managers of these funds. They could be an institution like a the trust department of a bank, an individual, or a number of trusted advisors. Their job is to make sure that the fund fulfills its duties spelled out by the governing law in the trust documents. Trustees typically receive small management fees. The trustee could manage the assets directly if the trust specifies this. In other cases, trustees have to pick out investment advisors who are qualified to manage money.

Trust funds come to life under the rules of the state legislature where the trust originates. Different states offer advantages to certain types of trusts. This depends on what the grantor wants to do by establishing the fund. This is why attorneys help to draft the trust documents to make sure they are correct and most advantageous. As an example, there are states which allow perpetual trusts that can continue forever. Other states make these illegal because they do now want to enfranchise a class of future generations who receive substantial wealth for which they did not work.

Special clauses may be inserted into these trusts. Among the most heavily used is the spendthrift provision. This keeps the beneficiary from accessing the fund assets to pay debts. It also allows parents to ensure that any irresponsible children they have do not find themselves destitute or homeless despite poor decisions they may make.

Trust funds provide a large number of benefits. They receive special protection from creditors. They ensure that family members follow wills after the grantor passes away. These trusts also help estates to avoid as many estate taxes as possible so that wealth can reach a greater number of generations.

Trusts can be an ideal way to ensure the continuity of a business. Sometimes business owners wish to protect a company and their employees after they die. They might still wish for the profits to benefit their heirs. In this case, the trustee would oversee the management of the business while the heirs reaped the financial rewards but could not break up or ruin the company through mismanagement.

Trusts can also be used with life insurance to transfer significant amounts of money which will benefit the heirs. A small trust could purchase a grantor life insurance. When the grantor dies, the insurance money funds the trust. The trustee will then buy investments and give the rents, interest, and dividends to the beneficiaries.

Trustee Savings Bank (TSB)

Trustee Savings Bank refers to a now defunct type of British financial institution. It is also known by its acronym TSB. These banks began as savings deposit institutions for those who had only meager financial means. The shares of these banks were not stock market exchange traded. Rather they were something like the mutually owned building societies of Great Britain. A key difference between the two types of financial institutions was that the depositors of the TSB's did not have any voting rights or ability to direct the organization's managerial or financial goals and direction.

In consequence for a lack of owner-voting rights, the boards of directors for the Trustee Savings Banks were appointed as volunteer basis trustees. This explains where the name for the TSB's came from in the first place. Reverend Henry Duncan from Ruthwell in Dumfriesshire established Britain's very first TSB in Scotland. He set this up to help out his poorest members of the congregation in 1810. The only reason for the organization lay in serving the local community members.

During the inter-war years a hundred years later, the Trustee Savings Bank model demonstrated that it could effectively compete throughout the retail banking model market with the major commercial banks and building societies throughout the nation. At one point by 1919, these types of financial institutions counted an impressive 100 million British pounds in combined deposits and assets. This amount reached 162 million pounds by 1929 and an incredible 292 million pounds at the outbreak of the Second World War in 1939.

Despite enjoying two centuries of success and growth as independent institutions, the Trustee Savings Banks became combined into one financial institution called the TSB Group plc from the years 1970 to 1985. Their stock traded on the famed London Stock Exchange until 1995 when the group merged with the Lloyds Bank to become the enormous conglomeration Lloyds TSB. At that moment, the new Lloyds TSB combined unit represented the largest bank in the United Kingdom by market share. It was second only to HSBC by market capitalization, as HSBC has absorbed Midland Bank in 1992.

The group which now represented the legacy of the Trustee Savings Banks expanded again in 2009 with the acquisition of the HBOS Halifax Bank of Scotland group. Its name changed again to the Lloyds Banking Group at this point. The TSB name was not lost, as the primary retail banking subsidiaries were Lloyds TSB Bank and Lloyds TSB Scotland. Lloyds again resurrected the TSB name and brand when it divested the 632 branches from Scotland, Gloucester, Cheltenham, and some of the Welsh and English Lloyds TSB bank branches into the TSB Bank plc.

The new operation came into being on September of 2013 and underwent an IPO initial public offering during 2014. The rest of the Lloyds Banking Group changed its name back to Lloyds Bank. This spin off happened because the Lloyd's Banking Group had to be bank rescued by Her Majesty's Government. Thanks to the 43.4% government stake in the group as a result of the Global Financial Crisis, European Union state aid rules required that it spin off a portion of the business.

Trustee Savings Bank plc did not continue for long as an independent entity. It began life in 2013 with a national network of 631 bank branches throughout especially Scotland, and also England and Wales. They counted over 4.6 million customers as well as more than 20 billion British pounds worth of customer deposits and loans. The group had its headquarters in Edinburgh, Scotland.

As the reestablished TSB, the group had a listing on the London Stock Exchange and remained a member of the FTSE 250 index of British based companies until it received and accepted a takeover bid from Spanish-based bank Sabadell. Sabadell made its offer for TSB Bank in March of 2015 and completed the acquisition of the last remaining Trustee Savings Bank on July 8, 2015. TSB Bank still operates as a wholly owned subsidiary of Sabadell, so the TSB brand name remains.

UBS

UBS is one of the major Swiss and international banking giants. The group is a global firm that has its headquarters in both Zurich and Basel. The bank offers a variety of financial services to corporate, private, and institutional customers. The bank recently celebrated its 150 year anniversary in 2012.

The UBS Group has a presence in every major financial center of the world. They maintain offices in more than fifty different nations. The bank employs around 60,000 individuals in these global locations. Around a third of the bank staff work in the Americas. Switzerland is home to 35% of its employees. Eighteen percent of them work in the Europe, Middle East, and Africa region, while 13% of the group's staff are located in Asia Pacific.

In 150 years time, UBS has merged with and acquired in excess of 300 different banks. The long history of the bank helps to explain why it has evolved into a gold standard in the international banking sector and remains a cornerstone of the legendary tradition of Swiss banking.

In Switzerland today, the country operates approximately 300 branches and maintains 4,500 employees. They serve one out of three households and reach 80% of all Swiss wealth. The bank also provides accounts and services to 120,000 companies and 80% of the banks that call Switzerland their home market.

The bank prides itself on the financial products and services it delivers to its corporate, wealthy, and institutional clients around the globe and to Switzerland. Besides its Corporate Center, the bank operates in five principle divisions. These are Wealth Management, Wealth Management Americas, Asset Management, Personal and Corporate Banking, and the Investment Bank. They focus all of their endeavors in the business areas in which they excel. Because of this, they have significant and competitive positions in each of their markets.

The UBS Wealth Management business offers advice to the bank's global wealthy clients besides those in its Americas' group. The group offers its clients many solutions. These include investment management, wealth planning, lending and banking services, advice for corporate finance, and special offerings.

Among the foremost wealth managers in the Americas is the group's Wealth Management Americas. They measure this based on the invested assets and productivity of their financial advisors. The sub-divisions include Canadian Wealth Management and U.S. Wealth Management businesses along with any international business that books within the United States. This business serves high net worth and ultra high net worth clients.

The UBS Asset Management operates in 22 different nations. It provides a range of investment styles and capabilities in both traditional and alternative classes of assets. These provide these offerings to global wealth management customers, wholesale intermediaries, and institutions. This group is the biggest mutual fund manager in Switzerland, a foremost European fund house, Asia's biggest international asset manager, and among the biggest managers of real estate on earth.

The UBS Personal and Corporate Banking business delivers a wide host of financial services and products to the institutional, corporate, and private customers who reside in Switzerland. It is a leader in this market. This business is key to their universal bank model in the country. It refers its clients to the Wealth Management business after it helps them to reach a certain level of assets.

The group's investment bank delivers services to its institutional, corporate, and wealth management customers. It offers them creative solutions, expert and professional advice, competitive execution, and all inclusive access to the world's global capital markets.

In 2015, the group boasted revenues of 30.6 billion Swiss francs and operating profit of 5.5 billion Swiss francs.

Underwriting

Underwriting refers to a means of determining if a consumer is eligible or not for a particular kind of financial product. These products vary depending on the person's or business' requirements. They might include home mortgages, insurance coverage needs, business mortgages, lines of credit, or financing for venture start up projects. The bank or other financial institution undergoing the underwriting evaluation procedure will look into the odds of the business transaction successfully providing them with a profit in exchange for their offer of financial help.

As banks and insurance firms go through the underwriting process, two different things will occur. The first of these is showing an interest in the project that the borrower is proposing for finance. They demonstrate this by offering the financial aid that the customer is requesting. Next, with a bank or institution underwriting an insurance policy, residential or commercial mortgage, or venture, they are looking to make money on their investment one day in the future. They might either gather these profits at one time in the form of a lump sum at a future date or little by little in monthly payments. In these underwriting activities, compensation is expected, which is commonly paid via finance charges or other fees.

Underwriters contemplate more than simply the amount of risk that an applicant demonstrates. They also consider the potential risk that working with the new customer might bring to other customers of their company. In order to ensure that the bank or firm does not suffer too much harm to keep up with commitments made to already existing clients, they have developed underwriting standards.

Insurance companies heavily rely on underwriting in performing their business. Health insurance is one example of this. Health insurance providers seriously look into the past and present health of a person applying. Sometimes their underwriting will show that they need to exclude various pre-existing conditions for a certain amount of time when they insure the person. Other times, underwriting will reveal a medical history that demonstrates too much risk for the company. In this case, a health insurance company will refuse to provide the requested health insurance coverage. Their goal is to not insure individuals who they believe will need significant medical treatment over time, so that they can provide a solid financial backing for their existing clientele.

In business, underwriting is commonly employed to determine if new ventures should be given financing. An example of this might be a company that has created a new technology that it wishes to sell. These underwriters will consider how marketable the product appears, the applicant's marketing plan, the expense of creating and selling the new items, and also the odds of the company realizing profits on every piece that they sell. Sometimes, underwriters of these business ventures will express an interest in having shares of stock in the start up company as a portion of their payment for services. Other times, they will only require a set interest rate for the dollar amount invested.

UniCredit

UniCredit turns out to be the largest Italian based bank and one of the biggest banks in the continent. This banking group is a major player throughout Western, Central, and Eastern Europe. As a leading commercial European bank, it operates in 17 different nations and maintains over 143,000 employees. The bank counts on its retail network of more than 7,500 branches as well as an international network that covers 50 different markets. This group's commanding position in Western, Eastern, and Central Europe helps them to have what is among the highest market shares in the region.

UniCredit is also unique in its commitment to keeping the local brands of the banks that they combined with when they formed their banking group. This is evident in such names for its banks in other countries as UniCredit Bulbank. Here the group merged the Bulgarian market leader Bulbank brand with its own name. They believe that their local brands are extremely valuable and worth preserving when they acquire them.

The banking group is headquarter registered in Rome while its general management offices are in the Italian commercial center of Milan. UniCredit's principle markets are Italy, Bulgaria, Austria, southern Germany, Russia, and Poland. They have divisions for investment banking internationally in such markets as London, New York, Hong Kong, Munich, Milan, Budapest, Vienna, and Warsaw.

This banking group concept is a fairly recent construct. It originated from the merger of a number of Italian banks back in 1998. The biggest of these were Unicredito from Verona, Turin, and Treviso and Credito Italiano that included Banca Popolare di Rieti and Rolo Banca. The new group initially went by the name Unicredito Italiano before this was changed to its present form. From 1998 to 2000, the group acquired four other significant Italian banks. In 1999, the bank created a new subsidiary named for the original component Credito Italiano.

This international bank is run as several different divisions. These include the CIB, CEE, and national divisions for Italy, Germany, Austria, and Poland. CIB has the responsibility of Global Division for the group. It handles multinational clients and large corporate clients. These have the potential needs for products in investment banking. CIB also carries the responsibility for the Financial and Institutional Groups clients, for the Global Transaction Banking, for the International Activities, and for the Global Financing and Advisory businesses.

The CEE division helps to coordinate the various activities of UniCredit in the markets of Central and Eastern Europe. Its main goal is to bring them into a unified and comprehensive vision for the region. Under this division, the various national businesses besides Germany, Austria, and Poland operate. This includes the bank subsidiaries in the Czech Republic, Slovakia, Romania, Bulgaria, Serbia, Slovenia, Croatia, and Russia.

The Italian division handles many different business located in Italy under its leadership responsibilities. These client segments include First, Business First, Family, Corporate Banking, Private Banking, Asset Gathering, and Public Sector. The Italian division breaks down into seven geographical regions, a Real Estate Network, and a Private Bank Network.

Each of the main national divisions has its own head that reports directly to the Deputy General Manager. These include the core markets of Austria, Germany, Poland, and the CEE. The banking group is a complicated organizational structure that somehow works together to form one of the largest banks in Europe and internationally.

UniCredit Bulbank

UniCredit Bulbank proves to be the biggest bank in the Republic of Bulgaria. Until 1994, this state-controlled and -operated bank bore the name of the Bulgarian Foreign Trade Bank or BFTB. It was in 2007 that the UniCredit Bulbank became formed when Bulbank, Hebros Bank, and Biochim merged together as individual subsidiaries of UniCredit Group from Italy.

Bulgarian Foreign Trade Bank first arose in 1964 in its headquarters of Sofia, Bulgaria. The at the time completely state-owned and -founded bank held an initial paid in capital of 40 million Bulgarian leva when it opened. This proved to be a large sum of capital in this day and age. At the time under the heyday of the communists in Bulgaria it specialized in foreign finance and foreign trade payments.

The bank realized that to effectively pursue foreign trade and finance, it needed several well placed good international branches. The bank then began to open important representative offices in London, Vienna, and Frankfurt throughout the subsequent decades. In 2015, the operation boasted substantially greater assets amounting to nearly 9 billion Euros and 2015 era equity of nearly 13 billion Euros.

Once Communism collapsed in Bulgaria during the successful national coup in 1989, the country established the Bank Consolidation Company in 1991 to operate the state- controlled banking sector and to help with the eventual privatizing of the various national Bulgarian banks. BCC owned 98 percent of the share capital of Bulbank at the time. It became the first Bulgarian bank operation to change over to international SWIFT codes. This helped it to massively improve its transaction reliability and operational performance as a direct result.

The bank's eventual privatization from 1998 to 2000 saw UniCredito Italiano gain control of 93 percent of the capital shares while German based re-insurance giant Allianz obtained another five percent of the remaining shares. Bulbank then sold its majority stakes in Corporate Commercial Bank and minor stakes in United Bulgarian Bank and HypoVereinsbank Bulgaria.

Bulbank has continuously worked on the merger of operations and branches between the old Bulbank offices and Hebros Bank and HVB Bank Biochim since UniCredit made the decision to merge the HVB Group back in 2005. The group was renamed UniCredit Bulbank officially at this point.

The same Chief Executive Officer has overseen the company's massive successes since the year 2001. This towering figure in Bulgarian banking and finance is Mr. Levon Hampartzoumian. He heads UniCredit Bulbank still as of end of 2016 in its second decade of existence in the present foreign owned-form of the financial institution.

Part of the leading in Bulgaria success that UniCredit Bulbank has consistently enjoyed in recent decades stems from the wide range of clientele they effectively serve. They offer bank checking, current, and savings accounts, insurance and investment products, land and home mortgages, and financing and credit for individual clients, private banking customers, small businesses, large corporate clients, other financial institutions, and even Bulgarian government and other public institutions as well.

UniCredit Bulbank is not only by far and away the largest bank in Bulgaria by branches, deposits, and assets; it is also a heavily award-winning financial institution. In 2016, it received the honors of "Bank of the Year" from the Association Bank of the Year and "Best Bank for 2016" from Global Finance Magazine. It is known as the "Best Digital Bank in Bulgaria for 2016" per Global Finance Magazine. Focus Economics ranks it as the "Most Precise Overall Economic Forecast for Bulgaria." Forbes Magazine labeled it the "Most Innovative Bank in Bulgaria". It received the "Best Bank in Bulgaria" designations from EMEA Finance Magazine and K10's Kapital Newspaper annual ranking. Global Finance Magazine called UniCredit Bulbank the "Best Trade Finance Bank in Bulgaria" in 2016, as did Euromoney Magazine as well.

US Trust

U.S. Trust today is the Bank of America Private Wealth Management division. It existed as an independent U.S. Trust Corporation from 1853 through 2000. At this time Charles Schwab and Co. acquired the bank and trust. They later sold it to Bank of America back in 2007. U.S. Trust today provides (as it has for two centuries) its clients with wealth structuring, investment management, and lending and credit facilities.

U.S. Trust has its headquarters in New York City on 114 West 47th Street in the United States. The firm counts more than 100 branch offices throughout the country across 31 different states plus Washington, D.C. They work to provide their ultra high net worth clients with specially tailored solutions and resources that help meet their needs for credit and banking, investment management, and wealth structuring. Teams of advisors serve the clientele through a wide variety of financial services. Chief among these offerings are financial and succession planning, investment management, specialty asset management, philanthropic asset management, customized credit products, family office services, family trust stewardship, and financial administration.

U.S. Trust arose in 1853 as a State of New York chartered bank. This makes it the original and also oldest such trust company within the United States. The new venture had the backing of a combination of wealthy investors who poured a million dollars into the firm which was called United States Trust Company of New York at that point.

Among the first board of trustees were thirty different influential and important New Yorkers. This included founding investor New York City Mayor Joseph Lawrence from the Bank of the State of New York who became bank trust president. Secretary of the trust went to United States Life Insurance Company of New York's John Aikman. Among the other important founders were industrialist, inventor, and philanthropist Peter Cooper; Marshall Field the department store founder; President Shepherd Knapp of Mechanics National Bank of the City of New York; and steel and iron manufacturer and railroad developer Erastus Coming.

The company became founded to serve clients of individuals and institutions as a trustee and executor of their money. This proved to be an innovative concept as trusts had not been fully conceived of at this point. It only took till 1886 for the firm to be well-established as a stable and highly regarded financial institution.

Thanks to this growing reputation, by the middle of the 1800's, the company had acquired a roster of super rich clients. It served a significant role in a number of nationally and internationally important construction projects like the Panama Canal and national American railroads. A great number of the firm's corporate clients floated securities to help finance such building project initiatives. The trust got to play the part of corporate trustee in the projects. Such a boom in enterprising and industrial projects aided the business in expanding into the management of personal trusts for the super rich as well. By the 1880's and 1890's, the firm counted such prestigious and ultra high net worth individual as William Waldorf Astor, Oliver Harriman, and Jay Gould.

The company successfully managed to survive and thrive despite a range of damaging financial crises in the last half of the 1800s and the early 1900s. In 1928, it counted over a billion dollars in trust assets. It stood well above its vastly smaller rivals. Thanks to the company's emphasis on stability, it managed to ride out the 1929 stock market crash and resulting decade long depression.

The company thrived by introducing additional specially tailored personal services in the next few decades. Among these were advising its ultra wealthy clients and families on careers, private schools, and universities for their kids. By 1958, U.S. Trust had begun its earliest ads in the newspaper society pages of The New Yorker. It was also advertising in the Metropolitan Opera and New York Philharmonic Society programs at this time.

Despite restructuring in the 1970s, 1980s, and 1990s, the company still became a takeover target by Charles Schwab and Co. in the year 2000. It ceased to be an independent prestigious outfit of nearly 150 years long at this point.

Variable Interest Rate

Variable Interest Rate refers to the applicable interest rate which comes with a security or loan. When such rates are variable, it means that they will fluctuate up or down in time. The reason for this is that a specific index or interest rate benchmark underlies them. This rate or index will change from time to time in the natural course of events. There is a potential great benefit to having such a variable interest rate when this index or interest rate goes down. This is because the interest payments of the borrowers will similarly decline. On the other hand though, when such underlying benchmarks go up, the interest payments will also rise, sometimes painfully.

Not every loan, mortgage, or security will utilize the same benchmark index or interest rate as its underlying comparison point with these Variable Interest Rates. In fact it actually comes down to the kind of security or loan in question. With credit cards, car loans, or mortgages, the Variable Interest Rates are often based on the prime rate for the nation in which the loan is based. Naturally the financial institutions, lenders, and banks will assess a spread between their rate and the true benchmark rate. The amount of this spread form of fee depends on many factors. Some of these are the credit rating of the individual getting the loan and the kind of asset to which the loan is attached.

Where credit cards are concerned, most of them work on a Variable Interest Rate arrangement. Their APR annual percentage rate happens to be fixed to a specific interest index. In most cases, this is the prime rate. With the prime rate, it generally moves up or down in lockstep alongside the federal funds rate that the United States Federal Reserve sets as part of their fiscal and monetary policy tools. A move up or down in this rate eventually leads to a net change in the underlying interest rate of credit cards across America. Such rates for these credit cards working off of variable interest rates are able to shift up or down at will. The credit card companies are not even required to provide written or verbal advance notice to their cardholding customers before adjusting the rates when the benchmark moves.

In the accompanying terms and conditions of such credit card accounts, the applicable interest rates will generally be described as the underlying prime rate added to a certain percentage rate. This specified additional percentage is always heavily based upon how credit worthy the card holding individual proves to be. As a real world example, many cards will assess an interest rate addition of 10.9 percent on top of the prime rate to come up with their credit card customer interest rates.

With other forms of loans that have Variable Interest Rates, the payment schedule proves to be different. The majority of non-credit card forms of loans are actually installment loans. These payments to repay them are fixed and pre-arranged. This leads to the loan reaching pay off on a pre-set specified day. All that changes as interest rates rise or fall is the amount of the payment. This will similarly increase or decrease per the amount of the interest rate change as well as the numbers of payments that remain to fully pay off the loan.

Mortgages have their own specific features. When they carry Variable Interest Rates, such loans are known as ARM adjustable rate mortgages. A great number of such ARMs actually begin their repayment life with a fixed lower interest rate during the initial years of the loan life. Once this pre-determined time frame expires, they will adjust up, sometimes steeply. The most typical periods of fixed interest rates on these adjustable rate mortgages turn out to be either three or five years. Loan officers refer to this as 5/1 or 3/1 ARMs.

Volcker Rule

The Volcker Rule is a controversial much loved or intensely hated part of the Frank-Dodd Wall Street Reform and Consumer Protection Act. This federal regulation made it illegal for banks to pursue specific investment activities using their own money and accounts.

It also restricted their relationship to and ownership of private equity funds and hedge funds. These so called covered funds engaged in a variety of speculative leveraged and high risk investments. Such investments and their ultimate massive failures played a major part in the American and ultimately global financial collapse of the 2008 financial crisis and Great Recession.

The Volcker Rule was originally named for Paul Volcker, the one time legendary Federal Reserve Chairman. This rule eliminates short term bank trading of derivatives, securities, commodity futures, and options on such futures. They may no longer use their own accounts for such trading that does not provide any benefit to the customers of the banks. The end result is that banks may not engage their own proprietary funds in order to participate in investments that may boost their own corporate profits.

This Volcker Rule is spelled out under section 619 of the massive Dodd-Frank Wall Street Reform and Consumer Protection Act. It amended the Bank Holding Company Act of 1956, also known as the BHC Act, by adding in a brand new section 13 that has become universally known as the Volcker Rule. All institutions which accept deposits, as well as any corporate entity that is affiliated with these insured depository groups, are prohibited from pursing this secretive proprietary trading.

They also may no longer have an interest in, acquire, or sponsor any private equity or hedge funds. There are some exemptions, definitions, and restrictions in the legal statute. It provided banking groups with some time until they had to prove they had conformed to the provisions of the rule. Originally this was July of 2014, but it was later extended to July 21, 2015 in order to provide banks with sufficient time to extricate themselves from these trades and practices.

The end form of the regulations had to be approved by five different federal agencies. These included the Federal Deposit Insurance Corporation, the Federal Reserve System Board of Governors, The Commodity Futures Trading Commission, the Office of the Comptroller of the Currency, and the SEC Securities and Exchange Commission. They approved these rules in December of 2013.

The rules became effective on April 1, 2014 and required banks' complete compliance by July 21, 2015. The Volcker Rule did not completely tie banks' hands. They are still allowed to keep making markets, hedging, and underwriting government securities. They may also engage in the activities of insurance companies and perform the roles of custodians, brokers, and agents.

They may offer customers private equity funds or hedge funds for their own accounts and benefit. All such services which they provide to their customers they may do in an effort to turn profits. The caveat is that banks may not pursue these activities when it leads to a dangerous conflict of interest, creates instability in the individual bank or the entire United States' financial system, or opens up the banking institution to dangerous trading strategies or involvement with risky assets.

Banks of certain sizes must report and disclose all of their covered trading activities to the appropriate government regulators. The bigger banks had to create programs that guaranteed they were abiding by the new rules. Besides this, their new compliance programs were subject to further independent analysis and tests. Institutions which were smaller were subjected to fewer reporting and compliance rules and regulations.

Western Union

Western Union proves to be a world-leading provider of global payment options and services. They help customers who range from individuals and families, to small businesses and not for profit NGOs, to international corporations. The company does more than simply help businesses and individuals to move money; they help national and international economies to expand and communities to experience a more prosperous and better life.

For the full reporting year 2015, Western Union transferred more than $150 billion dollars between customers and businesses around the globe. The firm boasts an impressive 500,000 different agents' locations, with more than 100,000 of their own ATM's and kiosks found around over 200 different countries and territories of the globe. They are constantly seeking to find smarter and better, more innovative and cutting edged means of sending money utilizing mobile, digital, and retail channels by providing a vast range of options for convenient pickup or payout to help their consumers and businesses with their cash needs.

Western Union is a major player in the world of currency translation as well. Their transactions happen throughout over 130 different currencies between more than a billion individual bank accounts around the world. They average an impressive 31 different transactions for every second (per the year 2015).

By simply going down to a retail outlet or utilizing the Western Union website or mobile app, customers are able to move money from almost any location to almost any other domestic or international location, from one currency to almost any other, and all in a matter of minutes. This helps their customers to be able to send money out to their family members or friends in almost every corner of the globe. They can offer financial support and encouragement, empower an education or entrepreneurial opportunity, or simply honor someone for a special accomplishment or occasion.

Their flagship service for individuals who wish to send money across the globe is called WU Connect. This international cross border system allows for peer to peer sending of funds to over 200 different nations and territories around the world. Pickup can be arranged via a wide variety of approved bank accounts, Western Union physical agent locations, and select mobile wallets.

Business customers also have access to a toolbox full of helpful services. The main category for this is the Western Union Business Solutions platform. This enables businesses to navigate their way through the challenging global economy. They can avail themselves of risk management, international payments, and cash management tools. More than 100,000 medium to smaller business clients, financial institutions, NGOs, and educational institutions are able to effectively transact in and make payment across national borders and through widespread geographical time zones.

Larger businesses and multinational corporations which require help in hedging international currency movements for the future are able to take advantage of their Leverage Forward Contracts. These help them to lock in an attractive current day exchange rate for specific time frames that extend up to 12 months out from the present date. This assists multinational corporations and big businesses in safeguarding their profit margins against currency movements over the short to medium term time frames. The WU system allows clients to place market orders in any time of the day or night. They can even set up a monitoring order to wait for a targeted advantageous exchange rate, whether or not they are sitting at their desk in the physical office or not.

The businesses can also avail themselves to the services Western Union offers to manage a company's exposure to foreign currency. Risk can be first identified and then addressed using a four step risk management protocol. The company maintains a staff of well-trained and knowledgeable specialists who are able to help set goals and develop a simple yet effective currency hedging plan to reduce and control currency exposures while protecting the important margins of profit.

Wholesale Banking

The concept of wholesale banking pertains to those banking services which are done between merchant banks or commercial banks and various other financial institutions. This form of banking services has to do with bigger bank clients like enormous corporations or other financial institutions. In contrast, retail banking concentrates on individual clients and small businesses. Such particular banking services cover financing of working capital needs, currency conversions, large trade transactions, and a range of alternative and specialized banking services.

There are so many different avenues which wholesale banking covers. This specialized department within the mega banks handles capital markets products, integrated credit, and a range of different advice and guiding for risk management, funding needs, and investment products and services for international and domestic major corporate clients. Such products and services run the gamut of structured transactions, specialized finance, credit structuring, loan syndications, project finance and securitization, merchant banking, wholesale equities, and public sector financing of infrastructure projects.

Among the many different types of wholesale banking clients are corporations which are medium sized to large, institutional investors and clients, pension funds, governmental departments and agencies, and other global banks and financial institutions both domestic and abroad. The services which they often need in day to day operations include equipment financing, cash flow management, large loans, trust services, and international merchant banking.

The concept also relates to lending and borrowing between larger institutional banks and other financial organizations. Such lending mostly goes on in the interbank market and revolves around huge sums of money in practice.

The majority of commercial banks function as such merchant bank operations, providing wholesale banking services besides the more usual retail customer banking services. It makes it more convenient for those customers who require wholesale banking services, as they will not be required to track down and go visit a specialized financial institution. Rather they are able to deal with the same bank which handles the customer's individual retail banking needs.

The most understandable means of comprehending this wholesale banking phenomenon is to draw parallels with a discount superstore chain such as Sam's Club or Costco. These outfits trade in such enormous quantities that they are able to feature special deals and lower fees per dollar of sales. For bigger institutions or organizations, this makes it advantageous for them who possess high dollars of assets and business banking transactions to participate in this banking wholesale instead of going the more traditional retail banking customer services route.

As an example, many businesses possess numerous locations throughout the country. They often times require a solution for their cash management, which wholesale banking can easily provide. Technology companies are an especially relevant business line for this type of banking. Perhaps an SaaS firm owns 10 sales offices throughout the U.S. It might be that every one of its 50 sales department members needs their own access to the company's corporate credit card. The company owners also insist on every one of the regional sales operations maintaining at least $1 million in cash reserves on hand. This amounts to $10 million worth throughout the various offices combined. Companies with these type of needs will be too big for the traditional format of ordinary retail banking.

The owners of this company might instead contact a significant sized bank and ask for a corporate account which will handle each of the company's financial accounts. These services function as a facility which will provide discounts to the company in exchange for meeting a minimum dollar level cash reserve requirements as well as a minimum level of monthly bank transaction requirements. It is in fact easy for the SaaS company to hit such targets each and every month. This is why the company will seek out such a corporate facility in order to properly consolidate together each of its financial bank accounts so that it may effectively reduce its total fees. This makes so much more sense for a larger company than instead having 10 different regional bank checking account and 50 separate retail bank corporate credit card accounts.

Wire Transfer

A wire transfer is the quickest, safest, most reliable means of sending money within the United States, in other countries, or around the world. They are often essential in the more critical financial activities of life such as purchasing a house. The reason larger transactions occur in this form of payment is because the recipient can receive and verify the funds transfer the same day it is done, or as near to immediately as possible (besides Western Union and Money Gram, which cost substantially more to utilize).

A wire transfer actually represents a means to electronically transfer money from one party to another via a bank as intermediary. A traditional and typical wire transfer starts at a credit union or bank and electronically processes through either Fedwire or SWIFT networks. Another common name for such a wire transfer is a bank wire, which also encompasses the standard bank to bank transfers.

Ultimately the wire transfers have become so successful and utilized throughout the United States and rest of world simply because they are capable of moving even enormous sums of money to any destination bank in the world in only a day or two. If they are affected within the same country such as the United States then same day wires can be done. For an international transfer via wire transfer, it often requires another day or even two to complete.

Since the funds move rapidly through the financial system, recipients are not required to wait a material amount of time for the funds to become cleared. This means they can access and utilize the money without significant delays. No holds are typically placed on wire transfer monies. The safety issue means that merchants prefer the wire mechanism. This is because checks can bounce because of insufficient funds, while wires never do so. In other words, these are guaranteed funds.

There are some particular requirements that wire transfers need in order to be possible to transact. At least in the United States, both parties would require a functioning bank account in order for a bank to act as intermediary. Since thieves can not open a bank account too easily, nor bank anonymously in the United States, it is difficult for them to carry out scams using bank wires. This is because it leaves a paper trail which is easy for law enforcement officials to follow.

This does not mean that wire transfer scams are unknown entirely. It is possible for a person to be tricked into wiring money to a fraudster for a purchase or service they never receive. Examples of this are fake insurance policies or false retirement or investment products. Once the wire has cleared the recipients account, they can either withdraw the funds in person or wire it to an offshore overseas account.

By the time the victims realize that they have been scammed, the funds sent by wire will be long gone. They would no longer be recoverable by traditional U.S. law enforcement or even court order methods once they have been transferred offshore. Pulling money back after it has been dispatched via bank wire is extremely difficult in any case. This is true even if the funds remain in the recipient's bank account.

Wire transfer fees can be significant. In many parts of the United States, they run as high as $40 to dispatch a bank wire. Many banks charge upwards of $10 in order for a bank wire to be received into an account. The costs to send one are higher if the wire is funded by utilizing a credit card cash advance. Cash advance fees would then apply, as well as typically large interest rates, plus the wire transfer fee. This is why it is typically most financially sound to effect a bank wire directly from the sender's bank account.

World Bank

The World Bank proves to be an institution in international finance. It offers developing countries of the planet leveraged loans to help out with funding capital programs. The major goal is to cut down on poverty. Every decision that the organization enacts is required to be carried out with the objectives of encouraging international trade, foreign investment, and facilitate capital investment.

The World Bank should not be confused with the World Bank Group. The World Bank is two of the five organizations within the World Bank Group. These two groups that make up the World Bank are the IDA, or the International Development Association, and the IBRD, or International Bank for Reconstruction and Development. The World Bank Group is also made up of MIGA, or the Multilateral Investment Guarantee Agency; the IFC, or International Finance Corporation; and the ICSID, or International Center for Settlement of Investment Disputes.

The World Bank's two organizations are widely supported by the nations of the world. The International Development Association contains one hundred and sixty-eight members, while the International Bank for Reconstruction and Development is comprised of one hundred and eighty-seven countries. Exclusively members of the IBRD may belong to the various other organizations in the World Bank. All IBRD members are supposed to belong to the IMF, or International Monetary Fund, as well.

The year 2010 saw significant revisions to the allocated votes of members of the World Bank. Developing countries, especially China, gained a larger voice. The nations that possess the biggest voting power currently are the United States at 15.85%, Japan at 6.84%, China at 4.42%, Germany at 4%, Great Britain at 3.75%, and France at 3.75%.

These changes are called the Phase Two of the Voice Reform. They also gave major votes percentages to countries such as India, Brazil, Mexico, and South Korea. To come up with the extra votes, the voting percentages of the majority of developed nations declined. Russia, the United States, and Saudi Arabia's votes did not change.

The World Bank focuses on reducing the poverty found in the poorest developing countries in the world. They do this analyzing a nation's economic and financial condition and comparing it against a snap shot of many local groups in the country. Then it comes up with unique strategies for addressing the problems of the given country. After this, the country's government lays out their biggest priorities for reducing poverty, so that the World Bank can line up its help to work together with this government.

Besides giving out money to the poorest countries on the earth, the World Banks heads several other initiatives. They are managers of the Clean Technology Fund. They also run the Clean Air Initiative.

Zero Balance Account (ZBA)

The zero balance account, also known by its acronym ZBA, refers to the type of checking account which maintains a permanent balance of zero. The account does this through an automatic transfer of funds out of a master account. The amount which transfers over only proves to be sufficient enough to cover any and all checks which other financial institutions present to the bank where the holder's account resides.

Corporations utilize these zero balance accounts in order to draw down excessive balances from separate accounts. It also helps them to keep better and stricter control over amounts they disburse in the ordinary everyday course of business operations.

These accounts will therefore only have a zero balance within them. The only exception to this zero balance account status is when checks are written against them and presented to the bank in question. In this way, companies are able to keep the balances as close to zero for accounts that do not have any reason to hold excessive reserves. The activity in these ZBA's is restricted to only processing payments. This is why they do not maintain any ongoing balances.

Because of this, a larger sum of funds will remain available for the company to deploy. They can instead put them to work in investments and company cash flow purposes rather than keeping low dollar amounts lying idly by in a number of sub-accounts. It does not present a problem when checks must be paid off from these special zero balance accounts, since the electronic clearing system recognizes that these accounts are in fact ZBA's and they will move the necessary funds over from the master account at the financial institution in the precise dollar amount needed to clear the check.

Companies and other organizations can also rely on a zero balance account to fund purchases which employees make with their debit cards. This allows them to carefully monitor all of the financial transactions and any activities which take place on the cards, since the debits must be pre-authorized. This works well for companies and charitable not for profit organizations which are protected by not maintaining any idle funds within the ZBA's.

The debit card transaction will not be approved by the bank which backs them until and unless the requisite funds become available to the account by a transfer from the authorized account representative at the firm or NGO. This means that debit card transactions simply can not be run without prior authorization by the appropriate superior in the organization. Businesses are able to reduce their risks of activities which are not approved of occurring.

This is critically important to especially larger organizations with many employees and numerous sub accounts and associated corporate debit cards. There is no better spending control oversight for these types of situations than the zero balance account. Incidental charges can be monitored throughout the sizeable operations.

Since incidental expenditures are variable in nature, it is harder to fund and control them without such an account. Large companies and not for profits effectively reduce rapid access to the company or charitable funds with these debit cards. In this way, they have put into place the best practices for approval procedures. It ensures that such procedures will be adhered to in advance of a purchase being made by an employee.

As budget monitoring tools, these ZBA's are also ideal. They may be established as one account per department or business operation. This allows the accountants at the company an easy and fast means of monitoring annual, monthly, and even weekly to daily purchases. The company book keepers are also able to effectively track particular shorter term projects and their financial expenditures by utilizing such a ZBA. Projects which are in jeopardy of running significantly and rapidly over budget also benefit from such accounts. The overseers can maintain control of all purchases by requiring proper approval and notification before the charges take place.

The master account of such zero balance accounts is the critical component of this entire concept. As the central operational center for all fund management in the organization, the account will be employed to disperse funds to all ZBA subaccounts as needed. These master accounts typically include other benefits like better interest rates for balances which they hold.

Zombie Banks

Zombie banks prove to be financial institutions that in reality have literal economic net worths of less than zero. They still keep running because they are able to continue paying their debts using government's real or implied support for their credit and balance sheet. Although this term has come to be heavily used in the financial crises of 2007 to 2010, it did not originate there.

Instead, Edward Kane coined the phrase Zombie Banks back in 1987. He used it to refer to and relate the perils of allowing a great number of banks that were actually insolvent to continue operating. The phrase came to be utilized for the Japanese banking crisis that began in 1993. It once again arose in popularity during the financial crisis of the last few years where hundreds of banks have failed in single years.

Zombie banks have many problems. Among these are bank runs from frightened depositors who are uninsured for their full account values. They also suffer from margin calls from their counter parties in derivatives contracts.

Zombie banks can be deceptive, as on the surface they may look like they are actually healthy and have the necessary level of capital to run. As investors learn the fair value of their assets, then they are suddenly looked at as insolvent institutions. This is to say that Zombie Banks keep operating in a regular manner as if nothing is wrong with their balance sheets. Yet the truth is that they will likely be seized by the Feds when the word becomes wide spread that they do not have the assets and money that everyone believed.

Healthy banks are able to make loans to new borrowers at the same time that they honor their obligations to lenders and share holders. Insolvent banks, or Zombie Banks, are incapable of generating new loans, since they lack the money and capital to make such loans while still performing on their obligations to lenders and share holders.

Comprehending what constitutes a Zombie bank requires that you know the basics of a bank balance sheet. One side of a balance sheet actually contains a bank's assets. The other side is comprised of the bank's liabilities as well as the bank's equity. The two sides are supposed to equal out, which is expressed in the equation assets equal liabilities plus the bank equity.

Zombie banks manage to hide their problems since no one is able to determine how much their assets are really worth. Asset backed securities and collateralized debt obligations are examples of assets whose values can not clearly be determined at any given moment. They might be worth as much as seventy-five cents for every dollar, or they could be valued as low as twenty-five cents per dollar.

The problem comes when Zombie banks have over valued their assets. If they later are forced to revalue them to correct and more appropriate levels, they quickly discover that they no longer have the assets to cover their future liabilities. Admitting to this causes them to become Zombie banks. At this point, the bank share holders are typically wiped out, while the depositors are given their money back by the Federal Deposit Insurance Corporation.

More books by Thomas Herold

www.ingramcontent.com/pod-product-compliance
Lightning Source LLC
Chambersburg PA
CBHW071543210326
41597CB00019B/3104